William Eleroy Curtis

The United States And Foreign Powers

William Eleroy Curtis

The United States And Foreign Powers

ISBN/EAN: 9783744725033

Printed in Europe, USA, Canada, Australia, Japan

Cover: Foto ©ninafisch / pixelio.de

More available books at **www.hansebooks.com**

Chautauqua Reading Circle Literature

THE UNITED STATES

AND

FOREIGN POWERS

BY

WILLIAM ELEROY CURTIS

Author of "The Capitals of Spanish America," "Trade and Transportation," "The Land of the Nihilist," etc., etc., etc.

MEADVILLE PENNA
FLOOD AND VINCENT
The Chautauqua-Century Press
1892

CONTENTS.

Chap.		Page.
I.	THE DIPLOMATIC SERVICE OF THE UNITED STATES	9
II.	THE CONSULAR SERVICE	27
III.	THE FOUNDING OF THE SOUTH AMERICAN REPUBLICS	36
IV.	DIPLOMATIC RELATIONS WITH THE OTHER AMERICAN REPUBLICS	47
V.	RESULTS OF THE INTERNATIONAL AMERICAN CONFERENCE	66
VI.	GENERAL RELATIONS WITH THE AMERICAN REPUBLICS	76
VII.	THE MONROE DOCTRINE	93
VIII.	NEGOTIATIONS FOR AN INTEROCEANIC CANAL	107
IX.	PROPOSED ANNEXATION OF SANTO DOMINGO AND ST. THOMAS. THE REPUBLIC OF LIBERIA	119
X.	A GENERAL VIEW OF EUROPE IN THE NINETEENTH CENTURY	136
XI.	GENERAL DIPLOMATIC RELATIONS WITH GREAT BRITAIN	149
XII.	DIPLOMATIC RELATIONS WITH GREAT BRITAIN—THE BERING SEA AND FISHERIES QUESTIONS	163

XIII.	Diplomatic Relations with France and the Purchase of Louisiana	178
XIV.	Diplomatic Relations with Spain and the Purchase of Florida	197
XV.	Relations with Russia and the Purchase of Alaska	211
XVI.	Relations with Italy	217
XVII.	Relations with Other European Powers	223
XVIII.	Relations with Eastern and Mediterranean Powers	239
XIX.	Relations with China	251
XX.	Relations with Japan	273
XXI.	Relations with Korea, Samoa, and Siam	283
XXII.	Relations with the Congo State and the Hawaiian Islands	296
	Index	309

PREFACE.

THE diplomatic history of the United States is a record of which any nation might be proud. Without a corps of trained diplomatists like those to whom the management of the foreign relations of the European governments are intrusted, without an army or a navy to enforce its claims, and with only a sense of justice and a consciousness of right, this country has succeeded through a century in maintaining its dignity and protecting its national honor. From the skillful and patient endeavors of Franklin, Adams, and Jefferson to secure the respect and recognition of the greater powers of the world for the feeble colonies then struggling for independence, to the able and courageous efforts of the present administration to protect the fisheries and sealing grounds of our citizens, it is a record of peaceful victories. There have been some incidents like those which led to the Mexican War, and the recent legislation against the Chinese, concerning which there may be a difference of opinion; but as a whole the influence of American diplomacy has had a wholesome and permanent effect upon the other nations of the world.

This little volume was not intended to be a complete

record of our foreign relations, nor has there been any attempt to treat the grave questions of dispute with other governments that have arisen from time to time in a technical or thorough manner, but the purpose has been to present a simple narrative of the principal incidents in our diplomatic history in a form that will enable them to be properly understood by those who are not versed in international law.

The author desires to acknowledge his obligations to Mr. George E. Vincent, of Buffalo, who prepared the chapter on The General View of Europe in the Nineteenth Century; Prof. Romyn Hitchcock, of the Smithsonian Institution, who prepared the chapter on China; to Mr. Winfield Scott Bird, of Philadelphia, who prepared the chapters on Japan, Korea, Samoa, and Liberia; to Mr. Henry L. Bryan, secretary of the Bureau of the American Republics, and Mr. Jesse Siddall Reeves, of Johns Hopkins University, who assisted in the preparation of the chapters on our relations with the European nations.

WILLIAM ELEROY CURTIS.

The required books of the C. L. S. C. are recommended by a Council of six. It must, however, be understood that recommendation does not involve an approval by the Council, or by any member of it, of every principle or doctrine contained in the book recommended.

THE UNITED STATES AND FOREIGN POWERS.

CHAPTER I.

THE DIPLOMATIC SERVICE OF THE UNITED STATES.

AFTER the Declaration of Independence, and under the Articles of Confederation, until October 20, 1781, the foreign correspondence of the government of the United States and the immediate management of its relations with other nations were intrusted to a committee of Congress. On the date mentioned Robert R. Livingston of New York, who had been elected secretary of foreign affairs by Congress, took the oath of office and served in that capacity until June, 1783, when he resigned, and Elias Boudinot of New Jersey, the president of Congress, performed the duties of this office as secretary *ad interim*. On the organization of the new Congress in the following November, Thomas Mifflin of Pennsylvania was elected to be its president, and he acted in this capacity until December, 1784, when John Jay of New York, who had been sent to Spain to secure the recognition of American independence by that government, was chosen to be secretary of foreign affairs. He served until March 4, 1789, under the Confederation. On the organization of the government under the Constitution, he continued in charge of its foreign relations, until March 21, 1790, having in the meantime been appointed and confirmed chief justice of the Supreme Court.

The act for the establishment of "an executive department, to be denominated the Department of Foreign Affairs" was passed by Congress and approved by the president, July 27, 1789. In the following September "an act to provide for the safe keeping of the acts and records and seal of the United States," was passed, which changed the name to the "Department of State," and provided that its principal officer should be called the secretary of state. Thomas Jefferson of Virginia was commissioned secretary of state in September, 1789, and entered upon the performance of the duties of the office on March 21, 1790, after his return from France, where he was our first minister plenipotentiary. Since the time of Jefferson there have been twenty-eight secretaries of state, not including undersecretaries of the department who have temporarily performed the duties of the office. They were: Edmund Randolph of Virginia; Timothy Pickering of Massachusetts; John Marshall and James Madison of Virginia; Robert Smith of Maryland; James Monroe of Virginia; John Quincy Adams of Massachusetts; Henry Clay of Kentucky; Martin Van Buren of New York; Edward Livingston of Louisiana; Louis McLane of Delaware; John Forsyth of Georgia; Daniel Webster of Massachusetts (twice, in 1841 and in 1850); Abel P. Upshur of Virginia; John C. Calhoun of South Carolina; James Buchanan of Pennsylvania; John M. Clayton of Delaware; Edward Everett of Massachusetts; William L. Marcy of New York; Lewis Cass of Michigan; Jeremiah S. Black of Pennsylvania; William H. Seward of New York; Elihu B. Washburn of Illinois; Hamilton Fish of New York; William M. Evarts of New York; James G. Blaine of Maine (twice, in 1881 and 1889); Frederick Theodore Frelinghuysen of New Jersey, and Thomas F. Bayard of Delaware. Of those who have served as secretaries of state six were subsequently elected presidents of the United States.

The Constitution authorizes the President, by and with the advice and consent of the Senate, to conduct the foreign policy of the government, and he, under the statutes of Congress, intrusts it to the secretary of state. He, in turn, directs the transactions of the officers of the diplomatic and consular service, who are stationed at the capitals and the principal ports and commercial cities of the world. These officers are appointed by the President and confirmed by the Senate, except in a few minor places when they are selected by the secretary of state.

The Senate of the United States has a committee on foreign relations, and the House of Representatives, committees on foreign affairs and expenditures in the Department of State. These committees are charged with the consideration of legislation that may be proposed affecting the intercourse of our government with foreign nations, and the Senate committee has also the duty of reviewing and reporting upon treaties with foreign governments, which require ratification by a two-thirds vote of the Senate before they can be proclaimed by the President and take effect. Under the rules of the Senate all nominations to the diplomatic and consular service, and all treaties are considered in secret session.

The discussions are never reported or published except in cases of extraordinary importance, but a record of the action of the Senate is preserved in what is known as the Executive Journal. The result is afterwards communicated to the President by the executive clerk, and published in the Congressional Record, after three sessions of the Senate have intervened. This postponement is for the purpose of enabling any Senator to enter a motion to reconsider whatever action may have been taken, should he desire to do so.

The House of Representatives may sit in secret session to consider questions affecting the foreign policy of the government, if a majority of the members of that body regard it expedient to do so. This provision is intended to enable

Congress to take action without the knowledge of foreign governments that may be interested, but it has very seldom been resorted to. The consideration of treaties in secret session by the Senate is for the same reason, and the rule requiring nominations to be considered behind closed doors is to protect the reputation of persons who have been appointed to office, and to enable the Senators to discuss their qualifications with greater freedom than public session would permit.

The word diplomacy, according to its modern meaning, as defined by Webster, is "the science or art of conducting negotiations between nations"; but it formerly had a very different signification. Several centuries ago a "diplomatist" was an official attached to a court, whose duty was to prepare diplomas, patents of nobility, charters, commissions, and other state papers. He was a sort of executive clerk to a king, and before the days of mails, ambassadors, and legations, sovereigns were in the habit of sending such officials as messengers to the courts of other nations, intrusted with delicate and important duties. From this practice the present meaning of the title was derived, and it was first used in its present sense by Count Vergennes in French, and Burke in English. Every independent nation has the right to send or receive agents or representatives to and from other governments with which it has relations, and this has been the practice since the beginning of civilization; but so many differences arose as to the rank and dignity of such agents that an international congress was held in Vienna in 1815, to prepare certain rules for their observance which have been adopted by all civilized countries. According to these rules diplomatic agents were divided into three classes:

(1). Ambassadors, who are sent by one sovereign to another; and legates or nuncios, who are sent by the pope alone.

(2). Envoys extraordinary, ministers plenipotentiary, and ministers resident.

(3). *Chargés d' affaires*, who are accredited not to sovereigns but only to ministers of foreign affairs.

Ambassadors are supposed to represent not only the country from which they come, but the person of the sovereign, and have the right to communicate personally with the sovereign to whom they are sent. Diplomatic agents of the two lower grades communicate with the sovereign through his or her ministers. There is very little difference however, between envoys extraordinary and agents of a lower grade, except in rank, for both have the same duties, functions, and privileges. During the absence of a minister the senior secretary of legation acts as *chargé d' affaires*, is entitled to the privileges and dignities of his principal, and under our laws is entitled to an allowance equal to one half his pay, which however is not deducted from the minister's salary and is in lieu for the time being of the salary provided for the secretary.

As the Constitution of the United States does not recognize the President as a sovereign, we have no embassadors in our diplomatic service, but the envoy extraordinary and minister plenipotentiary is the highest grade, and the laws of the United States authorize the appointment of twenty-nine officers of this rank, who are divided into classes, according to the importance of the nation to which they are sent and the compensation that is paid them.

The envoys extraordinary and ministers plenipotentiary to France, Germany, Great Britain, Russia, and Mexico are paid $17,500 each; to Austria, Brazil, China, Italy, Japan, and Spain, $12,000 each; to Chile, Argentine Republic, Colombia, Peru, Guatemala and Honduras, Turkey, and to Nicaragua, Costa Rica, and Salvador, $10,000; to Paraguay and Uruguay, Venezuela, Hawaiian Islands, Belgium, Netherlands, Sweden and Norway, and Denmark, $7,500; to Greece, Roumania and Servia (one), $6,500; to Bolivia, Ecuador, and Switzerland, $5,000.

There are ministers resident, who also act as consuls general, to Corea, $7,500; to Hayti, Persia, Portugal, and Siam, $5,000, and to Liberia with a salary of $4,000. The minister to Hayti is accredited as *chargé d' affaires* to Santo Domingo.

There are two secretaries of the legations at Berlin, London, Paris, China, and Japan. The first secretaries receive salaries of $2,625 a year; and the second secretaries, at Berlin, London, and Paris, $2,000. The second secretaries in China and Japan are required by law to devote their attention to the study of the languages of those countries, receiving yearly salaries of $1,600. There are also secretaries of legation at Bogota and Guatemala who also act as consuls general, and receive salaries of $2,000; in Austria, Brazil, Italy, Mexico, Spain, and Turkey, at $1,800; in Chile, Peru, Argentine Republic, Venezuela, and Corea, $1,500.

There are interpreters at the legations in Turkey and China, who receive a salary of $3,000; in Japan, $2,500; in Persia and Corea, $1,000; and in Siam, $500.

The secretary of state at his discretion allows additional clerical assistance at nearly all the legations, which is paid for out of a general fund. The ministers are allowed a certain amount of money each year for the rent of legations, offices, messengers, stationery, light, fuel, and other necessary expenses. There is also a fund for the payment of the funeral expenses of diplomatic officials who die abroad, and their widows are allowed an amount equal to their month's compensation.

As we have no diplomatic relations with the pope, the United States sends no minister to the Vatican and receives no papal nuncio.

The qualifications for employment in the diplomatic service of most countries consist of a thorough education in international law, history, and treaties, and a knowledge of French, which is recognized the world over as the language of diplomacy, but in the United States no special qualifications are required. In other countries also the diplomatic service is recognized as a profession, which is entered after special preparation in youth and followed through life, being attended with promotion from the lower to the higher grades according to ability and proficiency, and when by reason of age or infirmity the members become incapacitated they are retired on liberal pensions. But in the United States, where rotation in office is one of the fixed principles of political economy, every foreign minister is expected to tender his resignation with a change in the executive administration, and returns home to resume his previous occupation as soon as his successor is appointed. This practice is condemned by many people as a serious defect and an embarrassment, but there is much to be said on both sides of the question.

Among the first officials appointed after the inauguration of a new President and the installation of his cabinet, are the ministers to foreign nations, and it is customary for those who seek such honors to present their applications indorsed by the senators and representatives of the states in which they live, and other citizens who are supposed to have influence with the executive. These papers are filed at the Department of State and are there classified and briefed. When the President takes up the subject of appointments, the secretary of state lays the papers before him, and the friends of the candidates supplement the written testimonials by personal interviews with both the secretary and the President. The selections for the most important places are usually made, however, upon the personal acquaintance of the President with the candidates and he considers not only their qualifications, but their political services and influence and their geographical location, for it is an unwritten law that such appointments shall be distributed as fairly as possible among the several states. It is at the same time recognized as a privilege of the President to select his personal friends for the diplomatic service, as a diplomatic office is in no sense a political one, and like the members of his cabinet should be in sympathy with the policy he intends to carry out during his administration.

The selections having been made, the President sends the nominations to the Senate, where they are referred to the committee on foreign relations, whose duty it is to inquire into the character and qualifications of the appointee and to report the result of their investigations to their colleagues in executive session. It is a custom observed in almost every case that when a man who has once been a member of the Senate is appointed to office, his nomination shall be considered and confirmed without reference to a committee. This is called "senatorial courtesy," and is based upon the assumption that the qualifications of such a man must be known to every member of the Senate and that one who has once occupied a seat in that body is competent to serve his country in any other capacity. Nominations are, however, sometimes rejected by the Senate for either personal or political reasons; and there are some famous cases on record of the refusal of the Senate to "advise and consent to" the appointment of certain persons who have, in the press or in published volumes, criticised the official acts or attacked the personal character of members of the Senate. There is another practice in senatorial procedure that when a member of that body of recognized integrity and influence shall denounce a nominee as personally offensive to him and give good reasons for his objections, the nominee shall be rejected. But these instances are exceedingly rare, and such action is resorted to only in extreme cases.

The appointment having been confirmed by the Senate and accepted, the new minister takes the oath of office and receives his commission. He is then allowed thirty days' leave to make preparations for departure to his post and to receive his instructions. He is then furnished with credentials,—that is, a letter from the President to the ruler of the nation to which he is accredited, to the effect that the President, "reposing great confidence in the zeal, ability, and discretion" of the person named, has appointed him envoy extraordinary, etc., and that he hopes all faith and credit will be given him when he speaks for the United States. The President then reiterates his assurances of respect and confidence and his wishes for the welfare of the sovereign to which the letter is addressed, and signs the document "Your good friend, A—— B——" (President of the United States). Such letters are always addressed in a similar manner,

"*To Victoria, Queen of Great Britain and Ireland, and Empress of India:*

GREAT AND GOOD FRIEND—"

and are countersigned by the secretary of state.

No allowance is made for the expenses of a minister in traveling to his post, but his salary begins on the date when he takes the oath of office, and he is given a certain number of days to reach his destination, according to a fixed schedule of distances, which varies from fifteen days to Mexico to seventy days to China.

Upon his arrival at his post, if his predecessor is still there, the latter calls with him upon the minister of foreign affairs ; or he may be accompanied by the *chargé d' affaires*. After an introduction, he presents a certified copy of his credentials, and the draft of an address he intends to deliver when he is presented to the sovereign, with a request that the presentation may take place at the convenience of the latter. The retiring minister, if he has not already done so, presents his letters of recall, and asks an opportunity to take leave of the sovereign. There have been several instances in which the new appointee has not been what is termed a *persona grata* (an agreeable person) to the government to which he is accredited. This fact is usually made known to the secretary of state by the representatives at Washington of the country interested, and the commission is then revoked, as was the case in the recent appointment of a minister to China under the Harrison administration and a minister to Austria under President Cleveland. But usually the minister of foreign affairs receives the new appointee cordially and, after consultation, fixes a day and an hour for the official presentation. The ratification is accompanied by a copy of the address which the sovereign intends to deliver on the occasion. This exchange of speeches previous to their delivery is intended to avoid anything that may be offensive to either government and, as such addresses are purely formal and complimentary, no corrections are suggested, but there have been cases when the relations between two governments were "strained," that the presentation speeches have been revised by request before delivery.

In the United States there is no such officer as "the introducer of ambassadors," but he is generally found attached to all the courts of Europe, and the foreign officers of the Latin American Republics. He is the medium of communication between the minister of foreign affairs and the members of the diplomatic corps, officiates as master of ceremonies on occasions of festivity, attends the corps at public ceremonials, performs the very important duty of instructing new ministers in the etiquette and customs of the court, in the payment of their social obligations, and makes himself generally useful. These duties are usually performed in Washington by the chief clerk of the Department of State, and the new ministers obtain information as to official and social usage from the dean of the diplomatic corps.

The day and hour for the presentation of the new minister having arrived, he is waited upon at his legation by the official "introducer of ambassadors" and, attended by that gentleman, proceeds to the palace of the sovereign. There he is met by the minister of foreign affairs, who escorts him to the audience chamber or throne room. The doors being opened he sees the sovereign seated upon the throne at the opposite end of the apartment, and, with the minister of foreign affairs at his right and the "introducer of ambassadors" at his left and his secretaries behind him, he makes a low bow. Then the party march with slow and dignified strides to the center of the room, where they stop and make another bow. Then they resume their march to a respectful distance from the throne, make another bow, and the introducer of ambassadors announces the name of the minister, "envoy extraordinary and minister plenipotentiary from the United States." The latter then proceeds to read his address, and at its conclusion hands to the minister of foreign affairs the original copy of his credentials, which is passed up to the sovereign and received by some attendant. The sovereign then reads his reply to the address. In some countries, at its conclusion he descends from the throne, offers his hand to the new minister, and presents him to the queen, if she happens to be present, and to the other members of the court.

An envoy extraordinary is received in what is known as "public audience," that is, with full ceremonies and in the presence of members of the court, the sovereign wearing the robes of state. A minister resident is received in "private audience," that is, by the sovereign alone, without attendance and in ordinary costume. When a court is in mourning, all ministers are received in "private audience."

The United States is one of the few nations that has no "court dress." The ministers of other countries have a distinctive regalia according to their rank, wear swords, and sashes, and decorations, if they happen to have them, at their presentation and on all occasions of ceremony; but the representatives of the United States appear in simple evening dress (a swallow-tailed coat, a low-cut vest, and a white tie), but those who have served in the army are permitted to wear the uniform of their highest brevet rank. Some ambitious diplomatists from this country have appeared in militia uniforms, but this is simply tolerated, and is not recognized by the regulations.

The ceremonies of presentation having been completed, the minister, with his escort, makes a bow, and retires backward to the center of the room, bows again and continues to retire until the exit is reached, when he can turn and walk naturally; but it is very bad manners to turn one's back upon the sovereign of a nation. This, however, does not conclude the formalities. The new minister, within twenty-four hours after his presentation, is expected to pay a visit of ceremony to the minister of foreign affairs and other members of the cabinet, at their residences, and to his colleagues of the diplomatic corps. In these visits he is accompanied by the introducer of ambassadors and the secretaries of the legation, who present him.

The ceremony of presenting new ministers from foreign countries to the United States is very different and is in accordance with the "Jeffersonian simplicity" that is supposed to characterize the acts of all the officials of this government. At the hour appointed the minister goes to the Department of State, attended by his secretaries, and is escorted by the secretary of state to the White House. Then he is shown into the Red Room, and a messenger notifies the President. The latter leaves his desk and comes down to the Blue Room in his everyday garments. The new minister reads his address; the President reads his reply, the party shake hands all around, spend a few moments in familiar conversation, and retire.

The foreign legations in Washington are very much larger than those of the United States abroad, and the ministers and secretaries of legation receive much higher salaries. The British minister, for example, is provided with a residence owned by his government, almost as spacious as the Executive Mansion, and including the allowance for purposes of entertainment receives a compensation nearly equal to that of the President of the United States. Even his carriage and horses are paid for by his government and the wages of a certain number of servants, while the President of the United States provides his own carriage and pays his own servants with the exception of his steward, the gardeners, the messengers, and the watchmen. The British minister has five secretaries, a military *attaché*, and two naval *attachés*, besides several clerks.

The Mexican minister at Washington has six secretaries, while the United States minister at Mexico has one, and the legations of other countries have a similar number of assistants. It is a well-known fact that the diplomatic service of the United States is smaller in numbers and receives less compensation than that of any other of the great nations of the world. The annual cost of the entire service is about $400,000, while that of Great Britain is four times as much.

The duties of a minister are difficult to define, as they are so general in their character and depend entirely upon circumstances and the relations that exist between his own government and that to which he is accredited. He is expected always to keep the Department of State informed as to political events and public opinion, and their significance, especially when they have a bearing upon affairs at home. From him the secretary of state should learn, promptly, accurately, and fully, all that it is necessary to know about the affairs, the politics, and the policy of the nation to which he is sent, and in former times, before the days of telegraphic cables and newspapers, he was expected to send information concerning events of general interest. The communications of the ministers to England, France, and other countries seventy-five years ago were a continuous narrative of the history of the time.

These communications are called "dispatches," and all official correspondence is numbered consecutively, as a matter of convenience, so that in replying the secretary of state begins, "Referring to your No. 117, I have to say, etc." The letters from the secretary of state are known as "instructions." Each minister begins a new series with No. 1 and continues to the end of his term.

The secretary of state, when he desires to communicate with a foreign government, can do so either through the minister of the United States at the capital of that nation or through its minister at Washington. He can say to the minister of France at Washington, "I wish you would tell your government so and so," or he can write the minister at Paris, "You are instructed to inform the government of France that such and such is the case." But the ordinary practice is to confer with the minister of a foreign government concerning affairs that exist here, and with the minister of the United States concerning matters that are occurring near his post, on the theory that a minister should be most familiar with events that happen where he is located.

When a minister of the United States in a foreign country receives a message from the secretary of state he calls upon the minister of foreign affairs to deliver it. If it is a matter of importance, he prepares what is termed a "note," either a letter drawn in formal style or a mere memorandum containing a statement of facts, which he presents in person and accompanies with such oral explanation as may be necessary. To this "note" he expects to receive a prompt reply and if he requires additional information he calls to obtain it before communicating with his government. If it is a matter of minor importance he simply confers with the minister of foreign affairs in conversation and makes a memorandum of what has been said when he returns to his legation.

For the convenience of the diplomatic corps the minister of foreign affairs usually has a day when those who have business to transact with him can have an opportunity to do so, and the diplomatists are received in the order of their rank; or if they be of the same rank the first who comes has precedence; but ministers can call at any time at the Foreign Office, if their errand is urgent, or even at the residence of the minister of foreign affairs. At the Department of State in Washington, Thursday is "diplomatic day," and the secretary denies himself to ordinary visitors if any member of the diplomatic corps desires to see him.

If the minister does not converse fluently in the language of the country to which he is accredited or if the minister of foreign affairs does not understand his, he is at liberty to bring his own interpreter. There are official interpreters in the foreign departments of governments who may be called in on these occasions, but where the topic is of grave importance each has his own interpreter. When the minister of foreign affairs speaks, his interpreter makes the translation, and *vice versa*, and if any mistakes are made one has the right to correct the other.

Taking the affair of the riot in New Orleans in 1891 as an example of diplomatic controversy, Mr. Blaine conducted the correspondence with Baron Fava, the Italian minister at Washington, who received his instructions by cable from Rome. But Mr. Porter, our minister at Rome, was called upon by Mr. Blaine to make known to the government of Italy the provisions of the Constitution of the United States, the relations between the general government and the states, and the methods of criminal procedure that prevail in this country. He was instructed to explain to the Marquis Rudini that it was impossible for the federal authority to punish crimes committed in violation of the laws of the State of Louisiana, and to assure him, as Mr. Blaine had already assured Baron Fava, that the President would use all his influence to bring to justice those who had been guilty of the outrage.

When a treaty is to be negotiated, the first step usually taken by the minister is to call upon the minister of foreign affairs and discuss the subject in its several aspects in order that a general understanding may be reached. Then the representative of the government who proposes the treaty prepares a "note" or memorandum embodying the provisions he desires to have adopted. This he submits with whatever explanation or argument is necessary. Then the representative of the other power, having given the subject sufficient investigation and reflection, prepares a reply, which he forwards to the other, and the correspondence is continued, with frequent interviews, until an agreement in general terms is reached. Both prepare memoranda setting forth their understanding of the agreement. These are called protocols, and are usually submitted by the diplomatist to his home government for its approval. Then by further correspondence the details are agreed upon, two exact copies of the treaty are prepared and signed, for the ratification of the governments interested. When this ratification is completed, proclamation of the fact and the publication of the text of the treaty are made simultaneously at the capitals of both nations, usually at noon on a day agreed upon.

One of the gravest duties of a minister is the protection of the rights of his fellow-citizens, which are generally established by treaties. This is especially true of ministers of the United States in countries that have furnished a share of the immigrants that make up so large a proportion of our population. These immigrants often return to their former homes and get into trouble when they call upon the United States legation for protection. It is an unfortunate fact, too, that many of the "American colonies," as citizens of this country living in foreign lands are called, have representatives of the criminal class among their number, who are fugitives from justice and commit offenses against the laws of the nations in which they reside. They also appeal to the minister when they are charged with crime, and he is required to see that justice is done them. In each legation a register is kept, in which citizens of the United States can and should inscribe their names, professions, residences, etc., and at the same time have the minister indorse, or visé, their passports or naturalization papers, because the first thing required of people who are in trouble is to establish their citizenship. This can be done much more easily before than after they get into trouble, and the records of a legation are accepted as *prima facie* evidence of the fact.

Foreign ministers are also called upon frequently to perform the ceremony of marriage, to draw wills and administer estates, and to take charge of the property of citizens of the United States who die within their jurisdiction.

Social duties and pleasures also take up a large share of their time, and it is not only important that they should mingle freely in the society of the courts to which they are attached, but it is even more so that they should return the hospitality they enjoy, and entertain largely. The most successful diplomacy begins at the dinner table, and the social acquaintance and standing of a minister give him an influence that he could not otherwise obtain. For this reason the fact that a candidate for a diplomatic appointment is wealthy and can afford to spend money in entertaining is a powerful argument in his favor.

A minister who lives in an economical manner that would command respect at home, has little social standing or influence abroad, for he is recognized as the representative of a powerful and wealthy nation and is expected to maintain a corresponding style of living.

In the absence of great questions there is a multitude of routine duties to keep a minister busy, and he is expected to show some attention to his fellow-citizens who visit the country in which he is residing. They want to be presented at court or obtain admission to public and private places of interest, and they even ask him to recommend tailors for themselves and dressmakers for their wives. The legations have regular office hours, and their business is transacted with a great deal of formality. Their dispatches must be prepared according to a certain form; and copies made in a book kept for that purpose. All letters they receive must be preserved, registered, indexed, and filed, and a daily journal kept of the transactions of the legation.

CHAPTER II.

THE CONSULAR SERVICE.

THE consular service is entirely different and distinct from the diplomatic service. The envoy extraordinary and minister plenipotentiary is an agent of the government to conduct its business with another government. A consul is the representative of the people to look after the commercial interests of his country, and their business is with local officials, and exporters and importers. They have no diplomatic powers or privileges, and are stationed at commercial centers for the purpose of facilitating trade and preventing fraud upon the revenues of their country.

The consular service is the direct and necessary result of commerce, and in early times consuls were selected by mercantile associations and not by governments. They were formerly judges or arbitrators in the settlement of differences between merchants, and were known as judge-consuls, or consul-judges, taking their title from that of the municipal magistrates of the Roman Empire. This practice was continued for centuries. It is said that the first appointment of a consul by the government of England was at the request of a British commercial organization in an Italian city which could not agree in the selection of one of their own number, and the experiment was so successful that the government assumed the responsibility in other cases, and the practice became general among all governments. By the natural evolution of affairs the powers and duties of consuls became changed and enlarged, and the organizations of courts, and the adoption of codes of international law deprived them of their judicial duties.

The consular service of the United States was established by law in 1792, but before that date Washington had appointed seventeen consuls and five vice consuls. Under this law the secretary of state had the right of appointment, and no salaries were paid. The consuls got their compensation in the form of fees received for the services they performed, and were usually merchants or shipping agents at foreign ports. In 1816 an attempt was made to reorganize the system and establish a salaried corps, and it was repeated at subsequent sessions of Congress, but the present service was not established until 1856, when the President was empowered to make the appointments, subject to the approval of the Senate, and the consulates were graded according to their importance. The present establishment is awkward, and in many respects defective, and it is universally agreed by all who are familiar with the subject that its efficiency could be vastly increased by reorganization. At every session of Congress bills are reported for this purpose, but political influences and differences of opinion as to the best methods to be adopted have prevented the passage of a new law.

Under the laws of the United States no especial training or qualifications are required for the consular service, and appointments are made by the President for political and personal as well as for commercial reasons. Nor is there any specific term of office, the commission being revoked at the will of the President. But consuls are not expected to tender their resignations with a change of administration as diplomatic officers do. They continue to perform their duties until their resignations are tendered voluntarily or at the request of the Department of State. There have been several attempts in Congress to make the corps permanent and provide for appointments and promotions on the basis of special qualifications and efficiency, but political considerations have prevented, and the offices are still deemed proper rewards for political services. That the usefulness of the service is impaired by frequent changes and the appointment of inefficient and inexperienced men, there is no doubt; because it requires from six months to a year for a consul to become familiar with his duties, and his ignorance of the language of the country in which he is stationed detracts greatly from his efficiency.

To secure an appointment in the British consular corps a person must undertake a course of study and then submit to an examination. He must be able to read and write and speak fluently the language of the country to which he is sent; he must be familiar with commercial usages, have a thorough knowledge of commercial law, and be versed in statistics. Before he starts for his post he must serve at least three months in the consular bureau of the Foreign Office, and is usually required to serve as vice consul for a year or more before he is given a permanent place. In fact the greater portion of the British corps have commenced their career as consular clerks.

The French system is even more severe in its requirements. In France young men are educated especially for the consular service and must obtain a diploma from the national schools. The first appointment is made to the lowest grade, after an examination in international and commercial law, political economy, geography, statistics, tariff regulations, and the modern languages. Three years' experience in one grade is required before a consul can be promoted to the next, and a new examination is necessary each time.

Similar requirements govern appointments and promotions

in the German, Belgian, Austrian, Italian, and other European consular corps.

There are, however, a number of consuls in the service of the United States who have been retained for years, and promoted from time to time, because of their especial fitness and efficiency. The oldest officer holds a commission dated in 1848, and there are several who have served continuously for sixteen, eighteen, and twenty years.

Under the present law the service is classified into several grades : (1) consuls general; (2) consuls; (3) vice consuls; (4) deputy consuls; (5) commercial agents; (6) consular clerks. These are subdivided into three classes : (*a*) consuls who receive fixed salaries, are required to give their entire time to their duties, and are not permitted to engage in private business; (*b*) those who receive fixed salaries, but are allowed to engage in private business; (*c*) those who receive compensation from fees collected for official services performed and are allowed to engage in private business. All those included in classes *a* and *b* must be confirmed by the Senate.

A consul general is usually stationed at the chief commercial city of the country in which he resides, and has supervision over all the consuls in that country, but there may be two or more consuls general in the same country, each with his own district and jurisdiction. He may appoint his own vice consul and deputy consul and the consular agents in his district, subject to the approval of the secretary of state. The vice consul receives no salary and is not required to perform any duties except in the absence of his chief, but is generally a clerk in the office of the consul, and takes his place and receives his compensation during his absence. A deputy consul is a permanent official who receives a fixed compensation from the fees collected in the office, and assists the consul in the performance of his duties.

A commercial agent differs from a consul only in rank and grade, and is entitled to the same rights and privileges; he is appointed by the President without submitting the nomination to the Senate.

Consular agents, however, are only the representatives of the consul of the district in which they serve, and derive their powers from him and not directly from the government, although their duties are the same. They are not authorized to correspond with the Department of State, but make their reports to and receive their instructions from the consul.

There are two classes of consular clerks. There are thirteen clerks in the service who are appointed by the secretary of state, and hold commissions from him during good behavior, with salaries of $1,000 and $1,200 a year. It was designed by Congress when the law authorizing their appointment was passed, to make the corps of consular clerks a training school for the education of consuls, but the intention has not been carried out. The other class are temporary clerks, appointed by the consuls, with the approval of the secretary of state, and paid from the fees collected in the office.

The consuls of the United States may be described as trade sentinels stationed at the chief cities of the world, to keep their commander, the secretary of state, promptly and fully informed of all matters and events of commercial interest, to prevent frauds upon the revenues by certifying to the correctness of the invoices of goods exported to this country, and to notify the government at Washington of any attempt at smuggling which they may suspect or detect. They are charged in a general way to protect the interests of their fellow-citizens who may be residing in the district over which they have jurisdiction; to inform the government of the violation of treaties; to give advice and assistance to merchants and shipmasters that may visit their ports; to prevent the emigration of paupers and criminals to the United States; to look after sick and indigent citizens of their own country; and to take charge of the property of those who die. They are given police jurisdiction over the merchant marine of the United States, and have power to decide disputes between shipmasters and members of their crews, to arrest deserters from ships, to investigate shipwrecks, and send home discharged, disabled, or shipwrecked seamen. They are also required to investigate and report upon all arrests of American citizens charged with crime; to see that their interests are properly protected in the courts, and that the stipulations of treaties covering such cases are complied with.

A consul is also required to certify in triplicate to the accuracy of the invoices of all goods shipped to the United States. He not only takes the oath of the merchant or manufacturer who ships them, but must have an accurate knowledge of the value of the goods in order to prevent perjury and fraud in undervaluations. Of these triplicate invoices, one is filed in the consulate; one is forwarded to the collector of the port to which the goods are sent, and the third is given to the shipper, who sends it to the person for whom they are intended, for use in securing their admission through the custom house and in paying the duties assessed upon them. For this service he charges certain fees which are fixed by law. He must keep an accurate record of all invoices also, with the fees collected, and at the end of each quarter forward a copy to the secretary of the treasury at Washington.

He must register and report the arrival and departure of every ship that visits his port, inspect and sign the manifestoes of their cargoes; forward a list of passports issued or viséd; a list of the marriages and deaths of American citizens within his jurisdiction; and at stated times furnish the Department of State with a list of such citizens residing in his consular district. He must furnish quarterly, too, a report covering all the transactions of his consulate, his receipts and expenditures of money, etc. He must frequently inform the secretary of the treasury of the sanitary condition of the port at which he is located, notify him by cable of the departure of vessels infected with contagious diseases, and certify to bills of health.

He is required to keep pace with the progress of industry and commerce in his district, report promptly all important inventions and discoveries, all improvements in manufactures and agriculture, changes in tariff laws and regulations, tonnage and harbor dues and regulations, changes in lighthouses, buoys, beacons, shoals, and such other information as may be useful to those engaged in commerce and navigation.

At stated periods he must forward full reports and statistics concerning commerce, navigation, finances, immigration, agriculture, mining, fisheries, forestry, manufactures, population, the prices of merchandise, wages of labor, and such other matters as may be of interest to the people of the United States. At intervals the Department of State issues circulars to the officers of the consular service calling for specific information of importance to the various branches of industry and commerce in this country. This information and the regular reports of consuls are published by the Department in pamphlet form for free distribution to the public. Briefs or proof sheets are first furnished to the news agencies at Washington, and then the publications are issued in permanent form. They have proved to be of the greatest value.

There are thirty-four consuls general, who receive salaries varying from $2,000 to $6,000, one consul at Liverpool receiving $6,000, one at Hong-Kong receiving $5,000, eight receiving $3,500, twenty-one receiving $3,000, twenty-eight receiving $2,500, forty-eight receiving $2,000, eighty-two receiving $1,500, and the remainder $1,000 each. There are also 378 consular agents receiving fees limited to $1,000 a year.

The compensation of a consul, however, is not limited to his salary. He is authorized to collect two kinds of fees, official and unofficial. The services for which official fees may be charged are defined in the consular regulations and must be reported to the treasury. Consuls who receive fixed salaries may deduct the amount from the official fees they collect, and also whatever is allowed them for the expenses of their office. A consul whose compensation depends upon the fees of his office must report all his collections, but is not required to report his expenditures.

Unofficial fees may be collected for services not enumerated in the consular regulations, and need not be reported. The amount of such fees is variable and depends upon the location. They are derived chiefly from notarial acts: for preparing papers, attesting documents, witnessing signatures, taking depositions and other testimony, for collecting debts, managing estates, and for performing other service not strictly within the line of duty. In the larger cities of Europe these fees amount annually to a considerable sum, often greater than the salary of the consul.

The allowances to consuls for office expenses are very moderate, and are made under fixed regulations, dependent, however, upon the appropriations by Congress.

The salaries paid consuls by other governments are much larger than those allowed by the United States. Our consuls at London and Paris receive $6,000 a year, while the British consul at New York receives $12,500, and the French consul $12,000. Our consul at Berlin receives $4,000 and the German consul at New York, $10,000. Our consul at St. Petersburg receives $3,000 and the Russian consul at New York, $10,000. Our consul at Frankfort receives $3,000 and the German consul at Chicago, $5,000.

The consul, after his appointment, is allowed thirty days to close up his private affairs and to receive instructions, and a certain number of days, fixed by the regulations according to distance, for reaching his post. He is also allowed thirty days each year, or sixty days every two years, when he may be absent from his post. He cannot enter upon his duties until he has received what is called an *exequatur* from the government under which he is to reside. This is an official document given him by the Department of Foreign Affairs, acknowledging his appointment and recognizing his authority. Sometimes the *exequatur* is refused, perhaps on account of the personal character of the consul, or because he has said or done something offensive to the people among whom he is to reside.

His first duty upon receiving his *exequatur* is to receive the records and property of the consulate, and sign a duplicate inventory and receipt, for the protection of his predecessor. One copy is left on file in the consulate and the other is forwarded to the Department of State. He then makes calls of ceremony upon the officials of the city and upon the other members of the consular corps, and sends official notifications of his arrival to the other United States consuls in the vicinity of his post.

The social position of a consul depends entirely upon his personal character and attainments, exactly as it would at home. He receives invitations to participate in official ceremonies, but, unlike a diplomatic agent, he is not expected to entertain unless he cares to do so, and his social relations with the people where he resides are not governed by his official position.

CHAPTER III.

THE FOUNDING OF THE SOUTH AMERICAN REPUBLICS.

To UNDERSTAND properly the history and growth of diplomatic relations between the United States and the other nations of América, some knowledge of the events which led to the separation from Spain of her colonies on this continent is necessary. For nearly two and a half centuries the whole of South America, except Brazil, was governed by a viceroy residing at Lima, and the Spanish colonies in North America by a viceroy at the City of Mexico. Courts of justice, called Audiencias, were established in the several provinces, and their presidents, with the title of governor, or captain-general, exercised executive authority subject to the central power in Peru and Mexico. The Audiencia of Upper Peru, or what is now known as Bolivia, sat at Charcas; that of Chile at Santiago; that of Ecuador at Quito; that of Colombia, or New Granada, at Bogota; that of Central America at Guatemala; that of Venezuela at Carácas; and that of the United Provinces of the Rio de la Plata (Paraguay, Uruguay, and the Argentine Republic), sometimes at Asuncion, and often at Buenos Aires. Brazil, while under Spanish domination, from 1582 to 1640, was ruled by an Audiencia at Rio de Janeiro, but became a viceroyalty when the authority of Portugal was restored.

The policy of Spain was to restrain rather than to promote the development of her colonies in America; to strip them of everything that would bring profit to the crown, and to enforce a monopoly of commerce with the mother country. All industries that would compete with Spanish interests were prohibited; no goods could be imported from, and no products exported to any other country. The natives were enslaved, and citizens of Spanish birth were compelled to pay heavy tribute to the crown and to the church. But the growth of population made this form of government unwieldy, and the exclusive policy bred discontent. In 1740 therefore, a division of the southern continent was made, and a third viceroy was established at Bogota, in charge of the Northern Provinces of Ecuador, Columbia, and Venezuela. In 1776 a fourth was stationed at Buenos Aires to govern the Southern Provinces.

There were frequent, spasmodic attempts at resistance to Spanish tyranny during all these centuries, but they were directed only at unpopular governors or oppressive edicts. It was not until after the successful revolution in North America, and the establishment of the republic of the United States, that the thoughts of leading minds, and the efforts of patriotic statesmen were directed to actual independence.

Francisco Miranda, who was the leader of South American independence, was a native of Carácas, Venezuela. His family were of Spanish origin, and prominent among the colonial nobility. They had large estates and great wealth and, like other young men of his class, he was sent to Europe to complete his education. In Paris he met the Marquis de Lafayette, who had already been engaged in the war of the Revolution, and had returned to France for funds and reinforcements. Miranda, then about twenty-four years of age, was one of the first to enlist, and, reaching Boston, was given a position upon the staff of Washington. He fought through the war, and upon the organization of the government of the United States, having become inspired with the example of Washington, decided to attempt the liberation of his own country. Collecting a small company of adventurers from among his comrades of the continental army, he sailed from New York, and landed upon the coast of Venezuela, where he raised the standard of liberty and issued a proclamation calling upon his fellow countrymen to assert their independence. But public opinion had not been educated to a point favorable to such radical measures. Miranda was easily overcome by the forces of the Spanish governor. Some of his companions were shot, some were imprisoned, and his life was spared only through the intercession of his family and friends. Being banished, he returned to Europe, and remained for a time in France, where he endeavored to raise money and men to renew the attack. Then, attracted by the splendors of the court of Catherine the Great, he went to St. Petersburg, and spent several years as the favorite and acknowledged lover of that remarkable empress.

Miranda was a man of great accomplishments—a poet, a wit, and a musician; and behind the gay manners of a courtier he concealed the motive of his life. But he failed to enlist the sympathy of Catherine in his plan to liberate Venezuela, and when the French Revolution broke out, he returned to Paris, and was made a General of Division. Being defeated in battle he was deprived of his command, and went to London where he lived a miserable existence, in garrets and in gutters, writing songs and pamphlets, until he was rescued by Simon Bolivar.

The latter, thirty years younger than Miranda, was also a native of Carácas, a man of similar family and large estates. He also had gone to Europe to finish his education. Before leaving Venezuela, Bolivar had become infected with the revolutionary fever, and during a tour through the United States had visited the tomb of Washington, where, in a dramatic manner, he dedicated his life to the cause of Venezuelan independence.

The invasion of the Spanish peninsula by Napoleon in 1808, and the establishment of his brother upon the throne at Madrid, were the direct cause of the revolution in South America, for at Carácas the governor as well as the people declined to recognize the authority of Joseph Bonaparte. But a propaganda had been actively engaged since the ineffectual attempt of Miranda, and the people were now ready to throw off the yoke. Bolivar had been very active, with a number of other young men of aristocratic lineage, and in 1811, when he returned to Venezuela with Miranda, an organization was easily effected. On the 5th of July, 1811, a mass meeting of citizens was called in the Council chamber at Carácas, a declaration of independence was prepared and signed, and the republic of Venezuela was proclaimed with Miranda as military and political chief. The document, faded with age, still hangs in the room where it was written and signed, and beside it a massive painting representing the scene.

The Spanish governor at once abdicated, but Spain sent ten thousand men to Venezuela to recover authority. Miranda prepared to meet them, organized an army, and was about to take the field, when an awful earthquake occurred, which destroyed the greater part of Carácas, and buried several thousand of his soldiers in the ruins. The priests, always loyal to the crown, proclaimed the catastrophe as a righteous judgment of God upon the revolutionists, and the Spanish army took possession of the city before the moans of the dying had ceased. Miranda was captured and sent to Spain, where he died in prison. Bolivar escaped to the interior, and finally made his way to Jamaica, where he awaited developments.

The next revolution was in Chile, and was equally unfortunate; but in Buenos Aires the attempt was more successful, and in 1813 an independent government was established. General San Martin, the leader of the movement there, raised an army, which he led across the Andes to the aid of the Chilian revolutionists, and succeeded in driving out the Spaniards. But it was not until 1818 that the republic of Chile was organized. Before this time the epidemic of revolution had spread throughout all South America. Peru was the next point of attack, and the successful revolutionary party in Chile sent a fleet and an army there. In the meantime Bolivar had accomplished the independence of Venezuela, and had driven the Spanish army from Colombia. The republic of New Granada was formed by the two provinces with Bolivar as President. Ecuador was soon after added. Then Bolivar, at the head of his army, marched to the aid of the patriots in Peru, where he attacked the Spaniards from the north while San Martin and O'Higgins of Chile were following the conquest from the southward. In September, 1823, the two revolutionary forces met at Lima, where Bolivar was proclaimed Dictator, and the Spaniards withdrew. He then assembled the united armies for an attack upon Bolivia, the last of the provinces that remained under Spanish authority. On the 7th of December, 1824, on the little plain of Ayacucho, 11,600 feet above the sea, the last battle of the war for the possession of the continent occurred. The Spaniards were overcome, the independence of Upper Peru was declared, and a new republic formed, christened Bolivia in honor of the great Liberator. General Sucre was elected President, and Bolivar made a triumphant return to Lima. He soon afterwards resigned the presidency of Peru and returned to Bogota, where, after a turbulent administration of four years, he retired to the little city of Santa Marta, on the coast of Colombia and died impoverished in 1830.

The Republic of New Granada soon dissolved. Geographical conditions forbade its existence, and three independent states, Colombia, Venezuela, and Ecuador, were founded with the original colonial boundaries as their limits. Uruguay and Paraguay were separated from the Argentine Republic about 1828, and became independent nations.

When Napoleon took possession of Portugal in 1808, the king fled to Brazil and remained there until 1821. Then, upon his return to Lisbon, the independence of the colony was declared and Dom Pedro I., the eldest son of King Joam VI. of Portugal, was made emperor. In 1831 he was succeeded by his son, the late Dom Pedro II., who ruled until the republic was established in 1889.

Mexico had obtained her independence after a long and bloody struggle; in Central America the Spanish standard fell without a blow; but the far-reaching vision of Bolivar, who was the ablest man the southern continent has produced, saw the necessity of close political and commercial relations between the newborn republics in order that they might maintain their integrity and independence, for he said, "the will of God has not separated them without purpose, by the immensity of two oceans, from the rest of the world." He did not advise the consolidation of America under a single government or the establishment of a confederation, but his genius realized that a strong bond of union and sympathy between the recently created republics was necessary to preserve their peace, to promote their prosperity, and to protect them from the powers of Europe, who regarded their independence with the greatest apprehensions.

In 1815, Bolivar, then only about thirty years of age, was an exile in Jamaica. The cause of independence had suffered reverses throughout the entire continent. The revolutionary armies had been dispersed. The Spaniards had recovered control of most of their provinces, and seemed likely to resume their autocratical government over the remainder. To most of the patriots the future seemed hopeless. It was then that he wrote his famous "prophetic letter," addressed to some unknown friend. It is one of the most remarkable documents in history, not only from the clearness with which he explained the motives of the revolutionists and the reasons for the reverses they had suffered, but because of the wonderful accuracy with which he predicted the course of the struggle for independence, the final triumph, and the events that happened during the subsequent half century.

"It is difficult for me, or for any one else, to predict exactly the future condition of the New World, state the policy that it will pursue, or even prophesy the forms of government which will be adopted in it. . . . I consider the state of America, just at this moment, to be about the same as the state of Europe, when, upon the fall of the Roman Empire, each detached section constituted itself separately, according to its own interests or its geographical situation or perhaps the individual ideas or ambition of political leaders. . . . But in spite of these difficulties," Bolivar added that he would venture "a kind of guess about the future of America, mere conjecture," he said, "which at once I admit to be arbitrary, and dictated more by a reasonable desire than by probable reasoning."

The internal discussions and civil strife which he foresaw, and of which he had already no inconsiderable experience, found in his mind an easy explanation, in the fact that "the position in which the inhabitants of the American continent had been held for centuries had been purely passive, that they had been kept completely unacquainted with political life, and reduced to a state lower than slavery, which rendered it more difficult for them to raise themselves to the enjoyment of liberty." "Besides being deprived," he said, "of the rights which belonged to us, we were left, as far as public matters are concerned, in a state of permanent infancy . . . and in regard to matters of state, and to the science of administration of the government, we found ourselves as if absent, or cut off, from the rest of the world." . . . And now "we see ourselves called upon, suddenly, without any previous preparation, and what is more to be lamented, without any practical knowledge of public affairs, to act on the stage of the world the eminent part of legislators, judges, financiers, diplomatists, and generals, and to exercise authority in all degrees, from the supreme to the most subaltern position, filling all the offices which constitute the hierarchy of a well-regulated state. . . . Can it be expected that we may at once be able to keep the scale at its just equilibrium, and fulfil without difficulty the arduous task of conducting a republican government? Can it be imagined that a people, whose chains have just been broken, will enter the life of liberty, without being liable, like a new Icarus, to see its wings melted and to fall into the abyss? Such a prodigy would be inconceivable: and no reasoning or desire can ever induce us to entertain such hope."

The Liberator thought that Mexico would be a republic, with a tendency to a personal form of government, wherein the executive would be invested with great power, and where the stability of the institutions would depend primarily on the character of the individual into whose hands the management of public affairs would be placed.

"The states of the Isthmus of Panama," he said, "will form perhaps a union. That magnificent portion of America, situated between the two oceans, will be in due time the emporium of the universe. Its canals will shorten the distance which separates the nations of the earth, and will render the commercial ties which connect Europe, America, and Asia, closer and stronger. The yieldings of the four parts of the earth will be brought as a tribute to that happy section of the world. Perhaps the true capital of the earth might be established there, and be made exactly what Constantine desired that Byzance should be.

"New Granada may be united to Venezuela; and if they can agree to centralize their governments and form a republic, their capital must be Maracaibo, or, if not, a new city, which might be called Las Casas, in honor of that hero of philanthropy, and could be founded with advantage at the magnificent port of Bahia Honda, on the dividing line of the two countries. . . . The government of this republic will be shaped on the same plan as the British government, with the only difference that instead of a king the nation shall have at her head a chief executive magistrate, elected by the people, . . . a hereditary senate, which in all political storms, may interpose itself between the popular waves and the executive arm . . . and a popular house, consisting of members freely elected by the people. . . . But if New Granada does not consent to form with Venezuela a central government . . . the state formed by herself alone may be very happy and prosperous, because of the immense resources which she possesses.

"We know very little of what is going on in Buenos Aires . . . but judging by appearances the government will be centralized, and the military element will prevail in it, owing to its dissensions at home, and its wars abroad. It is possible for said government to degenerate into an oligarchy, or a more or less restricted monarchy, under some name which no one can guess. I have to say, however, that such result would be deplorable to the extreme, because the people of that country are entitled to splendid glory.

"The kingdom of Chile is called by nature, by its situation, by the habits and customs of its inhabitants, and by the example of its neighbors, the proud republicans of Arauco, to enjoy the blessings of just laws and republican institutions. If any republic is to last long in America, I am inclined to think that that one will be Chile. The spirit of liberty has never been extinguished there, and the vices of Europe and Asia will never come, or will come very late, to corrupt the habits of that remote corner of the universe. Its territory is limited, and always will be free from the infectious contact of the rest of mankind; its laws and usages will not be easily changed; the uniformity of its political and religious ideas will be preserved; and in a word, Chile will be free.

"Peru, on the contrary, has two elements which are thoroughly inimical to any kind of just and liberal system of government—gold and slaves. The former corrupts all things; the latter is itself already corrupted and rotten.

"From all the above stated the following conclusions can be easily reached. First: the American provinces now fighting for independence will succeed in securing it. Second: some of them will become in a regular way federal republics, where centralization will prevail; but monarchies will be founded, almost unavoidably, in those whose area is more extensive. Third: some of the new nations will be unhappy enough to exhaust in revolutions their great resources, rendering the establishment of a great monarchy difficult, and the establishment of a great republic impossible.

"It is a grand idea to try to make out of the whole New World only one nation, united by strong bonds, firmly connecting all its sections with each other and with the whole. As it has the same origin, the same language, the same habits, the same religion, it might have the same government, ruling over the different confederated states. But such a thing is an impossibility, because remote climates, different situations, conflicting interests, dissimilar characters, divide America. How beautiful would it be that the Isthmus of Panama should become for us what the Corinthian Isthmus was for the Greeks. Would to God that some day we may be fortunate enough to establish an august Congress of Representatives of the Republics, Kingdoms, and Empires of America, which will deal with the high interests of peace and of war between this continent and the other three parts of the world. An assembly of this kind may possibly be held at some future time, and mark a happy stage in the history of our progress. All other expectations are unfounded."

CHAPTER IV.

DIPLOMATIC RELATIONS WITH THE OTHER AMERICAN REPUBLICS.

WHEN the independence of the Spanish American colonies was established, and Bolivar returned to Lima, he wrote a proclamation of congratulation to his soldiers: "You have given freedom to South America, and a fourth part of the world is the monument of your glory." Almost at the same time and with the same pen he prepared his celebrated circular of December 7, 1824, inviting all the nations of America to send delegates to a conference at Panama. "After fifteen years of sacrifice," he said, "devoted to the liberty of America, to secure a system of guaranties that in peace and war shall be the shield of our new destiny, it is time that the interest and sympathy uniting the American republics should have a fundamental basis that shall perpetuate, if possible, their governments." He proposed a congress of plenipotentiaries from each state "that shall act as a council in great conflicts, to be appealed to in case of common danger, be a faithful interpreter of public treaties, when difficulties shall arise, and conciliate all our differences."

The first nation to accept was Colombia, then Mexico, Chile, and the others in order, but Bolivar sent no invitation to the United States. He foresaw opposition to such a conference from the slaveholding element in this country, for the principal features in his great plan of future operations were the liberation of Cuba, Puerto Rico and other European colonies, and the abolition of slavery upon American soil. But for this well-known purpose Bolivar and the other South American patriots would have received more substantial assistance from the United States in their struggle for freedom. Early in the revolution he had declared himself an abolitionist, and was one in practice as well as in theory. If he had been permitted to remain at the head of the government of Colombia, slavery would have been abolished immediately after the establishment of independence. When the new republic of Peru presented him with a million dollars for his services in its behalf, he devoted the money to purchasing the liberty of a thousand slaves, and in a famous message to the Congress of Colombia he said:

"There must be no caste on this continent. There is no blood less noble than other blood. All is the same in the sight of God. All are heroes who enter the camps of the battalions of liberty, and all, whether white or black, are equally entitled to the just recompense of valor, of honor, of intelligence, of sacrifice, and of virtue."

These sentiments did not find favor on the northern continent, and the movements of Bolivar were regarded with apprehension by the public men of the southern portion of the United States. But the governments of Mexico and Colombia asked the United States to send delegates to the proposed conference, and in a message to Congress on the 6th of December, 1825, President John Quincy Adams announced that the invitation had been accepted. The information was not received with approval. On the 26th of the same month, Mr. Adams transmitted another message to Congress in which he explained at length the purpose of the conference, and asserted that "the moral influence of the United States may perhaps be exerted with beneficial consequences at such a meeting, and a decisive inducement with me for according to the measure, is to show by this token of respect to the southern republics, the interest we take in their welfare, and our disposition to comply with their wishes. Having been the first to recognize their independence, and sympathize with them so far as was compatible with our neutral duties in all their struggles and sufferings to acquire it, we have laid the foundation of our future intercourse with them in the broadest principles of reciprocity and the most cordial feelings of fraternal friendship. To extend those principles to all our commercial relations with them, and to hand down that friendship to future ages, is congenial to the highest policy of this Union, as it will be to all those nations and their posterity. In confidence that these sentiments will meet the approval of the Senate, I nominate Richard C. Anderson of Kentucky, and John Sergeant of Pennsylvania, to be envoys extraordinary and ministers plenipotentiary to the assembly of American nations at Panama, and William B. Rochester of New York to be secretary to the mission."

This message was accompanied by a long and able letter

from Henry Clay, then secretary of state, setting forth what he deemed to be the just and proper policy for the United States to pursue toward the young republics which had been founded upon the same principles and were actuated by the same motives that had caused ours to exist. This communication and others upon the same subject, which preceded and followed it, were among the ablest public papers from the pen of Mr. Clay. He had been one of the earliest and most ardent advocates of the independence of the Spanish colonies in America, and both in Congress and upon the platform during their entire struggle had demanded, with his well-known fervor and eloquence, that the sympathy of the people and the government of the United States should not be limited to formal words, but should take the form of active co-operation with money, and arms, and men. His speeches on this subject are among the most brilliant examples of his eloquence, and it was largely due to his eloquence that this government was persuaded to recognize the belligerent rights of the Spanish colonists during the war, and their independence as nations when their victory was finally achieved. As early as 1818 he declared himself in favor of the establishment of "a human freedom league" in America, in which all the people "from Hudson's Bay to Cape Horn should be united for defense against the crowned despots of Europe." He declared that through the power of example, as well as by its moral influence, the United States should take an active part in promoting the liberty of the American people, "until the American hemisphere should become a haven for freedom and for the lovers of freedom, and a union of republics would be formed upon the soil that was wet with the blood of patriots"; and he regarded the Congress at Panama as "the boundary stone of a new epoch in the world's history."

The zeal and eloquence of Mr. Clay were not without their

effect upon the cooler temperament of President Adams, who in subsequent messages to Congress continued to advocate participation by the United States in the Panama Congress. He expressed a doubt whether "such a favorable opportunity for subserving the benevolent purposes of Divine Providence" and "dispensing the promised blessings of the Redeemer of mankind" would ever again in centuries be offered to this government.

But the opposition of the slaveholding element in Congress and the Southern States was equally determined. The slaveholders saw in the Congress at Panama peril to their "peculiar institution," and resisted every form of foreign policy that might point directly or indirectly to its destruction. In the invitations to the Congress Hayti had been mentioned, and it was a name of ominous sound to the slaveholding aristocracy of the United States. The story of the successful negro revolution on that island was read with apprehension through the entire South, and, as Hayne, the eloquent orator of South Carolina declared, "furnished an example fatal to our repose." "Those governments," he said, alluding to the South American Republics, "have pro-  claimed the principles of liberty and equality, and have marched to victory under the banner of universal emancipation. You find men of color at the head of their armies, in their legislative halls, and in their executive departments."

The proslavery party had a majority in the Senate committee on foreign relations, and Mr. Mason of Virginia, the chairman, made a report dated January 16, 1826, recommending that the Senate disapprove the action of President Adams in accepting the invitation to participate in the Panama Congress, and refuse to confirm the nominations of delegates he had selected.

This report covers about thirty printed pages of the usual size, and ends by recommending the passage of the following resolution :

"Resolved, That it is not expedient at this time for the United States to send any ministers to the Congress of American nations assembled at Panama."

The committee took the ground that the measure was "new and untried" and "in conflict with the whole course of policy uniformly and happily pursued by the United States from almost the very creation of this government to the present hour." And then, after discoursing at length on the "undefined objects of this Congress, so imperfectly disclosed in the vague descriptions given of them," disposes of the subject of slavery and slave trade in the following words :

"Some of the sovereign states here represented (the states of the Union) were the first in the world to proclaim their abhorrence of this traffic (the slave trade). . . . The United States, however, have not certainly the right, and ought never to feel the inclination, to dictate to others who may differ from them on this subject; nor do the committee see the expediency of insulting other states, with whom we are maintaining relations of perfect amity, by ascending the moral chair and proclaiming from thence mere abstract principles, of the rectitude of which each nation enjoys the perfect right of deciding for itself."

In regard to Cuba and Puerto Rico, the report said : "The

committee are well aware that the United States can never regard with indifference the situation and probable destiny of the neighboring Spanish islands of Cuba and Puerto Rico; but so far from believing it expedient to discuss these subjects at a Congress of all the American states, and especially at this time, the committee consider the great probability that such a discussion might be forced upon the United States if they are there represented, furnishing in itself the strongest objections to the adoption of the measures proposed. . . . The very situation of Puerto Rico furnishes the strongest inducement to the United States not to take a place at the contemplated Congress, since by so doing they must be considered as changing the attitude in which they have hitherto stood as impartial spectators of the passing scenes, and identifying themselves with the new republics."

In regard to the promotion of commerce, the committee said: "In considering these reasons (for the promotion of trade between the American nations) it cannot escape the observation of any, that in manifesting a disposition to establish such commercial relations, the Southern American nations must have been actuated by the only motive that ever operates either upon nations or individuals in regard to their mere commercial intercourse,—a desire fairly to advance their own interests and a belief that they could by such means properly accomplish that end. . . . The interests of commerce are necessarily peculiar: they grow out of numerous circumstances produced by locality, population, manners, times, and other causes, not one of which exists alike in any two nations on the globe. Few general principles, therefore, can ever apply with equal truth to so many peculiarities, and such as do apply need not the sanction of solemn compact to give them effect. It may be very safely confided to the natural disposition of man, promptly to discover, and eagerly to advance, his own best interests."

It must be said, however, that the plan of General Bolivar was received with greater favor in England than in the United States. This was due largely to the fact that her com-

mercial interests, which are always most influential in the foreign policy of Great Britain, were then endeavoring to secure the monopoly of the markets of the Spanish American nations that has since been so firmly held, and, although not formally invited to do so, Great Britain sent a delegate to the Panama Congress, to witness and report upon the proceedings, if not to participate in them. The same course was taken by the government of the Netherlands.

In his plan for the Congress, and in his instructions to the delegates from Peru, of which republic he was then president, General Bolivar defined at great length his purpose in calling it together and the results he desired it to accomplish. He proposed (1) a compact of union for defense against Spain, and all other European powers upon the American hemisphere. (2) A declaration of the policy to be pursued by the American republics in their relations with the other powers of the world, "friendship for all and strict neutrality." (3) The independence of Cuba and Puerto Rico; and "if the Congress, sensible to the true interests of the countries represented in it, believes it advisable to free those islands, you should enter into a treaty setting forth in detail what forces of land and sea and what sum of money each state of America shall contribute for that important operation." (4) He proposed a uniform system of treaties of friendship, navigation, and commerce, and defining the powers and prerogatives of diplomatic and consular offices. (5) "Such an energetic and efficient declaration as that made by the President of the United States in regard to further European colonization on this continent, and in opposition to the principles of intervention in our domestic affairs." (6) A plan for the settlement of disputes between the American nations. (7) Some declaration as to the relations to be established with Hayti and Santo Domingo, "which have emancipated themselves from their mother country, but have not succeeded in obtaining recognition by any power, whether European or American." (8) The permanent definition of the boundaries between the new American republics. (9) The inauguration of "such measures as shall be deemed most efficient for the suppression of the slave trade in America."

There were several other items of lesser importance in the great scheme of Bolivar, but these serve to show his purpose, and the object for which the conference was called. But the results did not meet his expectations, nor did the action of the Congress receive his approval. The proceedings were shortened and the adjournment hastened by an epidemic of yellow fever which broke out at Panama, and one of the delegates from the United States died of that dreaded disease on his journey homeward. The delegates to the conference lacked wisdom and experience. They failed to appreciate both the sublime purpose which had inspired Bolivar in planning the assembly, and the importance of the work in which they were engaged, and nearly all of them having recently been participants in the struggle for independence, the ruling idea in their minds was to form an alliance for mutual and united resistance to any attempt that might be made by Spain to recover her lost provinces in America. They agreed upon a plan for a league or permanent union of the new republics, for the purpose of defense only, but it was cumbersome and complicated in its details. This league they proposed to have represented by an international assembly to meet biennially. They also provided for a permanent army of defense to which each republic should contribute its quota of men, and which should be directed and controlled by a central organization, subject to the approval of the international assembly.

The most important topics the Congress was called to consider were deferred to another meeting which was appointed for the next year at the picturesque town of Tacubaya, three miles from the city of Mexico. But that meeting never took place, nor did the proposed international legislature ever assemble. Only one government, that of Colombia, ratified the action of the Congress, and the plan for an American union was temporarily postponed. But the ideas and the motives of Bolivar were immortal, and the failure of the Congress at Panama did not cause them to be abandoned. Subsequent efforts in the same direction were periodically renewed and the movement finally culminated in the International American

Conference which met at Washington in 1889, where the representatives of eighteen nations met to consider plans for the unification of their interests, and to promote their common welfare and prosperity.

Five years after the return of the plenipotentiaries to their homes from Panama, the government of Mexico issued invitations to a similar conference but for some reason it was not held. Seven years later in 1838, Mexico renewed the endeavor, with a view to "the union and close alliance of the American republics for the purpose of defense against European invasion, the acceptance of the friendly mediation of the neutral states for the settlement of all disagreements and disputes of whatever nature which may happen to arise between the sister republics, and for the framing and promulgation of a code of public laws to regulate their mutual relations." The invitations were repeated in 1839 and in 1840, but without effect.

At last, in 1847 five of the South American republics united in a conference at Lima, at the invitation of Peru, but the United States being at war with Mexico, was not represented. The results of this meeting were a treaty of confederation, another of commerce and navigation, and conventions for the regulation of consular and postal affairs.

In 1864 the government of Peru made a second attempt to bring the American nations together, and a Congress met at Lima on the 14th of November, the birthday of Bolivar, at which Bolivia, Chile, Ecuador, Colombia, Guatemala, Peru, Venezuela, and the Argentine Republic were represented. The sessions were secret and short, and were reported to have been turbulent, but nothing was accomplished.

In 1878, also at the invitation of Peru, another conference was held at Lima, "to oppose the aggressions of foreign force, and to formulate the tables of the American Decalogue." Peru, the Argentine Republic, Chile, Bolivia, Ecuador, Venezuela, and Costa Rica were represented, and also Cuba, whose independence had been recognized by some of the South American republics. The results of the conference were treaties of international law and extradition which were afterwards ratified by Guatemala and Uruguay.

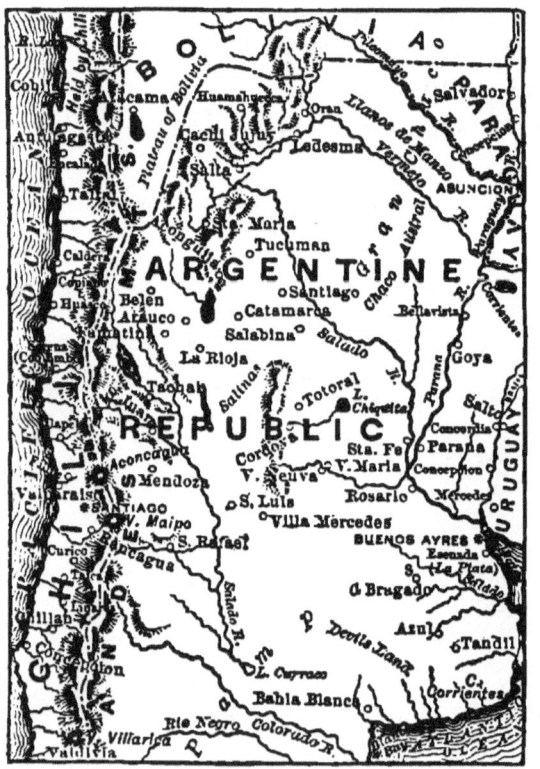

In 1880 the government of Colombia issued invitations to a conference at Panama, the chief object of which was to secure the adoption of some mode of arbitration to settle international differences; but the war in which Chile, Peru, and Bolivia were then engaged caused an indefinite postponement.

In the following year, however, the government of the United States issued similar invitations for a similar conference, to meet at Washington on the 24th of November, 1882, "for the purpose of considering and discussing methods of preventing war between the nations of America." "The President," said the secretary of state in his invitation, "desires that the attention of the congress shall be strictly confined to this one great object; that its sole aim shall be to seek a way of permanently averting the horrors of cruel and bloody combat between countries, often of one blood and speech, or the even worse calamity of internal commotion and civil strife; that it shall regard the burdensome and far-reaching consequences of such struggles, the legacies of exhausted finances, of oppressive debt, of onerous taxation, of ruined cities, of paralyzed industries, of devastated fields, of ruthless conscription, of the slaughter of men, of the grief of the widow and the orphan, of embittered resentments, that long survive those who provoked them and heavily afflict the innocent generations that come after.

"The President is especially desirous to have it understood that in putting forth this invitation the United States does not assume the position of counseling, or attempting, through the voice of the congress, to counsel any determinate solution of existing questions which may now divide any of the countries of America. Such questions cannot properly come before the congress. Its mission is higher. It is to provide for the interests of all in the future, not to settle the individual differences of the present. For this reason especially the President has indicated a day for the assembling of the congress so far in the future as to leave good ground for hope that by the time named the present situation on the South Pacific coast will be happily terminated, and that those engaged in the contest may take peaceable part in the discussion and solution of the general question affecting in an equal degree the well-being of all.

"It seems also desirable to disclaim in advance any purpose on the part of the United States to prejudge the issues to be presented to the congress. It is far from the intent of this government to appear before the congress as in any sense the protector of its neighbors or the predestined and necessary arbitrator of their disputes. The United States will enter into the deliberations of the congress on the same footing as the other powers represented, and with the loyal determination to approach any proposed solution, not merely in its own interest or with a view to asserting its own power, but as a single member among many co-ordinate and co-equal states. So far as the influence of this government may be potential it will be exerted in the direction of conciliating whatever conflicting interests of blood or government

or historical tradition may necessarily come together in response to a call embracing such vast and diverse elements."

Venezuela, Guatemala, Brazil, Salvador, Nicaragua, Honduras, Bolivia, Ecuador, and Mexico accepted, but in August, 1882, the invitations were withdrawn by Mr. Frelinghuysen, who had succeeded Mr. Blaine as secretary of state upon the death of General Garfield and the accession of Mr. Arthur to the presidency. The motive for the abandonment of the plan has been the subject of much controversy. The reason given in the circular issued by the secretary of state, was that "the peaceful condition of the South American republics, which was contemplated as essential to a profitable and harmonious assembling of the congress does not exist,"—Chile, Bolivia, and Peru being still engaged in war,—but the actual cause for the withdrawal of the invitation was the failure of the Congress of the United States to make the necessary appropriations for the expenses of the conference, and to grant authority for the appointment of delegates to represent this country.

President Arthur at no time desired or intended to prevent the consummation of the plan, which for sixty years had been discussed with so much favor among the American republics, but at once took measures to carry it into effect upon a scope much more comprehensive than had previously been proposed. He awaited the termination of the war upon the west coast of South America, and then introduced into the original plan of Bolivar a commercial feature which was very gratifying to the merchants and manufacturers of the United States who were beginning to feel the necessity of more extended and profitable markets for the disposition of the surplus products of the farms, the mines, the forests, and the factories of this country. Upon his recommendation, Congress authorized the appointment of a commission to visit the other American republics for the purpose of conferring with their governments as to the propriety of again calling together such a conference as had been so often proposed, and also as to the topics that should be considered by it. This commission consisted of George H. Sharpe of New York, Thomas C. Reynolds of Missouri, and Solon O. Thacher of Kansas, with William E. Curtis of Illinois as secretary. Afterwards, upon the resignation of Mr. Sharpe, Mr. Curtis was appointed a member of the commission.

Having visited each of the republics and the empire of Brazil in order, the commission made its report; recommending the assemblage of a conference, and enumerating the topics which it should be called to consider. Bills were introduced into both Houses of Congress to carry out these recommendations, and finally a law was passed authorizing the President to issue invitations, and providing for the expenses of the gathering.

The conference met at Washington upon the 2nd of October, 1889, every independent nation in America being represented except Santo Domingo; and afterwards, by special resolution of Congress the Hawaiian Kingdom was asked to participate. The government of Spain informally suggested that her American colonies, Cuba and Puerto Rico, would accept invitations, but none were extended.

Mr. Blaine was elected president, Mr. Romero of Mexico and Mr. Zegarra of Peru, vice presidents, William E. Curtis, executive officer, and Remsen Whitehouse, Fidele E. Pierra, and José Ignacio Rodriguez, secretaries; and the delegates from the United States were Messrs. John B. Henderson of Missouri, Cornelius N. Bliss of New York, Clement Studebaker of Indiana, T. Jefferson Coolidge of Massachusetts, William Henry Trescot of South Carolina, Andrew Carnegie of Pennsylvania, Morris M. Estee of California, John F.

Hanson of Georgia, Henry G. Davis of West Virginia, and Charles R. Flint of New York.

Immediately after the organization of the conference the foreign delegates, with their secretaries and *attachés*, to the number of 78, were conducted on a special train of Pullman cars through the country, and visited most of the principal educational, commercial, and manufacturing cities, where they were received with great attention and hospitality. The objects of this excursion were: (1) to give the visiting delegates, who included the leading men of the nations of America, an opportunity to study the institutions of the United States and witness the magnitude and the prosperity of our industrial and commercial interests; (2) to enable them by familiar contact to become thoroughly acquainted with each other before proceeding to the serious duties they had to perform; and (3) finally to awaken among the people of the United States an interest in the purpose of the conference and the objects it was desired to accomplish.

The sessions were resumed on the 18th of November, and continued until the 21st of April. The conference was only a deliberative body. It was authorized to discuss and recommend propositions for the subsequent ratification of the governments represented; and its conclusions took the form of a series of reports which embodied the views of the delegates—and in almost every case with unanimity—as to the best measures to promote the peace and prosperity of the American republics. These reports, which were able and voluminous, recommended:

1. The adoption of a plan of arbitration for the settlement of international differences, which was also earnestly recommended to the powers of Europe.

2. The denial of the right of conquest.

3. The adoption of a code of international law for the pro-

tection of the rights of citizens of one country residing in another.

4. The adoption of rules of procedure for the adjudication of claims of citizens of one country against the government of another, and to regulate diplomatic intervention.

5. The negotiations of treaties for the free navigation of all rivers on the American hemisphere.

6. The adoption of a uniform system of weights and measures throughout America.

7. The adoption of a uniform standard of value, and a common silver coin.

8. The establishment of an international banking system similar to the national banking organization of the United States.

9. The negotiation of treaties for the protection of patents and trademarks.

10. The negotiation of a uniform system of treaties for the extradition of criminals.

11. The survey of a route for an intercontinental railway to connect the roads of the United States with those of Chile and the Argentine Republic.

12. The negotiation of reciprocity treaties for the free interchange of the products of the American nations so far as is consistent with the raising of revenues for the support of their governments.

13. The establishment of more frequent lines of communication by steamship and telegraphy under governmental subsidies.

14. The preparation and publication of a uniform code of nomenclature to define articles of merchandise exported and imported.

15. The adoption of a uniform system for the classification and appraisement of merchandise imported.

16. The adoption of uniform consular fees and regulations.

17. The adoption of uniform harbor fees and regulations.

18. The adoption of uniform sanitary regulations to prevent the spread of contagious diseases.

19. The establishment of a Bureau of Information for the dissemination of intelligence of a useful character concerning the resources, progress, and commerce of the American republics.

CHAPTER V.

THE RESULTS OF THE INTERNATIONAL AMERICAN CONFERENCE.

THE International American Conference recommended the adoption of a uniform standard of value by the republics of this hemisphere, and the issue of common coins which should be coined by each to an amount proportionate to its population; to be of uniform design and of uniform weight and fineness; and to be legal tender in commercial transactions between the citizens of all; but, owing to the failure of the delegates from the United States to agree upon the weight and fineness of the coins and their relative value to gold, the details of the arrangement were deferred to the consideration of another conference to be held within one year at Washington.

In accordance with these recommendations, what is known as the International Monetary Conference was held at Washington in February, 1891. Nearly every one of the American republics was represented, but, after a protracted session, the assemblage was compelled to adjourn without accomplishing anything more than the passage of a series of resolutions acknowledging the usefulness, and commending the adoption, of a common standard of value and a uniform system of coinage. The reason for the failure of this Conference was the inability of the delegates from the United States to agree upon what is known as the "silver question." All of the other American nations urged the issue of an international coin of a value similar to that of the standard silver dollar of the United States, but to this the delegates from this government would not agree, and the subject after much discussion was postponed, as one of the foreign delegates observed, "until the United States had determined upon a silver policy."

The International Conference also recommended the survey of a route for an intercontinental railway, under the direction of a commission representing the several governments through whose territory it would pass. According to the recommendations of the Conference, which were ratified by all the American republics, the route of this proposed railway shall be always regarded as neutral ground; the property shall be always exempt from taxation; and all material for its construction and maintenance shall be admitted free of duty.

Commissioners were appointed by each of the republics, who met at Washington in January, 1891, and organized by the election of Mr. Alexander J. Cassatt of Pennsylvania as president, and by the appointment of the necessary committees. A chief engineer, W. F. Shunk of Pennsylvania, was selected, and under his direction three parties of surveyors were sent into the field. One party commenced work at the termination of the surveys already made by the government of Mexico at the Guatemala boundary (see map, page 57), and proceeded southward toward the Isthmus of Panama. A second party began at Quito (see map, page 48) and sought a route northward through Ecuador and Colombia, while a third started southward from Quito toward Peru and Bolivia. At this writing all of the parties are still in the field, making rapid progress and forwarding regular reports which indicate that the topographical difficulties are not so serious as were supposed.

It is the intention to continue these surveys until a route has been selected for a grand trunk line to connect the railway system of Mexico on the north with that of the Argentine Republic, which already extends to the boundaries of Bolivia. Then branch lines will be surveyed from some convenient point in Colombia to the populated section and seacoast of Venezuela and the head of free navigation on the Orinoco River. Another line will be surveyed from some point in Peru or Bolivia, eastward to Rio de Janeiro; and several western branches are planned from the main trunk, which will pass along the great basin between the two ranges of the Andes.

After the several routes have been surveyed, and the cost of construction determined, private enterprise will be given an opportunity to undertake the work of building the railway, with the assistance of the governments through whose territory it will pass. The amount and nature of this assistance has not been determined, but it is expected that each country will grant a liberal allowance of its public lands to those who engage in the promotion of the enterprise, and also financial assistance in the form of cash subsidies, to be governed by the mileage, or a guarantee of a certain rate of interest upon the investment required. It is the universal opinion that the construction of this railway will aid in the development of the natural resources of the countries of the southern continent to a greater degree than any other means that can be adopted; and that it will have the same effect upon the southern continent, with its vast mineral and agricultural wealth, that the building of the transcontinental railways has had upon the United States.

The Bureau of Information recommended by the International Conference was established in November, 1891, and has proved to be a very useful agency in promoting the social and commercial relations of the American republics and colonies. The institution is known as the Bureau of the American Republics and it is supported by contributions from the several countries participating in its advantages, assessed annually upon each in proportion to their respective populations. The purpose of the Bureau is to publish regular bulletins containing intelligence concerning the resources, products, industries, crops, commerce, laws, customs tariffs and regulations, and such other information as may be of educational and commercial value. It is its duty also to answer specific inquiries upon these and other subjects and to serve as a medium of communication for merchants and manufacturers who desire a knowledge of commercial opportunities and facilities for trade between the United States and the other countries of the American hemisphere.

The Bureau prepares and publishes annually in the English and Spanish languages a general handbook to the American republics; and is issuing a series of special handbooks to each of the countries south of the Gulf of Mexico and the Rio Grande. It has also issued a series of Commercial Directories, containing classified lists of merchants in the southern countries for the use of merchants and manufacturers in the United States in sending out catalogues and circulars; and a series of bulletins containing the customs tariffs and regulations of the several nations and colonies, and other bulletins containing codifications of their laws relating to patents, copyrights, trademarks, public lands, mines and mining, railway concessions, and other subjects of interest to persons engaged in commerce or desirous of making investments in the Latin-American countries.

The Bureau also prepares and furnishes daily to the newspapers and press agencies in Europe as well as in America articles containing information of general and current interest, which reach the readers of some fifteen thousand periodicals. The purpose in general is to awaken and promote an interest in the affairs of the other American republics, concerning which the people of the United States have hitherto had little knowledge.

What is known as the "reciprocity policy" was inaugurated by President Arthur in 1882. There had been reciprocity treaties between the United States and Canada, and the Hawaiian Islands, previous to this time, but the present movement to extend the export trade of the United States in the Latin-American republics and colonies began at that time. Railway communication having been opened with Mexico, it was believed that the geographical and political relations between the two countries, as well as their commercial welfare, justified mutual concessions in customs duties. Therefore General Ulysses S. Grant and Mr. William Henry Trescot, representing the United States, and Mr. Matias Romero and Mr. Estanislao Cañedo, representing the republic of Mexico, negotiated a treaty under which certain merchandise from this country was to be admitted into Mexico free of duties, and certain products from that country were to be admitted free into the United States. The ratifications were exchanged on the 20th of May, 1884, and formal proclamation of that fact was made on the 2d of June following. But although the limit of time was twice extended by diplomatic negotiation, the Congress of the United States failed to enact the legislation necessary to carry it into effect, and the treaty fell valueless on the 20th of May, 1887.

In 1884 Mr. John W. Foster, then minister to Spain, negotiated a similar treaty with that government, acting in behalf of its American colonies, Cuba and Puerto Rico. A third treaty was negotiated by Mr. Frelinghuysen, then secretary of state, with Mr. Manuel J. Galvan, a plenipotentiary appointed for that purpose by the government of Santo Domingo. Both of these treaties failed to receive the sanction of the Senate of the United States.

During the same year, as has been related, the South American Commission visited the several Latin-American republics, and in addition to its other duties it was instructed to initiate treaties with their governments similar to those already arranged with Mexico and Spain. With a single exception the governments visited expressed not only a willingness but a desire to enter into reciprocal commercial arrangements with the United States, and in several cases a preliminary understanding was reached.

Congress, in the act authorizing the meeting of the International Conference, designated as one of the topics for conservation "measures toward the formation of an American customs union, under which the trade of the American nations with each other shall, so far as possible and profitable, be promoted."

The Conference, having met, referred this proposition to a committee, which, after due consideration, reported that the systems of taxation and the condition of the public revenues of the Latin-American republics made such a customs union as had been proposed—that is a free interchange of merchandise—impracticable; but recommended the negotiation of commercial treaties embracing mutual tariff concessions, so far as could be done without impairing the revenues necessary to sustain their several governments.

On the 10th of June, 1890, the secretary of state handed this report and recommendation to the President with a letter in which he said:

"Fifteen of the seventeen republics with which we have been in conference have indicated, by the votes of their representatives in the International American Conference and by other methods which it is not necessary to define, their desire to enter upon reciprocal commercial relations with the United States; the remaining two express equal willingness, could they be assured that their advances would be favorably considered."

The last clause of this paragraph refers to Chile and the Argentine Republic, whose chief export is wool, and they would enter into reciprocity treaties with the United States only upon condition that wools of the coarser grades should be admitted free into the United States or at a rate of duty considerably below the present tariff on that article.

"To escape the delay and uncertainty of treaties," the secretary suggested "an amendment to the pending tariff bill authorizing the President to declare the ports of the United States free to all the products of any nation of the American hemisphere upon which no export duties are imposed, whenever and so long as such nation shall admit to its ports free of all national, provincial (state), municipal, and other taxes, our flour, corn meal, and other breadstuffs, preserved meats, fish, vegetables and fruits, cotton-seed oil, rice, and other provisions, including all articles of food, lumber, furniture and other articles of wood, agricultural implements and machinery, mining and mechanical machinery, structural steel and iron, steel rails, locomotives, railway cars and supplies, street cars, and refined petroleum. I mention these particular articles, because they have been most frequently referred to as those with which a valuable exchange could be readily effected. The list could no doubt be profitably enlarged by a careful investigation of the needs and advantages of both the home and foreign markets.

"The opinion was general among the foreign delegates that the legislation herein referred to would lead to the opening of new and profitable markets for the products of which we have so large a surplus, and thus invigorate every branch of agricultural and mechanical industry."

In conclusion the secretary of state observed, "Of course the exchange involved in these propositions would be rendered impossible if Congress, in its wisdom, should repeal the duty on sugar by direct legislation, instead of allowing the same object to be attained by the reciprocal arrangement suggested."

The suggestions contained in the letter of the secretary of state were not entirely new to Congress, having been offered to the committee on ways and means of the House of Representatives several months previous. The foreign delegates to the International American Conference had been observing with the greatest solicitude the progress of that committee in the preparation of what is popularly known as the "McKinley tariff bill." The voluminous and conflicting reports in the newspapers of what had been, or would be done with the tariff schedules in which were included the staple products and chief exports of the countries from which they came, afforded a topic of daily conversation more interesting and important than the questions under consideration in their own councils.

A protracted discussion in Congress finally resulted in what is known as the "reciprocity section" of the tariff bill, by which, although sugar, coffee, tea, and hides were included in the free list, the President was required after January 1, 1892, to impose a tax on those commodities when imported from countries whose tariff regulations "were reciprocally unequal and unreasonable"; or in other words, the United States proposed to favor those nations and those only that would grant something like equivalent favors in return.

Immediately upon the passage of this measure, diplomatic negotiations that had been interrupted by the tariff agitation in Congress were resumed. It may be said that such negotiations with special plenipotentiaries from the emperor of Brazil had been commenced as early as August, 1889, and that upon the establishment of the republic, they were immediately renewed. It was not so long, therefore, before an arrangement was concluded under which the Brazilian government authorized the admission into its ports, free of all duties, of the products of the farms and mines of the United States, all forms of machinery and railway supplies, agricultural implements, labor-saving machinery, and a considerable number of other articles, and the admission of a long list of other manufactured articles including wearing apparel, hardware, preserved meats, fruits and vegetables, lard, dairy products, lumber, furniture, wagons and carriages, at a rate of duty twenty-five per cent less than was imposed upon similar merchandise imported from other countries.

During the following months similar arrangements were entered into by Mr. John W. Foster, representing the United States, with the government of Spain, representing her American colonies, Cuba and Puerto Rico, and the ministers plenipotentiary of Mexico, Guatemala, Salvador, Nicaragua, Costa Rica, Colombia, Ecuador and Peru, and with the British minister representing the British colonies of Jamaica, Trinidad, British Guiana, Barbadoes, the Leeward Islands, and the Windward Islands.

It is too early clearly to demonstrate the results of the "reciprocity" policy, and the whole question is so closely connected with current partisan politics that it cannot appropriately be discussed in a book of this character. It is safe to say that the people as a whole heartily desire closer relations with the republics of South America, and unqualifyingly approve many of the plans that have been carried out. All favor "reciprocity" in so far as it means an increased demand for American products and manufactures. Those who have been the means of putting reciprocity to the test are confident of its great success and already point to statistics in support of their position. Certain it is that the people of the

United States are interested in the southern continent as never before. The political opponents of those who advocate the present "reciprocity policy," acknowledge the soundness of the general theory as far as it goes, but maintain that if a lowering or abolition of the tariff in the cases of certain countries is beneficial, the extension of reciprocal relations to all nations without distinction would be still better. The experience of the future must be the arbitrator in this as in many other questions.

CHAPTER VI.

GENERAL RELATIONS WITH THE AMERICAN REPUBLICS.

The independence of the Spanish American colonies was not recognized by the United States until 1822. As early as 1816 agents from Venezuela, Chile, Colombia, and the La Plata Provinces—now known as the Argentine Republic—arrived in this country, seeking the recognition of the several revolutionary organizations they represented, but their credentials were irregular and the President declined to receive them officially. Distrustful of the representations of these agents, but at the same time desirous of giving all lawful encouragement to the colonies that were struggling to attain their independence, the government sent a commission to inquire into their condition and to report upon the propriety of acknowledging the belligerent rights of the revolutionary parties. The reports were not encouraging. They declared that there was organized resistance to the Spanish authority, but no complete or regular government anywhere.

Not discouraged by the inquiries of the first commission, the government dispatched a second in 1820 to Chile and Buenos Aires, which were represented to have made the most substantial advance toward emancipation and constitutional government. Commodore Perry and Commodore Morris of the navy were also sent with fleets to both coasts of South America to keep the government posted as to the condition of

affairs, and the progress of events. At the close of the year 1821, the reports of these agents left little doubt as to the ultimate success of the provinces in their struggle for independence, and on the 8th of March, 1822, President Monroe sent a message to Congress in which he recited the history of that struggle and recommended their recognition as independent states. The message was referred to the appropriate committees, which shortly after submitted favorable reports, with the following resolutions :

"*Resolved*, that the Senate and House of Representatives concur in the opinion expressed by the President in his message of March 8, 1822, that the American provinces of Spain, which have declared their independence and are in the enjoyment of it, ought to be recognized by the United States as independent nations.

"*Resolved*, that the committee on ways and means be instructed to report a bill, appropriating a sum not exceeding $100,000, to enable the President to give due effect to such recognition."

These resolutions were passed and, accordingly, on the 4th of May following, Congress made the appropriation.

The Spanish minister at Washington immediately entered a protest, declaring that such action "can in no way now or at any time lessen or invalidate in the least the right of Spain to said provinces, or to employ whatever means may be in her power to reunite them to the rest of her dominion."

John Quincy Adams, who was secretary of state, replied at length to this communication, concluding his note with the words: "We (the United States) confidently rely that the time is at hand when all the governments of Europe, friendly to Spain, will not only concur in the acknowledgment of the independence of the American nations, but in the sentiment that nothing will tend more effectually to the welfare and happiness of Spain, than the universal concurrence in that recognition."

This was followed by a manifesto on the part of the king of Spain, protesting against the action of the United States as a violation of the best known maxims of the law of nations and as the unjustifiable sanctioning of the undefined right of revolutionary insurrection.

Under the authority of Congress above recited, the President, on the 27th of January, 1823, appointed Cæsar A. Rodney of Delaware as minister to the Argentine Republic; Herman Allen of Vermont to Chile; and Richard C. Anderson of Kentucky to Colombia, which then included Venezuela, Colombia, and Ecuador.

The first regular diplomatic representative to arrive in the United States from the Latin-American nations was Señor Don Manuel Torres, who was received as the minister of Colombia on the 17th of June, 1822.

On the 30th of October, 1823, Great Britain recognized the independence of the South American republics and in 1825 they were recognized by France.

On the 3d of October, 1824, the first treaty between the United States and a Spanish American nation was concluded at Bogota. On December 5, 1825, a treaty was made with the Central American States and shortly after similar conventions were entered into with the other American republics. The independence of Brazil was recognized in 1825, and that of Mexico in the same year.

The Navigation of the La Plata.

The Rio de la Plata, or the River Plate, as it is often but improperly termed (for the name means "The Silver River"), is the great artery of commerce by which the products of Southern Bolivia, the interior provinces of Southern Brazil, the northern provinces of the Argentine Republic and

Uruguay, and the republic of Paraguay reach the sea. (See map, page 58.) The Rio de la Plata itself is but a few hundreds of miles long, but with its great estuaries, the Uruguay, the Parana, and the Paraguay Rivers, furnishes nearly five thousand miles of navigable waters, and drains about one third of the great southern continent.

After attaining its independence in 1821, the Argentine Republic, then known as the United Provinces of Rio de la Plata, claimed the right to control navigation upon this great system, and to open or close it to commerce at will. This authority was disputed by Paraguay and Brazil, and resisted by England and France. But General Rosas, the Argentine dictator, was stubborn, and it was not until he was overthrown by General Urquiza, the governor of the Province of Entre Rios, with the assistance of Brazil, in 1851, that the navigation of these rivers was declared free to the ships of all nations.

The United States was the first country to avail itself of the privilege, and Lieutenant Thomas Jefferson Page, of our navy, was directed to explore and survey all of the rivers emptying into the Rio de la Plata. He sailed in the steamer *Water Witch*, and was accompanied by Robert C. Schenck of Ohio, then minister to Brazil and afterwards a famous statesman and general in our Civil War, and Mr. John S. Pendleton, *chargé d'affaires* at Buenos Aires. They concluded a commercial treaty with Paraguay, and at Buenos Aires met the ministers of England and France, who had instructions to make similar arrangements. But the Argentine Republic was again convulsed by civil war, the province of Buenos Aires having refused to submit to the authority of General Urquiza. The three plenipotentiaries undertook to settle the difficulty by acting as arbitrators, but failed. They then concluded with the two contending factions two treaties, identical in terms and text, which were signed on the 10th of July, 1853. Then a new difficulty arose. The province of Buenos Aires claimed the right to fortify a little island called "Martin Garcia," near the mouth of the Parana River, which Urquiza, representing the other provinces of the confederation, insisted should not be permitted on the ground that such fortifications would impede navigation. Finally the governments of Great Britain, France, and the United States agreed " to use their influence to prevent the possession of said island being retained or held by any state on the Rio de la Plata or its confluents which shall not have given its adhesion to the principle of free navigation."

After the treaty had been signed and ratified, the province of Buenos Aires protested, declaring that it was an independent power ; but the three governments declined to recognize the protest on the ground that Urquiza represented the other thirteen provinces of the Argentine Republic, which had consented to the treaty.

In the meantime the *Water Witch* had made careful surveys of all the rivers, even into the interior of Brazil, and the reports of Lieutenant Page, which were published by Congress, were received by all the commercial nations of the world as a most important contribution to the art of navigation.

A series of unfortunate incidents shortly afterwards brought the government of the United States into hostile relations with Paraguay. Mr. Edward A. Hopkins, a citizen of Vermont, resigned his commission in the navy to accept an appointment as the first consul of the United States in that republic. He was permitted to engage in business and, obtaining capital in the United States, started several cigar factories and other enterprises, including a steamboat company. He soon became obnoxious to the President, familiarly known in that country as the Tyrant Lopez I., and with other citizens of the United States, who had joined him in Paraguay, he was driven out of the country. His property was confiscated and some of his buildings destroyed. He afterwards presented a claim against Paraguay for damages amounting to several millions of dollars, and this claim has ever since been a subject of diplomatic correspondence. Mr. Hopkins was in Washington as late as 1891, urging the government to insist upon the payment of his claim, but in that year died at an advanced age.

The treaty that had been made with Paraguay, when presented for ratification, was found to be so defective, through the carelessness of Mr. Pendleton and an Englishman who had acted as his clerk and interpreter, that it was returned to Lieutenant Page in Paraguay for correction. Our government had been described in the document as "The United States of North America," and as "The North American Union," and there were thirty-two other similar errors.

Being angered at the transactions of Mr. Hopkins and other citizens of the United States, the Paraguayan tyrant declined to correct the treaty and returned the notes of Lieutenant Page unopened, on the ground that they were written in English and he was unable to read them. Page insisted upon the use of his own language and Lopez, claiming that this was an insult, commanded him to withdraw the *Water Witch* from Paraguayan waters, and issued a decree forbidding all foreign vessels of war from entering the rivers of the country. In descending the Parana in February, 1855, the *Water Witch* was fired upon by the garrison of a Paraguay fort and the helmsman was killed.

Our government then sent Mr. Richard Fitzpatrick as a commissioner to Paraguay to enter a remonstrance and at the same time to secure a correction of the treaty. He reached Asuncion, the capital, in November, 1856, but Lopez refused to receive him. Whereupon there was a long continued investigation by Congress, and President Buchanan in June, 1858, sent Mr. Jas. B. Bowlin as a second commissioner, with a fleet of nineteen vessels, and a force of 2,500 men. This show of force had its effect. The original treaty of 1853 was ratified, as corrected; another treaty for the protection of the rights of American citizens in Paraguay was negotiated, and an apology was offered for the attack upon the *Water Witch*.

Mr. Charles A. Washburn was sent to Paraguay as minister from the United States shortly after, and remained until 1868, when that republic and Uruguay were placed in charge of the same legation.

The Navigation of the Amazon.

In 1851 Lieutenants Herndon and Gibbon of the United States Navy were sent to Peru with instructions to explore the river Amazon (see map, page 60) for the purpose of ascertaining the extent of its facilities for navigation and the opportunities it afforded for commerce. As soon as their mission became known at Rio de Janeiro, the Brazilian government sent a commissioner to Peru and Bolivia to negotiate treaties "by which the citizens of the United States should be excluded from all participation in the navigation of the Amazon and its branches, and in the trade of the interior of South America." This movement on the part of Brazil was inspired by the influence of an English company which at that time was establishing trading posts along the Amazon under a concession which gave it a monopoly of the commerce. The treaty proposed was not negotiated with Peru, but another was concluded, which stipulated in general terms that the navigation of the great river should be controlled and regulated by the nations through whose territory it passed.

Lieutenant Herndon, who was in Bolivia at the time, succeeded in frustrating the designs of the Brazilian minister, and secured the promulgation of a decree granting to the subjects of all nations the free navigation of all waters flowing through Bolivian territory, and at the same time offering a subsidy or reward of $10,000 to the first steamer that should reach any town in that republic from the sea. The Brazilian government also attempted, but without success, to persuade Ecuador, Colombia, and Venezuela to extend to the Amazon Steamship Company a monopoly of the navigation of the branches of that river which flowed through their territory.

The United States remonstrated against the action of Brazil, and was soon joined by Great Britain and France, who demanded the free navigation of the Amazon and its branches and the abolition of any monopoly that might affect its commerce. The Brazilian government resisted, whereupon Mr. Marcy, who was secretary of state, wrote the United States minister at Rio de Janeiro, "Should you discover any reluctance on the part of the government to yield to this just claim, you will impress upon it the determination of the United States to secure it for their citizens. The President is desirous to cultivate the most amicable relations with that government, and would much regret to have these relations disturbed by a persistence in a policy that is so much at variance with all the liberal views of civilized and enterprising nations."

President Pierce made the controversy the subject of a message to Congress in 1853, in which he took firm ground in favor of the free navigation of all rivers, and announced that the United States would insist upon and enforce its rights upon the waters of the Amazon.

The Brazilian government replied that "it was not the intention of the imperial government to keep the Amazon forever closed to foreign commerce, but its opening does not seem to be as yet called for"; that Brazil believed it to be to her advantage as well as her right to afford the navigation of the river to individual nations, under treaty stipulations, rather than by general permission to all; that the western boundaries of the empire were still undefined, and that until they were determined delay was necessary.

The correspondence continued until 1861 when it was suspended by reason of the Civil War in the United States. In the meantime the monopoly of commerce upon the Amazon was maintained. In 1866, however, the emperor issued an edict which opened its waters to the commerce of the world.

The Annexation of Texas and the Mexican War.

The treaty of April 30, 1803, by which the United States acquired what was known as the "Louisiana territory" from France, said nothing of its extent, except that it was the territory which Spain had ceded to France in the treaty of San Ildefonso in 1800. The consequence of this omission was a long controversy with Spain. The United States claimed that the Rio Grande was the southwestern boundary, but the French ambassador, De Neuville, to whom the question was referred, decided in favor of the Sabine River—the present boundary between Louisiana and Texas. John Quincy Adams, then secretary of state, objected, but President Monroe and the remainder of the cabinet decided to accept the decision, so Mr. Adams was compelled to yield and a treaty to this effect was signed in February, 1819. This treaty caused great dissatisfaction in the Southern and Southwestern States, and particularly among the inhabitants of Texas, which was almost exclusively settled by emigrants from the United States.

In 1824 the constitution of the new Mexican republic united Coahuila, hitherto a separate province, and Texas as a single province, and a Mexican was placed in power as governor. He had much trouble with the American residents, and in 1830 President Bustamente of Mexico issued a decree forbidding further immigration from the United States. In 1833 the

American residents, then numbering from 20,000 to 25,000, held a convention and asked the Mexican government to permit them to organize a separate state. This was declined, and Colonel S. F. Austin, who carried the petition to Santa Anna, was thrown into prison. This was followed by a revolution and the organization of a republic under General Sam Houston in December, 1835. Santa Anna marched into Texas with a large army, captured the Alamo, a fortress at San Antonio, and massacred the entire garrison. The Mexican troops were finally driven out. A constitution was adopted in 1836, and in March, 1837, the United States recognized the new republic. Two years later England, France, Holland, and Belgium also recognized the independence of Texas. In 1841 and 1842 the Mexicans again attempted to recover the lost province without success, and in 1843 President Tyler made a treaty with the authorities of Texas for the annexation of the disputed territory to the United States. This treaty was denounced by Mexico, protests were made by the powers of Europe, and the Senate of the United States in 1849 refused to ratify it. But during the following year a joint resolution was adopted by Congress authorizing annexation, the Texan government accepted it and in December, 1845, Texas was formally admitted into the Union, the entire territory being ceded to the United States for the sum of $10,000,000, which was applied to the payment of the debts of the republic. This was the cause of the war between Mexico and the United States.

Mexico having formally protested against the annexation of Texas, Mr. Slidell was sent to the capital of that country to attempt a reconciliation, but the government declined to receive him, and in January, 1846, General Taylor was ordered to advance his army to the Rio Grande and fortify himself.

In February Captain John C. Fremont, who was conducting

a scientific investigation in the far West, entered Monterey, California, with his men and asked permission of the Mexican authorities to spend the winter there. Consent was originally granted, but, under instructions from the federal government at Mexico, it was afterwards withdrawn and an order was issued expelling all Americans from Mexican territory. Fremont withdrew to the neighboring mountains with the United States citizens then residing at Monterey, and fortified himself. This was considered by Mexico as an affront, and in April hostilities were begun on the Rio Grande. A few weeks later General Kearney took possession of Santa Fé and proclaimed the annexation of New Mexico and all territory north of the Rio Grande to the United States. After a series of engagements the city of Mexico was captured, and in February, 1848, the treaty of Guadalupe Hidalgo was signed, which ended the war and ceded New Mexico and California to the United States in return for the payment of $15,000,000.

In 1853 an expedition of filibusters was organized in California for the invasion of Lower California and other portions of Mexico. This called out a proclamation from President Pierce warning the citizens of the United States against all such undertakings and threatening the guilty with the utmost severity of the laws. But the popular cry of "manifest destiny" was too loud to be unheeded, and the annexation of new territory to the United States was advocated by many politicians. In compliance with this demand the President appointed James Gadsden a plenipotentiary to Mexico to negotiate with Santa Anna for the acquisition of certain lands along the Mexican border. He visited the city of Mexico and succeeded in concluding a treaty by which that part of Arizona lying south of the Gila River, which was the boundary fixed by the Guadalupe-Hidalgo treaty, was annexed to the United States upon the payment of ten millions of dollars.

The Filibusters in Nicaragua.

One of the most dramatic incidents in the relations between the United States and the other American republics was the attempt of William Walker to secure control of Nicaragua (see map, page 111). In 1854 an expedition was organized in New York and Philadelphia under the leadership of H. L. Kinney, ostensibly to establish a colony upon the Mosquito Coast of Nicaragua, but really to obtain control of the governments of Central America. Remonstrance was made to the United States and the plans of the conspirators were defeated. In the following year an American named Byron Cole arrived in Nicaragua, and entered into a contract with the revolutionary party, then endeavoring to overthrow the government, to bring to their assistance an army of foreigners under the guise of colonists. Cole went to California to obtain recruits, and there transferred his contract to William Walker, a native of Tennessee. Walker was a man of small stature, but great personal courage. He possessed marked natural abilities, which were developed by a classical education and the study of the law, which he practiced at Philadelphia for some years. Having a taste for adventure, he went to California in 1849 and commenced the practice of his profession at Marysville. In 1852 he went to Lower California and conceived the idea of establishing an independent republic on that peninsula; but his plans were frustrated. Having failed in that direction he entered eagerly into the projects of Cole and organized an expedition of reckless adventurers, with whom he landed in Nicaragua and joined the leaders of the revolution. He soon obtained command of their army, and after a long and bloody struggle secured control of the government. The people of Nicaragua however appealed to the United States, and President Pierce issued a proclamation denouncing him. The legitimate government also appealed to the other Central

American nations. The call was responded to by all of them, who united their forces against Walker. The latter's army numbered about 1,200 men, largely adventurers from the United States. The rest were Englishmen, Frenchmen, and Germans. These foreigners could not endure the climate, and their army was rapidly weakened by sickness and death. They were driven to the northern coast of the country, where they finally surrendered to Commander Charles H. Davis of the United States Navy, commanding the U. S. Corvette *Saint Mary*. Walker escaped, but 400 of his followers were transported to the United States by Commander Davis. The war being ended, the allied forces departed for their homes, and Walker finally reached the United States.

But he was not satisfied with his defeat, and, taking advantage of a rupture between Nicaragua and Costa Rica, he organized another expedition, eluded the vigilance of the United States authorities, and sailed from New Orleans. Upon his arrival in Nicaragua he was immediately arrested by Commodore Paulding of the United States Navy, and sent home. But he at once organized a third expedition of filibusters, and landed at Truxillo, Honduras, where he seized the funds in the custom house. The British war vessel *Icarus*, however, entered the port, and Walker fled to the interior, where he was overtaken and arrested by the British commander, and delivered to the local authorities, who tried him and sentenced him to death. He was executed at Truxillo on the 12th of September, 1860.

The War between Chile, Bolivia, and Peru.

After the separation of her colonies in South America from Spain, the viceroyalty of Peru was divided into two republics, one of which retained the old name. The other was called Bolivia, in honor of Bolivar, the leader in the war for independence. In the division of territory Bolivia was given a long strip of desert on the coast, which was supposed to be worthless, but half a century later it was found to be stored by nature with immense deposits of nitrate of soda. A Chilean company, whose headquarters were at Valparaiso, was working these deposits on a large scale, within the territory of Bolivia, when the government of that republic in 1879 imposed an export tax upon the product. The company refused to pay the tax, and was sustained by the government of Chile, which contended that it was in violation of a treaty made in 1874. Bolivia responded by seizing the property of the company, and ordering its sale at auction for failure to pay the tax. Chile at once sent her fleet to the port, and landed an armed force to prevent the sale. Some years before, Peru had entered into a secret treaty of alliance offensive and defensive with Bolivia, and the latter country having declared war against Chile called upon Peru for assistance. Thus the three nations became involved in a struggle which assumed grave dimensions.

Under the direction of President Hayes the United States in October, 1880, offered its good offices as an arbitrator to settle the difficulty, and representatives of the three belligerent powers met on board the man-of-war *Lackawanna* to arrange terms of peace. After a conference of three days a treaty was formulated, which was accepted by Peru and Bolivia, but was finally rejected by Chile.

When General Garfield became President in March, 1881, Mr. Christiancy, who had been minister to Peru, was replaced by General Hurlbut, and the latter at once renewed the offer of mediation on the part of the United States; but its form and language were declared offensive by Chile, which by that time had conquered Peru, and was occupying the country with its victorious army. General Kilpatrick, who had been sent as minister to Chile, expressed his sympathy with the protest entered by that government against General Hurlbut's proposition, and Mr. William Henry Trescot was sent from Washington in December, 1881, to see if he could adjust the controversy and exert a pacific influence upon both governments. But he failed to accomplish what was desired, and a treaty of peace was finally negotiated, under which Peru and Bolivia forfeited to Chile as an indemnity for the war a large tract of territory along the Pacific coast.

The Trouble between Chile and the United States.

In the winter of 1890-91 a dispute arose between the President and the Congress of Chile over their respective constitutional powers, and a revolution for the overthrow of the former began. The naval forces of the republic took the part of the Congress, which retired from the capital and organized a provisional government at the city of Iquique in the northern part of the country. The steamship *Itata*, which had been sent to San Francisco by the Congressional party for a cargo of arms, was seized by the United States officials and held for alleged violation of the neutrality act. The Congressional party felt and expressed great indignation at this act of our government, which was augmented by a belief that the United States had shown unjustifiable sympathy with their President, and had refused to recognize their belligerent rights. When this party succeeded in their attempts to overthrow the President, and organized a new government at Santiago, their sympathizers expressed in various ways a resentment toward the United States. In October, 1891, a party of sailors from the man-of-war *Baltimore* having been given "liberty" at the port of Valparaiso, went on shore and became involved in a quarrel with a number of citizens, which resulted in a serious riot in which several were killed and wounded. The police of the city, instead of endeavoring to suppress the riot, and protect the American seamen, joined in the assault upon them, and it was alleged that the sailors who were killed met their death at the hands of the police.

The United States' demand for redress was responded to by an insulting circular, signed by the Chilean minister of foreign affairs, addressed to the diplomatic officers of that republic throughout the world, in which the grievances of Chile against our government were set forth at length. President Harrison demanded an apology for the circular, and reparation for the attack upon the sailors of the *Baltimore*, which the government of Chile after a long and bitter controversy consented to grant.

The Union of Central America.

After the achievement of their independence, the five states of Central America united in a confederation, which was dissolved about ten years later because of local jealousies. Repeated attempts have since been made to reunite the five republics under a single government, and that is still the desire of the wisest men in all of them. General Barrios, who for twelve years was President of Guatemala, and was the greatest soldier and most progressive statesman that republic has produced, cherished the ambition to accomplish the reunion, and died in the attempt. In 1884 he secured the adhesion of Honduras and Salvador to the plan, and with the approval of the Presidents of these republics, issued a proclamation announcing the union of Central America, with the expectation that Nicaragua and Costa Rica would ultimately signify their assent. But the President of Salvador, after the proclamation was issued, repudiated the agreement, and Barrios declared war against that republic. In one of the first engagements in March, 1885, he was killed. Four years later delegates from the five republics met in Salvador and agreed upon a plan for reunion, but it was not carried into effect. The policy of the United States has been to encourage the plan, provided it can be peacefully accomplished, but always to oppose coercion.

Claims against the American Republics.

Citizens of the United States residing in the several American republics have repeatedly invoked the aid of this government to collect claims against them for damages suffered, and losses sustained from various causes. These claims have usually been settled by the appointment of commissions to make investigations and to award such damages as the evidence has justified.

The United States has frequently exercised its good offices in determining disputed boundaries between the other American republics.

CHAPTER VII.

THE MONROE DOCTRINE.

THAT popular feature of the foreign policy of the United States known as the "Monroe doctrine," is based upon certain declarations made against European interference in American affairs or occupation of American territory by President Monroe, in a message to Congress on the 2nd of December, 1823.

In 1815, after the downfall of Napoleon, the great powers of Europe organized what was known as the Holy Alliance, the object of which was to maintain the "divine right of kings" and preserve the territorial integrity of the continent. At a congress of delegates representing this alliance, sitting at Verona, Italy, in October, 1822, it was proposed that the other European nations should assist Spain in recovering her lost provinces in America. Great Britain had already secured commercial supremacy in the new American republics, and fearing that the re-establishment of the Spanish power would close their markets to her merchants, entered a vigorous protest through her delegate, the famous Duke of Wellington. Shortly after, Mr. Canning, then premier of England, proposed to Mr. Richard Rush, the United States minister, that the governments of Great Britain and the United States should unite in a declaration against the designs of the Alliance in regard to this continent. Mr. Rush consented, provided England would formally recognize the independence of the Spanish American republics, as the United States had done some months before. This, however, Mr. Canning declined to do, and the declaration was never made.

The proposition and the correspondence relating to it, together with a detailed account of the supposed designs of the Holy Alliance, were promptly forwarded to Washington by Mr. Rush, and Mr. Monroe considered the matter of such gravity that he solicited the advice of ex-Presidents Jefferson and Madison, and made it the subject of a message to Congress in which he said :

"The occasion has been judged proper for asserting, as a principle in which the rights and interests of the United States are involved, that the American continents, by the free and independent condition which they have assumed and maintained, are henceforth not to be considered as subjects for future colonization by any European powers. . . . . We owe it therefore to candor and to the amicable relations existing between the United States and those powers to declare that we should consider any attempt on their part to extend their system to any portion of this hemisphere as dangerous to our peace and safety. With the existing colonies or dependencies of any European power we have not interfered and shall not interfere; but with the governments that have declared their independence and maintained it, and whose independence we have on great consideration and on just principles acknowledged, we could not view any interposition for the purpose of oppressing them or controlling in any other manner their destiny, by any European power, in any other light than as the manifestation of an unfriendly disposition toward the United States."

A few days afterwards Henry Clay, then speaker of the House of Representatives, took the floor to offer the following resolution :

"Resolved by the Senate and House of Representatives of the United States of America in Congress assembled, that the people of these states would not see, without serious inquietude, any forcible intervention by the allied powers of Europe in behalf of Spain, to reduce to their former subjection those parts of the continent of America which have proclaimed and established for themselves independent governments, which have been solemnly recognized by the United States."

No action was ever taken by Congress upon the resolution of Mr. Clay. None was necessary. The positive and patriotic utterances of President Monroe, when published in Europe, terminated the discussion of the proposition to aid Spain in the recovery of her American provinces, and the independence of Mexico and the Central and South American republics was shortly after recognized by Great Britain and other European powers.

It should be said, however, that the message of Mr. Monroe on this subject is believed to have been prepared by John Quincy Adams, then secretary of state.

The Clayton-Bulwer Treaty.

Although the announcement of the Monroe doctrine was nowhere more cordially received and approved than in Great Britain, it is an interesting coincidence that the first direct application of the policy it involves was to prevent the establishment by that nation of a protectorate over the Mosquito nation of Indians that occupy a tract of land along the north coast of Nicaragua between Costa Rica and Honduras. This tribe of Indians was one of the few native races that were not subjugated during the occupation of Central and South America by the Spaniards, and, although frequent and determined attempts were made to subdue and civilize them, they managed to maintain their independence. During the constant struggle between the English and the Spaniards for supremacy in the western seas, the Mosquito Indians, recognizing the latter as their natural enemies, gave aid and comfort to the British seamen, and their ports were always open as an asylum for British ships. There the British buccaneer found supplies of food and water, and in the dense forests along the Mosquito Coast they concealed the treasure captured from the Spanish galleons. As a natural consequence many English adventurers took up their residence among the Mosquito villages and intermarried with the natives. In 1848 serious differences arose between the Indians and the government of Nicaragua, when Great Britain espoused the cause of the Mosquitos, established a protectorate over them, and forced the Nicaraguans to recognize their independence. The British men-of-war took forcible possession of the port of San Juan del Norte (Greytown) and fortified the place (see map page 111).

As this port was regarded as the necessary terminus of any railway or canal that might be constructed across the Isthmus, and as the action of England was regarded as an unjustifiable interference with the affairs of Nicaragua, the United States entered an earnest protest, and a special commissioner was sent to Central America to make an investigation and report. The relations of the United States with Great Britain began to assume a threatening aspect and the correspondence between the two nations was very active and earnest. But the difficulty was adjusted by diplomatic negotiations conducted by John M. Clayton, then secretary of state, and Sir Henry Bulwer, the British minister at Washington, who signed at Washington, the 19th of April, 1850, what is known as the Clayton-Bulwer treaty, "for the purpose of setting forth and fixing the views and intentions of the two governments with reference to any means of communication by ship canal which may be constructed between the Atlantic and Pacific Oceans by way of the River San Juan de Nicaragua or both of the lakes of Nicaragua or Managua to any port or place on the Pacific Ocean."

As this treaty has been the subject of protracted controversy in the past and is likely to be the subject of serious discussion in the future it is important that the entire text should be given, as follows:

"ARTICLE I. Neither government will ever obtain or maintain for itself any exclusive control over the said ship canal; nor erect nor maintain any fortifications 'or occupy or fortify or colonize or assume or exercise any dominion over Nicaragua, Costa Rica, the Mosquito Coast, or any part of Central America; nor make use of any protection which either affords or may afford, or any alliance which either has or may have to or with any state or people,' for any of the above purposes, nor use any alliance or influence that either may possess with any state or government through whose territory the canal may pass for the purpose of acquiring for the citizens or subjects of the one any rights of commerce or navigation, 'which shall not be offered on the same terms to the citizens or subjects of the other.'

"ARTICLE II. Vessels of both countries, in case of war between them, shall, while traversing the canal, or at such a distance from the two ends thereof as may hereafter be established, be exempted from blockade, detention, or capture.

"ARTICLE III. Those constructing the canal under the authority of the local governments are to be protected in person and property.

"ARTICLE IV. The contracting parties will use their influence with local governments to facilitate the construction of the canal; and also their good offices to procure the establishment of two free ports.

"ARTICLE V. When completed, the contracting parties

guarantee the protection and neutrality of the canal; which may be withdrawn by either party upon six months' notice to the other, if the regulations concerning traffic 'are contrary to the spirit and intention of this convention.'

"ARTICLE VI. The contracting parties engage to invite friendly states 'to enter into stipulations with them similar to those which they have entered into with each other'; also to enter into treaty stipulations with the Central American states 'for the purpose of more effectually carrying out the great design of this convention'; and also to use their good offices to settle differences between the states of Central America 'as to right or property over the territory through which the said canal shall pass.'

"ARTICLE VII. The contracting parties agree to give their support to such reliable persons or company as may first offer to commence the construction of the canal; priority of claim to protection to belong to any person or company having made preparations therefor.

"ARTICLE VIII. Both governments 'agree to extend their protection, by treaty stipulations, to any other practicable communications, whether by canal or railway across the isthmus,' and especially to those 'which are now proposed to be established by the way of Tehuantepec or Panama.' Both governments shall approve of the charges or conditions of traffic. Equal privileges shall be granted 'to the citizens and subjects of every state which is willing to grant thereto such protection as the United States and Great Britain engage to afford.'"

It was only a few months after the ratification of this treaty that a claim of the British government to Honduras and its occupation of the Bay Islands, caused another serious controversy with the United States which was settled by a supplementary treaty negotiated by Mr. Dallas and Lord Clarendon.

This was ratified by the Senate of the United States with some amendments to which the British government would not agree, and the discussion was continued until 1859, when Great Britain signed treaties with Guatemala, Honduras, and Nicaragua in which were renounced the claims she had made to Central American territory. With this the government of the United States expressed satisfaction.

Controversies over the Island of Cuba.

The fertile island of Cuba has also caused the Monroe doctrine to be invoked. Early in the century, when Louisiana was ceded to the United States by France, and Florida by Spain, Cuba was regarded as an equally natural and necessary acquisition, but Spain declined to part with so valuable a colony. In 1825 the French government made overtures for the purchase of Cuba and Puerto Rico which caused Mr. Clay, then secretary of state, to send a very positive dispatch to Mr. Brown, the American minister at Paris, in which he said: "With the hope of guarding beforehand against any possible difficulties on that subject that may arise, you will now add that we could not consent to the occupation of those islands by any other European power than Spain under any contingency whatever."

Mr. Clay was assured that the French government had no desire to acquire the Spanish possessions in America, but this did not allay apprehensions, and their possible occupation by France, Germany, or England was a familiar topic of discussion for a quarter of a century. In 1848 President Polk directed our minister at Madrid to negotiate for the purchase of Cuba and Puerto Rico by the United States, but the secretary of foreign affairs replied that "sooner than see the islands transferred to any other power they would prefer them to be sunk in the ocean."

The history of Cuba is the recital of a series of political disturbances, and the revolutions which have continually agitated and impoverished the people by requiring them to sustain a large standing army, have frequently been organized by Cuban conspirators, who have found a temporary asylum in the United States. Although our government has consistently endeavored to prevent these disturbances, they have been a constant source of irritation. In 1852 when Mr. Fillmore was President and Mr. Webster secretary of state, it was proposed that the United States should enter into a treaty with England and France, disclaiming forever any intention to obtain possession of Cuba, and pledge themselves to assist Spain in sustaining her authority over the island.

The governments of Great Britain and France asserted their adherence to the principle enunciated by Mr. Clay in 1825 against the occupation of the island by any other power than Spain, and argued that if the United States would enter into a perpetual obligation to sustain the Spanish authority, that government would be relieved of great expense in maintaining an army in Cuba, and could thus more easily meet her engagements with her French and English creditors. But the United States declined to enter into the treaty on the broad ground that the oldest tradition of this government was an aversion to political alliances with European powers, and in 1854 President Pierce instructed Mr. Soule, Mr. Buchanan, and Mr. Mason, our ministers to Madrid, London, and Paris, to renew negotiations for the purchase of Cuba. They met at Ostend and drew up a form of agreement, which was, however, never formally presented to Spain, for at the meeting of the Spanish Cortes not many weeks after, the subject was alluded to, and the Spanish prime minister, in reply to an inquiry, declared that "to part with Cuba would be to part with the national honor." As this sentiment was approved by a vote of the Chamber of Deputies, it was considered impolitic to submit a proposition that was certain of rejection.

In 1859 the subject was revived in the Congress of the United States by Senator Slidell of Louisiana, who introduced a bill appropriating $30,000,000 for the purchase of Cuba. An animated discussion followed, but the bill was not acted upon.

There have been several similar propositions since introduced in Congress, and our ministers to Spain have frequently, under instructions, approached the Spanish government on the subject, but without success.

The Maximilian Episode in Mexico.

The most vigorous application of the Monroe doctrine in recent years was when the French government attempted to establish and maintain a monarchy in Mexico. In 1861 Benito Juarez, having become President of Mexico, instituted a series of reforms which were directed chiefly against the Roman Catholic Church. They were intended to destroy the influence of the priesthood, which was alleged to be against the progress and development of the country and the education of the people. All the religious orders were expelled, the parish schools were closed, and the property of the church, valued at over $300,000,000, was confiscated for the benefit of the government. Since the independence of the republic was achieved there had been a constant warfare between the clerical or conservative party with monarchical tendencies, on the one hand, and the liberal, or progressive party on the other, which resulted in a series of most disastrous and bloody revolutions, and such frequent changes of government that there were thirty-six rulers in Mexico within a term of thirty-three years. Juarez was the first President of the republic who was permitted to retain the office to the end of the term for which he was elected.

The governments of Great Britain, Spain, and France presented to the Juarez administration large claims for damages alleged to have been suffered by their subjects in Mexico during these revolutions, which he refused to pay; and in 1861 a joint convention was held in London, at which it was determined to take possession of the Mexican customs houses and apply the revenues toward the payment of the claims. In January, 1862, British, French, and Spanish troops were landed at the port of Vera Cruz, but it was soon after arranged to settle the English and Spanish claims by diplomatic negotiations, and the forces of those governments were at once withdrawn. But Napoleon III. refused to accept the terms of settlement and, at the solicitation of Mexican exiles of the clerical party in France, declared war against the Juarez government. His purpose to occupy Mexico permanently and restore a monarchy there, was soon disclosed, but it is the prevailing opinion that the French emperor would never have committed himself to this unfortunate undertaking had he not believed that the leaders of the Confederacy would be successful in their design to dissolve the Union of the United States.

Although this government was involved in the greatest war of modern times, President Lincoln immediately asserted his adherence to the Monroe doctrine and solemnly protested against the invasion of the American continent by a European power. The French government was equally serious in its assurances that the only purpose of its army in Mexico was to enforce reparation for losses sustained by its subjects; and the United States for the time being was powerless to interfere. After a series of engagements the French army occupied the city of Mexico, and summoned a "Congress of Notables"—leading citizens belonging to the church party—to organize a government. This assembly proclaimed a hereditary monarchy, under a Roman Catholic emperor, and the crown was accepted by the Archduke Maximilian of Austria, in 1863.

Mr. Seward, then secretary of state, promptly protested in the name of the United States, on the ground that the people of Mexico favored a republican form of government of domestic origin, and that it was essential to the progress of civilization on the American continent. He was sustained by our Congress, which, without a dissenting voice, passed a resolution declaring that "it does not accord with the policy of the United States to acknowledge any monarchical government erected on the ruins of any republican government in America, under the auspices of any European power."

The passage of this resolution created great excitement in France, and war seemed imminent, but the United States was not then in a condition to enforce its declaration, and was compelled to be a passive witness of the overthrow of the Mexican republic. At the close of our Civil War, however, Mr. Bigelow, the United States minister to France, was instructed to demand the immediate withdrawal of the French troops from the territory of Mexico. It has been asserted that he gave an assurance that the authority of Maximilian would be recognized if this was done, but this assurance was promptly disapproved by the President, and the demand was renewed without any conditions or qualifications, and Mr. Seward instructed the American minister to inform the French government:

"1. That the United States earnestly desire to continue and cultivate sincere friendship with France.

"2. That this policy will be brought into immediate jeopardy unless France can deem it consistent with her interest and honor to desist from the prosecution of armed intervention in Mexico to overthrow the domestic republican government existing there, and to establish upon its ruins the foreign monarchy which has been attempted to be inaugurated at the capital of that country."

To emphasize the declarations of this government, General Sheridan was sent to the southwestern frontier with a large portion of the army that had been engaged in the Civil War, and on the 5th of April, 1866, the French emperor ordered his troops to evacuate Mexico. Being left to his own resources the ill-fated Maximilian was soon overcome. He appealed to Napoleon, to Austria, and to the pope, without success, and in June, 1867, was captured and shot.

The Northwest Boundary Dispute.

The occupation of the northern portion of the continent of North America by Great Britain and Russia was a source of great irritation to the United States during the first half of the present century, and the limits and boundaries of the territory acquired by purchase from France and Spain were so indefinite as to be the cause of constant friction. By a treaty between the United States and Great Britain, signed in 1818 and renewed in 1827, all disputed territory was left free and open to citizens of both nations. Finally, in 1846 the 49th parallel of north latitude was fixed as the boundary line between the United States and the British possessions. There was some earnest discussion in this country as to the application of the Monroe doctrine, and the forcible annexation of Canada and British Columbia to the United States was frequently suggested, but it was maintained by the conservative sentiment of the people that the spirit of that doctrine only applied to the invasion of the American continent by European powers, and the extension of foreign authority, and as stated by Mr. Monroe not to the peaceable occupation of territory already occupied.

Early in the century claims were made by the United States to the entire Pacific coast from Bering Strait southward to and beyond the mouth of the Columbia River, and in 1821 the government of Russia created some consternation by asserting its territorial rights as far south as the 51st degree of north latitude. Both the United States and Great Britain were emphatic in their expressions of dissent, and diplomatic correspondence on this subject continued for several years until the boundaries between Alaska and British Columbia were determined by a treaty signed at St. Petersburg in 1825. In 1865 these boundaries were recognized by the United States by the purchase of the territory of Alaska from Russia for the sum of $7,200,000.

The Monroe Doctrine in Santo Domingo.

The Monroe doctrine was again invoked to protect the republic of Santo Domingo against the designs of Spain. That island, upon which was established the first civilized government in the new world, was a Spanish colony until it was ceded to France in 1795, but in 1844 it achieved its independence under the influence of that remarkable negro, Toussaint L'Ouverture. In 1861 a revolutionary leader by the name of Pedro Santana overthrew the legitimate government, and proclaiming himself dictator, invited Spain to resume its ancient relations with the island. A few Spanish troops were sent over to sustain Santana, but the government at Madrid was very much engaged with its own domestic disturbances, and never attempted to take formal possession. The people of the republic applied to the United States for aid and protection, but being occupied with the war the government could do no more than offer sympathy and forward a remonstrance to the king of Spain. As a result the Spanish army was withdrawn from Santo Domingo in July, 1865, and the Santo Dominicans proclaimed that "the United Dominican people, without regard to rank or color, have planted the white cross of the republic on the principle enunciated by the Great Mother of free nations, that America belongs to the Americans, and we will endure all our trials over again sooner than desert it."

In 1864 a war broke out between Spain and her former colonies on the west coast of South America. It was caused by the forcible seizure by Spain of the Chinca Islands, which were rich with guano, to indemnify certain Spanish residents in Peru for losses suffered during a revolution in the latter country. The citizens of the United States residing in Peru called a meeting, which was attended by the subjects of other nations, and passed a series of indignant resolutions, embodying the principles of the Monroe doctrine, and calling upon the United States government to enforce them as "the safeguard and only defense of the sister republics of this continent." The neighboring republics of Ecuador, Bolivia, and Chili joined with Peru in a treaty of offense and defense against Spain, and the fleet of the latter nation responded by bombarding Valparaiso on March 31, 1866. The United States entered a remonstrance, hostilities were suspended, and a peace conference was held at Washington, which was presided over by Hamilton Fish. Its deliberations resulted in a treaty for a permanent armistice, which "cannot be broken by any of the belligerents, until three years after express and explicit notification shall have been given by one to the other of the intention to renew hostilities. In such case notification must be made through the government of the United States."

CHAPTER VIII.

NEGOTIATIONS FOR AN INTEROCEANIC CANAL.

THE great purpose of all the early explorers in American waters was to discover a western passage from Europe to India, China, and other countries of the East. The Portuguese voyagers found a pathway around the Cape of Good Hope, and, when Columbus started from Palos upon his memorable voyage, he had no expectation of finding a new world, but sought only to demonstrate the accuracy of the theory that the world was round, and that India could be reached by sailing westward as well as to the east. On his last and most disastrous voyage he cruised up and down the northern coast of Central America, searching each inlet and creek and bay for the navigable passage his genius taught him should be there, but which nature, by some Titanic convulsion, had closed ages before his time.

The discovery of the Straits of Magellan, and the circumnavigation of the globe by the seamen who followed Columbus proved the truth of his theories, but the enormous distance that must be sailed before the Pacific Ocean could be entered made it necessary to shorten the route by artificial means. As early as 1513, when the Pacific Ocean was discovered by Vasco Nuñez de Balboa, a proposition for a canal through the isthmus was made, but several years passed before the Spaniards abandoned the attempt to find a natural channel across the continent. As late as 1523, Emperor Charles V. admonished Cortez to search carefully along the western as well as the eastern shores of New Spain for what was termed, *El secreto del estrecho*—the secret of the straits.

In 1528, however, the fact that no passage existed became very well established, and a Commission of Engineers was appointed by the court of Spain to consider a plan for artificial water communication across the Isthmus of Darien (Panama), but there is no record of further action until 1534, when Charles V. instructed the governor of Panama (see map, page 48) to make an exploration and report the result. The governor, Pascual Andagoya, replied that the scheme was impracticable, but in 1540 the investigation was resumed under the direction of Philip II., and Bautiste Antonelli reported in favor of a canal across Nicaragua (see map, page 111). In 1550 Antonio Galvao proposed four different routes, of which he considered that across Nicaragua the most practicable, and the subject was extensively discussed, but the superstitious monks, who still controlled the policy of Spain, condemned the plan as contrary to the will of the Divine Providence that had placed a barrier there to restrain the fury of the seas.

The project was frequently revived, not only in Spain but in other parts of Europe, and finally in 1695, William Patterson, the founder of the Bank of England, organized the first company that was ever established to construct an interoceanic canal. Money was freely subscribed in England, Holland, Belgium, and other European countries, and a colony of twelve hundred men in five ships sailed to the isthmus from Leith, Scotland, in July, 1698, to commence work. Spain sent a fleet and an army to prevent the enterprise, and, after four months of resistance and distress, the colonists surrendered, and returned to England.

Various subsequent attempts were made to undertake the work, with no better success, and it was not until after the republic of New Granada (Colombia) had achieved its independence that even a scientific survey was made to determine a route for a canal. Then, in 1827, Simon Bolivar employed two English engineers, who spent two years on the isthmus, and reported in favor of the route that was afterwards adopted for the line of the Panama railway. In 1838 the government of New Granada gave a concession to a French company to construct the canal, but they did no more than make a survey.

The project was first proposed in this country in 1825 by Antonio Jose Cañaz, minister at Washington from the republic of Central America, who, in the name of his government, invited the United States to undertake the construction of a canal across Nicaragua. Henry Clay, who was then secretary of state, replied in a communication that stands as one of the noblest state papers ever issued from the Executive Department of this government, accepting the invitation and announcing that the United States minister to Central America had been instructed to make the necessary examination. Mr. Williams, the minister, reported favorably on the subject, and the result was the formation of a company, under a charter from Congress, to construct the canal. DeWitt Clinton, then governor of New York, and the father of the Erie Canal, was the most conspicuous member of the corporation, which secured a concession from the government of Central America and made a series of surveys, but was unable to obtain the necessary capital.

This company having dissolved, the king of the Netherlands agreed to undertake the work, but the dissolution of the Central American Confederacy caused him to abandon the project.

No further action was taken by the government of the United States until 1835, when Congress passed a resolution directing the President to open negotiations with the governments of New Granada and Central America for the purpose of securing treaty stipulations for such individuals or companies as might undertake the construction of a ship canal across the isthmus. On the first of March following, President Jackson appointed Charles H. Biddle of Philadelphia as commissioner to confer with the authorities of Colombia and Central America, and to make such investigations as were necessary fully to inform the government on the subject. Mr. Biddle visited Central America, but died shortly after his return to the United States, leaving a partially completed report, which pronounced the Panama route impracticable.

In 1838 a memorial was submitted to Congress by citizens of New York and Philadelphia for a renewal of the negotiations, and the committee on roads and canals of the House of Representatives made an elaborate report on the subject, which was illustrated by maps, charts, plans, and profiles showing the several proposed routes and discussing their respective advantages. The report concluded with a resolution requesting the President to reopen negotiations; it was adopted by the House, but no further action was taken.

In 1839, however, Mr. John L. Stephens, accompanied by Mr. Catherwood, a skillful artist and draughtsman, was sent to Central America, ostensibly to visit the ruined cities there, but really to make a confidential report to the President on the subject of an interoceanic canal. In Nicaragua he met Lieutenant Bailey of the British Royal Engineers, who had surveyed a canal route for the Nicaraguan government, and secured from him copies of all his reports and maps, which were afterwards submitted to Congress; but owing to the unsettled condition of political affairs in Central America, the negotiations were postponed.

In 1848, during the negotiations that followed the war with Mexico and resulted in the annexation of New Mexico and Arizona to the United States, it was proposed to purchase a right of way for a canal or railway across the Isthmus of Tehuantepec, but the offer was rejected by the Mexican authorities.

During the same year a treaty, which is still in force, was negotiated with New Granada, under which the United States was guaranteed the right of free transit across the Isthmus of Panama, and permission to construct a railway or canal or any other means of transportation under the same rights and privileges that might be enjoyed by the citizens of that country.

About this time occurred the incident of the occupation of the city of Greytown, Nicaragua, by the British government, and the establishment of a protectorate over the Mosquito Indians, which led to the negotiation of the Clayton-Bulwer treaty. The circumstances are fully related in the chapter on the Monroe doctrine (page 93).

Under the provisions of the treaty the government of Nicaragua granted a concession for the construction of a canal to Cornelius Vanderbilt and his associates, under the corporate name of the American Atlantic and Pacific Ship Canal Company, and a survey was made by the United States Topographical Engineer Corps, under the direction of this government.

The discovery of gold in California had greatly stimulated public interest in the canal question, and the immense traffic across the isthmus, made necessary by the lack of transportation facilities overland, caused the organization in New York of a company, under the leadership of General Aspinwall, for the construction of a railway between the two oceans. A concession was obtained from New Granada, with a stipulation on the part of the government of the United States that it would guarantee free and uninterrupted traffic across the isthmus, and the protection of the property of the company. The road was constructed and is still in operation, but the project of building a canal was not abandoned, although the Vanderbilt Company did not undertake the work. From 1850 to 1860 repeated surveys were made under the direction of the United States government, covering all possible routes from the Isthmus of Tehuantepec to the Isthmus of Darien (Panama), and several canal companies were organized, but nothing further was accomplished. Soon after, the Civil War diverted the attention of the public.

When General Grant became President he revived the plan with great earnestness, for he was a strong advocate of the practicability and necessity of an interoceanic canal. Several expeditions were organized under his direction, and both military and naval engineers were engaged in the search for a more economical route than had hitherto been discovered. A new treaty was negotiated with Colombia for the construction of a canal by the United States government across the Isthmus of Panama, and was submitted to the Senate in 1870, but failed of ratification. President Grant was not discouraged, but in 1872 appointed a commission to take the subject again under consideration, which ordered new surveys and reported three years later in favor of the Nicaragua route.

The report of the commission was submitted to Congress by President Hayes, but no action was taken.

The government of Colombia, having taken offense at the report of this commission in favor of a canal across Nicaragua by way of the River San Juan and Lakes Nicaragua and Managua, entered into negotiations with the French government, and granted a concession to a company, of which Ferdinand de Lesseps, who had just completed the Suez Canal, was president, to construct a canal across the Isthmus of Panama. This company immediately organized and commenced operations, but the undertaking was regarded with great disfavor in the United States, and several resolutions were proposed in Congress asserting that the Monroe doctrine was a cardinal principle in our national policy, and that no canal across the isthmus could be permitted unless constructed under the auspices and protection of the United States. The committee on foreign affairs of the House of Representatives made an elaborate report on the subject, in which they held that the construction of a water way upon the American continent by foreign capital, under the charter of a foreign government, was in violation of the spirit of the Monroe doctrine, and that the United States "would assert and maintain control over any such water way by whomsoever constructed so far as was necessary to protect its national interest, means of defense, unity, and safety, and to advance the prosperity and augment the commerce of the Atlantic and Pacific States of the Union."

President Hayes, in transmitting to Congress various documents relating to the subject, expressed the sentiment of the country in his message when he said:

"1. The policy of this country is a canal under American

control. If existing treaties or the rights of sovereignty or property of other nations stand in the way of this policy, negotiations should be entered into to establish the American policy consistently with the rights of the nations to be affected by it.

"2. The capital invested in the enterprise must look for protection to one or more of the great powers of the world. No European power can be allowed to intervene for such protection. The United States 'must exercise such control as will enable this country to protect its national interests and maintain the rights of those whose private capital is embarked in the work.'

"3. Such a canal would virtually be 'a part of the coast line of the United States'; and its relations to this country 'are matters of paramount concern to the people of the United States. No other great power would, under similar circumstances, fail to assert a rightful control over a work so closely and vitally affecting its interest and welfare.'"

President Garfield, in his inaugural address, alluding to the De Lesseps enterprise, said: "We shall urge no narrow policy, nor seek peculiar or exclusive privileges in any commercial route; but, in the language of my predecessor, I believe it to be 'the right and duty of the United States to assert and maintain such supervision and authority over any interoceanic canal across the isthmus that connects North and South America as will protect our national interests.'"

One of the first state papers of the Garfield administration was devoted to this subject and was addressed to Mr. Lowell, the United States minister to England.

It asserted that this government did not desire exclusive privileges for American ships in time of peace and would not interfere with the enterprise as a commercial one, but would insist that the political control of the canal must be in this country, for the reason that the possessions of the United States upon the Pacific coast are imperial in extent and would supply the larger part of the traffic. Nor would the United States consent to an agreement between the powers of Europe to guarantee the neutrality and control of the political character of the canal, on the ground that such an agreement affecting the political condition or the commerce of the American continent would be attended with danger to the peace and welfare of this nation. "The position of the United States on this question," the paper continued, "had been long and well understood, and the principles of the doctrine which had been enunciated a century before are familiarly interwoven into our national policy."

Earl Granville replied that the position of England toward the canal was based upon the terms of the Clayton-Bulwer treaty; but this government retorted that the Clayton-Bulwer treaty was made thirty years before, under conditions that were temporary in their nature, and that the remarkable development of the Pacific coast of the United States required modifications in the terms, which practically conceded to Great Britain the control of any canal that might be constructed. The fact that Great Britain maintains a vast naval armament, gave that country an advantage over the United States which would be decisive in case of a possible struggle for the control of the water way, because the treaty binds this government not to use military force, while it leaves the naval power of Great Britain free and unrestrained. If no American army was to be allowed on the isthmus, no war vessels of Europe would be permitted to control the waters at either entrance of the canal. The United States, it was argued, was simply seeking to defend its interests as Great Britain defended hers, and it would be equally reasonable for the United States to demand a share in the fortifications that commanded the Suez Canal as for Great Britain to make a similar demand in reference to the canal across the isthmus. Great Britain, therefore, should not object to the United States assuming absolute control of any canal which shall unite the two oceans, and which this government will always regard and treat as a part of our coast line.

The United States then proposed a modification of the Clayton-Bulwer treaty in five particulars as follows:

(1) Every part which forbids the United States fortifying the canal and holding the political control of it in conjunction with the country in which it is located, to be canceled.

(2) Every part in which Great Britain and the United States agree to make no acquisition of territory in Central America, to remain in full force.

(3) No objection to maintaining the clause looking to the establishment of a free port at each end of the proposed canal.

(4) The clause to the effect that treaty stipulations should be made for a joint protectorate of any railway or canal never having been perfected, to be regarded as obsolete.

(5) The distance from either end of the canal where, in time of war, captures might be made, to be as liberal as possible.

The correspondence was continued for several years, Great Britain holding that the declarations of the United States were distinctly at variance with the terms of the Clayton-Bulwer treaty.

In the meantime work was commenced upon the Panama Canal and continued until the funds of the company were exhausted, when it was abandoned for lack of capital. During the intervening years another company was organized in the United States, with General Grant as president, for the construction of a canal across Nicaragua. A charter was sought from Congress and a new concession was obtained from Nicaragua, but it was found impossible to raise the necessary capital. The next step was the negotiation in 1884 of a treaty between the United States and Nicaragua for the construction of a canal by the government of the United States along a route located by Mr. A. G. Menocal, an engineer of the navy. This treaty was submitted to the Senate by President Arthur; and its terms were as follows:

The canal was to be built by the United States, and to be owned jointly by the United States and Nicaragua.

The United States was to protect perpetually the integrity of the territory of the republic of Nicaragua.

Privilege was given the United States to construct across the territory of Nicaragua a railway between the termini of the canal, and telegraph lines, in its discretion.

A belt of land was granted, two and one half miles wide, of which the canal was the central line, and a belt two and one half miles wide around the southern end of the lake.

The canal was exempted from taxation.

The United States was to have exclusive control of construction.

The net revenues were to be divided between the owners in the proportion of one third to Nicaragua and two thirds to the United States, and accounts were to be liquidated quarterly.

The United States was to loan Nicaragua $4,000,000 for works of internal improvement, to be refunded out of Nicaragua's share of the revenues.

The treaty was laid before the Senate, but failed of ratification under the two-thirds rule, and shortly after, it was withdrawn.

In October, 1886, a meeting of persons interested in the construction of the canal was called at New York, and a new company was organized which sought a charter from Congress. In the meantime Captain Eads had obtained a concession from Mexico for a ship railway across the Isthmus of Tehuantepec, and had introduced into Congress a bill providing for the charter of his company. The antagonism between the two interests delayed both bills so that they were not acted upon, but in March, 1887, the new Nicaragua company sent Mr. Menocal to Nicaragua to obtain a new concession in their behalf, which was ratified by the Nicaraguan government in April of that year. At the meeting of Congress in December, a bill for the incorporation of the Maritime Canal Company of Nicaragua was introduced, and reported to both Houses with a favorable recommendation. Final action was reached in February, 1889, and the bill, approved by the President, became a law. A construction party consisting of forty-seven engineers and their assistants was immediately sent to Nicaragua and work was begun.

The government of Costa Rica having claimed riparian rights along the San Juan River was also induced to grant a concession similar to that already secured from Nicaragua, and the work began under most favorable conditions. The harbor at Greytown, which had long been useless, was improved by the erection of a breakwater and pier, and a railway was constructed some distance up the San Juan River for the use of the canal company, which is now actively engaged upon the enterprise.

CHAPTER IX.

PROPOSED ANNEXATION OF SANTO DOMINGO AND ST. THOMAS. THE REPUBLIC OF LIBERIA.

ONE of the most interesting episodes in our diplomacy and an event that caused a serious political commotion, was the proposition made during the first year of the administration of President Grant, to annex the island of Santo Domingo to the United States. Being the cradle of American history, the scene of the first civilized settlement in the new world, and for half a century the center of affairs on this side of the Atlantic, there has always been a sentimental interest attaching to Santo Domingo that has not been felt in any other part of our continent. Then, too, the dramatic and furious fight that was made there for emancipation, the successful issue of the struggle, and the foundation of a republic of black men, for black men, and by black men, have made the soil of the picturesque island holy ground to the lovers of human freedom.

"Soon after my inauguration as President," said General Grant in his message forwarded to Congress in 1871, "I was waited upon by an agent of President Baez with a proposition to annex the republic of Santo Domingo to the United States. This gentleman represented the capacity of the island, the desire of the people, and their character and habits, about as they have been described by the commissioners whose report accompanies this message. He stated further that, being weak in numbers and poor in purse, they were not capable of developing their great resources, that the people had no incentive to industry on account of lack of protection for their accumulations; and that, if not accepted by the United States—with institutions which they loved above those of any other nation—they would be compelled to seek protection elsewhere. To these statements I made no reply, and gave no indication of what I thought of the proposition. In the course of time I was waited upon by a second gentleman from Santo Domingo, who made the same representations, and who was received in like manner.

"In view of the facts which had been laid before me, and with an earnest desire to maintain the Monroe doctrine, I believed that I would be derelict in my duty if I did not take measures to ascertain the exact wish of the government and inhabitants of the republic of Santo Domingo in regard to annexation, and communicate the information to the people of the United States. Under the attending circumstances I felt that if I turned a deaf ear to this appeal I might, in the future, be justly charged with a flagrant neglect of the public interests and an utter disregard of the welfare of a downtrodden race praying for the blessings of a free and strong government, and for protection in the enjoyment of the fruits of their own industry."

In the July following, General Grant sent General Babcock, his private secretary, to Santo Domingo upon a secret mission. He bore a letter of instructions from Secretary Fish to ascertain the facts about the condition of the government, its standing with the people, the financial condition, resources and industries of the island, and particularly the public sentiment with reference to the annexation proposition. His report to the President was confidential, and has never been made public, but it must have been favorable, for within a very short time after his return Secretary Fish negotiated a treaty with an agent of the Dominican government by which that portion of the island under its control and jurisdiction—not including the western shore which constitutes the republic of Hayti—was annexed to the United States. The area of this territory was 28,000 square miles, equal in size to Vermont, Massachusetts, Connecticut, and Rhode Island combined.

There was also a separate treaty negotiated, which granted to the United States the perpetual lease of the peninsula and Bay of Samana, at the eastern end of the island, as a supply station for the use of our navy in the West Indies.

In his message to the Senate, transmitting this treaty, General Grant expressed the opinion that the island, if properly cultivated, would yield to the United States all the sugar, coffee, tobacco, and other tropical products that would be required to supply the needs of our people, and would cut off at least a hundred million dollars' worth of our imports annually. He expressed great interest, too, in the benefits which annexation would confer upon the people of Santo Domingo, who for years had been plundered by thieves and adventurers.

But to the surprise of General Grant, when the annexation treaty was submitted to the United States Senate, it was rejected by a tie vote, 28 to 28, although a two-thirds vote was required for its ratification. There was great excitement in political circles, for some of the most famous and influential leaders of the Republican party, including Senator Sumner, were determined in their opposition to the treaty. It was charged that there were large private interests involved, and that the treaty was intended to protect and enrich a few citizens of the United States who had acquired large plantations in Santo Domingo, and to enable them to import sugar, tobacco, and other products into this country without the payment of duty. It was also charged that the people of the island had been intimidated to obtain their consent to annexation, that the government officials had been bribed, and that all forms of corruption had been used in securing the treaty.

Although the treaty was rejected by the Senate, President Grant was not discouraged. In his annual message six months later he called attention to the subject again, giving new and powerful arguments in favor of the acquisition of the republic. "I firmly believe," he said, "that the moment it is known that the United States has entirely abandoned the project of occupying as a part of its own territory the island of Santo Domingo, a free port will be negotiated for by European nations in the Bay of Samana, and a large commercial city will be built up, to which we will be tributary without receiving corresponding benefits." He recommended that a commission be appointed to negotiate a new treaty.

This proposition at once led to a bitter discussion in both Houses of Congress, Mr. Sumner and other Republicans leading the opposition. Senator Morton of Indiana offered a resolution, which was adopted by the Senate, authorizing the President to send to Santo Domingo such a commission as he had proposed, but it was not adopted by the House of Representatives without the addition of an amendment declaring that nothing in the resolution should be construed as committing Congress to the annexation policy.

The commission which went to Santo Domingo was composed of Benjamin F. Wade of Ohio, Andrew D. White of New York, and Samuel G. Howe of Massachusetts, with Frederick Douglass and Allan A. Burton as secretaries. Robert R. Hitt, afterwards assistant secretary of state and now a member of the House of Representatives, was one of the stenographers. The party was accompanied by several scientific men instructed to investigate the resources of the island. The commission was carried to its destination by a man-of-war, and reached Samana Bay on the 24th of January, 1871.

A thorough inquiry was made into the resources and condition of the republic, its products and commerce, and the expediency of annexation. A public investigation as to the charges of corruption and intimidation, and as to the sentiments of the people was conducted and the testimony and views of many prominent citizens were secured. The report was submitted to Congress in the following April, and in every particular sustained the statements and opinions of President Grant. Strong reasons and arguments were given in favor of a treaty of annexation, and they had much influence upon public sentiment in the United States. In forwarding the report to the Senate, General Grant sent a message in which he defended his motives and explained his reasons for negotiating the original treaty. He said:

"Under these circumstances I deemed it due to the office which I hold, and due to the character of the agents who had been charged with the investigation, that such proceedings should be had as would enable the people to know the truth. A commission was therefore constituted, under authority of Congress, consisting of gentlemen selected with special reference to their high character and capacity for the laborious work intrusted to them, who were instructed to visit the spot and report upon the facts. Other eminent citizens were requested to accompany the commission in order that the people might have the benefit of their views. Students of science and correspondents of the press, without regard to political opinions, were invited to join the expedition, and their numbers were limited only by the capacity of the vessel.

"The mere rejection by the Senate of a treaty negotiated by the President only indicates a difference of opinion between two co-ordinate departments of the government, without touching the character or wounding the pride of either. But when such rejection takes place simultaneously with charges openly made of corruption on the part of the President, or those employed by him, the case is different. Indeed, in such a case the honor of the nation needs investigation. This has been accomplished by the report of the commissioners herewith transmitted, which fully vindicates the purity of the motives and action of those who represented the United States in the negotiation.

"And now my task is finished, and with it ends all personal solicitude upon the subject. My duty being done, yours begins; and I gladly hand over the whole matter to the judgment of the American people, and of their representatives in Congress assembled. The facts will now be spread before the country, and a decision rendered by that tribunal whose convictions so seldom err, and against whose will I have no policy to enforce. My opinion remains unchanged; indeed, it is confirmed by the report that the interests of our country and of Santo Domingo alike invite the annexation of that republic.

"In view of the difference of opinion upon this subject, I suggest that no action be taken at the present session beyond the printing and general dissemination of the report. Before the next session of Congress the people will have considered the subject and formed an intelligent opinion concerning it; to which opinion, deliberately made up, it will be the duty of every department of the government to give heed, and no one will more cheerfully conform to it than myself. It is not only the theory of our Constitution that the will of the people, constitutionally expressed, is the supreme law, but I have ever believed that 'all men are wiser than any one man'; and if the people, upon a full presentation of the facts, shall decide that the annexation of the republic is not desirable, every department of the government ought to acquiesce in that decision.

"In again submitting to Congress a subject upon which public sentiment has been divided, and which has been made the occasion of acrimonious debates in Congress, as well as of unjust aspersions elsewhere, I may, I trust, be indulged in a single remark.

"No man could hope to perform duties so delicate and responsible as pertain to the presidential office without sometimes incurring the hostility of those who deem their opinions and wishes treated with insufficient consideration; and he who undertakes to conduct the affairs of a great government as a faithful public servant, if sustained by the approval of his own conscience, may rely with confidence upon the candor and intelligence of a free people, whose best interests he has striven to subserve, and can bear with patience the censure of disappointed men."

But Mr. Sumner, Mr. Schurz, and other senators who had originally opposed the proposition, were even more determined in their hostility than before, and the first-named, who for some real or fancied grievance, had conceived a strong personal dislike for the President, denounced the treaty as "a measure of violence," a "dance of blood," and used other equally severe terms. He alluded to the president of Santo Domingo and his cabinet ministers as "political jockeys," and reiterated the charges of corruption, bribery, and fraud.

Although the President was stoutly defended by his friends the influence of Sumner and others was sufficient to defeat the adoption of the recommendation of the commission, and the President reluctantly abandoned the project. The question was, however, one of the principal reasons for the division of the Republican party in 1872, and it became a political issue in the presidential campaign of that year.

The Annexation of St. Thomas.

The kingdom of Denmark owns three small islands of the Virgin group of the Leeward Islands, lying between 17° and 18° north latitude, and in about 64° west longitude. They are St. Croix, or Santa Cruz, which has an area of 74 square miles and a population of 18,430, St. Thomas with an area of 23 square miles and a population of 14,389, and St. John with 21 square miles and a population of 944. Two thirds of the inhabitants are black, but they are well educated, and the Lutheran creed is the established religion of the country. The products are small, consisting of sugar, rum, and molasses, but the foreign commerce of the three islands is comparatively very large and amounts to about $3,000,000 a year, a greater part of which are imports of supplies intended for the use of passing ships.

St. Thomas is known as the keystone of the West Indies. It stands at the apex of the arc which forms the wall between the Atlantic Ocean and the Caribbean Sea, known as the Windward and Leeward Islands. It lies in the track of all vessels from Europe, Brazil, the East Indies, and the Pacific Ocean, bound to the north coast of Central and South America, the east coast of Mexico, the gulf ports of the United States and the West India Islands, and also in the track of all vessels sailing from the United States and Canada to Brazil and other countries in South America. It is a point where all vessels touch for coal, water, and other supplies when needed, and is a central rendezvous or focus for the commerce of the West Indies. All mail intended for ships that frequent those waters is sent to St. Thomas, for every ship is pretty sure to touch there either going to or returning from its destination. In a military sense St. Thomas is a central point commanding all of the West Indian Islands, and is so situated that it can be fortified to any extent. The bay on which lies the town of Charlotte Amalie, the principal city, is almost circular, the entrance being narrow and deep, and guarded by two heavy forts which could be so strengthened and protected that no foreign power could ever hope to take it. There is no other landing place, for the island is surrounded by reefs and breakers which constitute a natural protection, and the surf runs so high that it would be impossible for a boat-load of sailors or soldiers to land anywhere outside of the harbor. There is no harbor in the West Indies better situated for commerce or for military purposes, and it is large enough to shelter all the vessels in the world.

The Civil War demonstrated that the greatest military weakness of the United States was the lack of a harbor of refuge and a source of naval supplies in the West Indies. The sovereignty of these islands, more than a thousand in number, is divided among nearly all of the great nations of the earth, but the United States has no foothold there. England, France, Holland, Spain, and other countries have ports in which their vessels can seek supplies and protection at any time. In case the United States should become involved in war with any of those nations we should be at a great disadvantage because our vessels would be compelled to return frequently to our Atlantic ports for coal and provisions. It is the universal opinion among naval experts that the lack of such a station in the West Indies prolonged the late war at the cost of millions of dollars and the loss of thousands of lives; therefore, at the close of hostilities, Mr. Seward, who was secretary of state, endeavored to secure a base of supplies.

After considering the various questions involved, in January, 1865, he conveyed to the Danish minister at Washington, General Rassloff, an intimation that the United States would consider a proposition to purchase the possessions of Denmark in America. Although the communication was informal, the subject was widely discussed, both in the United States and in Copenhagen, and informal but very earnest protests were received by the Danish government from England, France, Germany, and other foreign powers. The assassination of President Lincoln caused the proposition to be temporarily abandoned, but during the winter of 1866 the negotiations were resumed.

Secretary Seward, after his recovery from the wounds of the assassin on the night when Lincoln was killed, sailed through the West Indies for the purpose of restoring his health, and made personal investigation of the advantages of St. Thomas, which were afterwards the subject of a report to the President. Consequently, in July, 1866, a formal proposition was made to Denmark, through General Rassloff, for the purchase of the three islands for the sum of $5,000,000. The latter arrived in Copenhagen with the proposition just at the moment of the defeat of the conservative party, whose late leaders had rejected the original overtures from the United States. The new ministry, which was military in its instincts, did not show any greater favor toward the American proposition, but, for fear of offending the United States, the government decided to make no answer to the proposition. General Rassloff resigned, and the Danish mission in the United

States was vacant. Mr. Seward telegraphed Mr. Yeaman, the United States minister to Copenhagen, to obtain a definite' reply, but he failed to secure from the Danish government any expression either of assent or dissent. He was informed, however, that there were many interests, sentiments, and conditions that must be considered and conciliated before any action could be taken.

Ten months later the Danish minister of foreign relations informed Minister Yeaman that while the government declined the offer of $5,000,000 for its American provinces it would agree to cede them to the United States for $15,000,000, the transfer of Santa Cruz, however, to depend upon the consent of France, as this was required by a treaty stipulation of two hundred years' standing. Or, if this proposition was not acceptable, St. Thomas and one other island would be ceded to the United States for $10,000,000, provided the inhabitants would approve the proposition by ballot. This offer was met by the United States with a counter-proposition to purchase two of the islands for $7,500,000, which was accepted by Denmark, with the condition that the inhabitants might express their assent to the measure. Senator Doolittle of Wisconsin, who happened to be in Europe at the time, was requested to proceed to Copenhagen and there conclude the negotiations. The purchase of Alaska from Russia was pending at the same time, and it was suggested that the endorsement of Russia upon the St. Thomas proposition would have a favorable effect. Thereupon, Senator Doolittle secured from Chancellor Gortchakoff an assurance that Denmark would have the moral support of Russia in the transaction. All of the papers having been signed on the 24th of October, 1867, the treaty, together with a history of the case and the documents, was sent to the Senate when Congress met in December.

In the meantime the Danish government appointed Edward Carstensen as a commissioner to take the vote of the people of St. Thomas on the proposition to transfer them from subjects of his majesty the king of Denmark to citizens of the United States. The United States sent Reverend Doctor Hawley, who was pastor of the church attended by Secretary Seward at Auburn, N. Y., as a commissioner to observe the election and answer any questions of a general character, or give any desired information in regard to the purposes of the United States that might be demanded by a people who were about voting upon a measure that affected their interests so deeply. Dr. Hawley found the people earnestly and amiably inclined, but the merchants desired an assurance that in the event of the transfer to the United States no duties would be imposed upon articles imported into St. Thomas for at least a stated length of time. He was unauthorized to meet this question, and Commissioner Carstensen could not proceed with the vote until it was settled. Rear Admiral Palmer at once dispatched a vessel to the United States with the Danish commissioner and Dr. Hawley, to lay this important matter before the government, but they arrived in Washington in the midst of the quarrel between President Johnson and the Senate which resulted in the impeachment of the former. Commissioner Carstensen returned alone to St. Thomas, and informed the merchants that he was not authorized to give them any assurances about the continuance of St. Thomas as a free port. On the 9th of January the vote was taken amid great ceremonies and festivities. The result was almost unanimity in favor of annexation, there being but 22 votes cast against the proposition in St. Thomas, and not one dissenting vote in St. John. When the news reached Copenhagen the parliament ratified the treaty without debate, and the king signed it on the 1st of January, 1868; but no notice was taken of it in Washington. The treaty lay buried in a pigeon-hole of the desk of Mr. Sumner, the chairman of the committee on foreign relations. Official notice was sent to the Senate of the result of the vote on the islands, and the action of the Danish parliament and the king, and attention was called to the fact that the limit of time for ratification would expire on the 24th of February; but that produced no effect. The Senate was otherwise engaged. On the 21st of February the proceedings in the impeachment of President Johnson began, and amidst the political excitement St. Thomas was not thought of.

In the following August, our government proposed to Denmark that the time for the exchange of ratifications be extended one year from October 14, 1868, which was agreed to, and the treaty was revived. The Danish government soon became indignant at the delay of the United States and sent Mr. Rassloff to demand that either the treaty should be ratified by the United States Senate, or just cause shown for the failure to do so. But during the busy session of Congress in 1869 the treaty remained suspended, and although a third opportunity was offered for the extension of the time for ratification no action was ever taken upon it. The failure of these negotiations caused the downfall of the first liberal ministry that ruled in Denmark, and the friendly relations between the United States and that country were impaired for several years by the unexplained neglect of the United States to carry out a solemn compact of its own seeking.

The Republic of Liberia.

By the terms of paragraph 1, section 9, of article 1 of the Constitution of the United States, the admission of African slaves into our country was, in effect, prohibited after the year 1807. This period expired near the termination of the administration of President Jefferson, who, anticipating the capture of slave ships subsequent to that date and the necessity of returning their cargoes to Africa, desired to negotiate for some port upon the western coast of that continent to which the captured slaves might be returned. With this object in view it occurred to him that Sierra Leone, a colony established by Great Britain, to which American slaves captured during the Revolution of 1776 were transported, was the most favorable point for the purpose; and he therefore suggested a treaty with that country which should designate that place as an asylum. But before any steps could be taken for the realization of his purpose, the United States and Great Britain were again at war and the project was indefinitely deferred.

The importance of the establishment of such a colony again suggested itself at the commencement of the administration of President Monroe, since it became evident that these miserable creatures, when captured and returned unprotected to their native land, were liable to be seized again and sold into slavery. In response, therefore, to petitions upon the subject, the Congress of the United States passed an act on March 3, 1819, authorizing President Monroe to return all such persons to the coast of Africa and to provide for their temporary relief and protection by the establishment of an agency or freedman's bureau there under the patronage and authority of the government of the United States. This is the only colonizing scheme that has ever been undertaken by our country.

In pursuance of the purposes of this act, Lieutenant Stockton of the American navy was instructed to proceed to the African coast in October, 1821, to carry out the designs of the government. This officer, touching first at Sierra Leone, sailed down the coast on a voyage of discovery in search of a favorable spot for the location of the colony. Upon his arrival at Cape Mesurado, a bold promontory some eighty feet above the level of the sea, he was attracted by its topographical features, and, after landing and exploring the vicinity, resolved to purchase the land and found the settlement there. While, however, he was visiting the neighboring chiefs and endeavoring to arrange the necessary preliminaries, some slave traders were actively engaged in thwarting his purposes by slander and misrepresentation; so that, when a council of their chiefs had assembled to consider the proposals of Lieutenant Stockton, their disapproval of his scheme was manifested in such threatening terms that he found it necessary to call in an armed force that had been prudently posted near at hand. This opportune display of arms promptly wrought a change in the conduct of negotiations; so much so that the African warriors were easily induced to make a grant of the desired territory and a treaty to that effect was forthwith formulated and executed. A few American colonists who had accompanied the expedition were disembarked and, with the personal aid and material assistance of Lieutenant Stockton and his crew, they began to organize and build up the settlement. Thus was founded the city of Monrovia, so called in honor of President Monroe, at Cape Mesurado.

The negro republic of Liberia lies wholly within the torrid zone or between the fourth and seventh degrees of latitude north of the equator. Its territory extends from the San Pedro River at 4° 20′ latitude north to the Manna River at 6° 80′ latitude north or about six hundred miles, and from the Atlantic coast on the west to an undefined boundary about two hundred miles distant in the east. It is thus west of Soudan, south of Sierra Leone, and north of the negro monarchy Ashantee.

The constitution of the republic is closely modeled after that of the United States. The executive power is vested in a president who is elected for the term of two years. The legislative council is composed of a senate of eight persons elected each four years and of a house of representatives of thirteen members elected every two years. The cabinet of the executive consists of five members. The average annual revenue, most of which is derived from customs duties, amounts to about $175,000, and the average annual expenditure, chiefly incurred for the general administration of the government, amounts to the sum of $165,000. The unpaid principal and interest of the national debt, contracted in England in 1871, amounts to $200,000. The chief exports consist of coffee, palm oil, palm nuts, cocoa, sugar, arrowroot, ivory, and hides. The annual coffee crop reaches about one million pounds. The combined annual exports and imports are estimated in the sum of one million dollars.

The native population of Liberia, comprising about 800,000 souls, has been reinforced by about fourteen thousand negro colonists from the United States and the West Indies and by nearly six thousand recaptured African slaves that have been sent there, from time to time, by the United States government. Although the country is a democracy yet the emigrants from America are exclusively the governing class and they have built up among themselves a sort of aristocracy, that is rigidly maintained to the entire exclusion of the natives. This latter class cannot aspire to any social equality with the American-born negro and is subjected to all the menial service that people of their race are accustomed to perform in the United States. The aristocrats are absolved from all anxiety in reference to their social status by the fact that their government is a negro republic where white persons cannot hold property nor be admitted to citizenship.

Liberia, under the patronage and protection of the American colonization society, occupied a peculiarly anomalous position, since it had no rank among the states of the world and, though established as a colony in due and legal form by the government of the United States, received small sympathy and encouragement from our country. Hence its intercourse with the world was attended with inconveniences and embarrassments and the colonists grew restive under this condition of affairs until 1848, when, with the approval of the American society, they resolved upon measures of self-government. To this end a declaration of independence was adopted in which, after reciting the wrongs to which their race was subjected in America, Liberia was declared to be a free, sovereign, and independent state. A constitution was soon after ratified, a president elected, and the new government formally inaugurated.

The black republic has thus far escaped any serious complication with foreign powers and has demonstrated, although in a feeble way, its capability for independent existence. While it has probably failed in every sense to justify the expectations of its promoters and founders, yet, as an outpost of civilization upon the dark continent, it may serve as a foothold for future efforts toward the humanizing and christianizing of the African race. If it had been founded forty years later, when the slave was the innocent cause of the great civil contest that cost our country so much blood and treasure, it is not unreasonable to suppose that it would have become an asylum for a very large portion of the black Americans and thus have mitigated if not entirely removed the conditions that have so long operated to disturb peace and order in the southern states.

CHAPTER X.

A GENERAL VIEW OF EUROPE IN THE NINETEENTH CENTURY.

AT THE very time when the colonies in America were forming a stable government, Europe was approaching a crisis and a new order. A general acquaintance with European affairs during the century is helpful to a clear understanding of the relations which have existed between the United States and the older nations.

In 1789 France was the scene of a significant, popular uprising, and for the next twenty-five years she played the leading part in social and governmental changes which extended to almost every quarter of Europe. Louis XVI. inherited in 1774 the throne of France, with its responsibilities, made serious by years of arbitrary and extravagant rule. The taxes fell heavily on the peasant and merchant, but rested lightly on an exempted nobility and clergy; an unjust system of land ownership, brought down by the nobles from feudal times, oppressed the common people cruelly; monopolies of staple articles granted to the rich and powerful were a further irritation to the masses. Strange, new notions about the "equality of men" and the true nature of governments were set going by a certain class of writers. The news of the successful revolt of the American colonies from England and of the share which Lafayette and other Frenchmen had taken in the struggle came as a suggestion and an encouragement. All these and many other things combined to bring about the French Revolution, but the immediate cause was national bankruptcy. Every plan to restore the finances was tried in vain. Only one resort remained. The national parliament, or "States General," which the absolute monarchs of France had ignored since 1614, must be summoned and made to vote increased taxes. The call was issued, but the States General, quickly controlled by the representatives of the middle class, began to complain of abuses, to demand reforms, and in other ways to show a spirit new to French subjects. Louis, naturally benevolent and devoted to the best interests of his people, was hampered by antecedents and education, and urged to arbitrary acts by his courtiers. He resisted the demands of the parliament, tried to dismiss it, but finally had to yield. Thus he lost not only his power but the chance to surrender it gracefully.

American sympathies were heartily with the French people during the early stages of the revolution. When the hated prison, the Bastille, was destroyed, Lafayette sent one of its keys as a present to Washington. But the excesses of 1792 and 1793 caused a revulsion of feeling, and the United States decided upon a policy of neutrality.

The attack in France upon the "divine right of kings" alarmed the monarchs of Europe. The doctrine that the people are the source of authority was deemed hardly less dangerous than are anarchist teachings to-day. Austria was the stronghold of absolute monarchy. Her ruler, Francis I., was the father of his people, who were kept in ignorance and denied the right to think for themselves. Germany was a mosaic of some three hundred states and free cities, all loosely combined with Austria into the "Holy Roman Empire," a fancied perpetuation of the old Roman rule, sanctified and strengthened by an alliance with the pope. There was no national spirit; Germany was a "geographical expression." Russia, as a result of Peter the Great's policy, was emerging from semibarbarism and taking part in the affairs of Europe. Italy, like Germany, was a composite of kingdoms, principalities, papal states, and republics. Spain fallen upon evil days still dreamed of her ancient glory under Charles V. and, though poor, priest-ridden, and misruled, cherished a national pride and patriotism unknown outside of England.

England had long been a constitutional monarchy, but the suffrage was very limited, dissenters and Catholics were discriminated against, the representation in Parliament was unjust and corrupt, and the criminal law, almost barbarous. Such in outline was the state of the Europe which France had for an enemy during twenty-five years.

The French Revolution was a series of steps from absolute monarchy to complete democracy, and back again to one-man rule. First a constitutional throne was established, but Louis by his insincerity, secret correspondence, and attempted flight, lost his crown and soon after his life. A republic followed, but fanatical leaders were not satisfied, and demanded more direct rule by the people. Thousands of those who resisted met death during the "reign of terror" in 1793-94. At last a reaction came; the people were sickened by the sight of blood. There was a demand for a stronger government, both to restore order in France and to drive back the invading armies of hostile Europe. The Directory, with five executive directors and two legislative chambers, was now established. Its administration was extremely corrupt. Bribery existed to a scandalous extent. The American commissioners sent to negotiate a treaty refused to pay the customary fees, and were rudely repulsed. The new government failed to meet the emergency, and was first influenced, then controlled by a young Corsican, Napoleon Bonaparte, who had won great and sudden fame by driving the Austrians out of Italy. In the year 1800, Napoleon was virtually master of France, and in 1804 he was crowned emperor.

The career of this wonderful man, however selfish and unworthy its motives and methods may have been, brought about the reconstruction of Europe. The French armies between 1796 and 1800 carried the principles of the revolution and the republic into Belgium, Germany, and Italy. Under the empire foreign conquests were followed by the establishment of better local governments, which the common people appreciated. Thus ideas were disseminated which no power could destroy, and in spite of opposition they finally prevailed.

Napoleon's triumphs followed each other in brilliant and rapid succession. Austria was three times beaten and despoiled of territory; Italy was entirely controlled by France; Prussia suffered a crushing defeat; and the German states were reduced to vassalage; Russia became an ally; England, protected by the channel, was attacked through the exclusion of English goods from continental markets; Spain was invaded, although not with the wonted success of French arms.

The commercial war between Napoleon and England was attended with serious results to American shipping. Both sides claimed extraordinary rights over neutral vessels, and many American ships were seized in French and English harbors and on the high seas. England asserted also the right to "impress" British seamen, wherever found, into her own service. In some cases American vessels were stopped and searched for deserting sailors.

In 1810 the French empire included a vast area and claimed the direct or indirect loyalty of nearly fifty million people. But this magnificent power was doomed to swift destruction. Spanish national spirit, sustained by English troops, made headway in the peninsula. The czar of Russia, realizing that he had been victimized, became first a cool ally, then an avowed enemy. Napoleon, determined to crush the only country he had not yet invaded, prepared for his ill-fated Russian campaign, in which he lost three hundred and seventy thousand men.

The Prussians had been waiting for such a chance as now presented itself. A coalition was formed and war declared. Napoleon, nothing daunted, raised a new army and took the field. Austria, for a time neutral, finally joined the enemy. The great general fought with his utmost skill, but in vain. Gradually the allies advanced to the French border, and early in 1814 entered Paris. Napoleon abdicated and retired to the island of Elba off the Italian coast, while the brother of Louis XVI. was restored to the throne of his family. Less than a year later Napoleon appeared once more in Europe for the brief, final scene of his active career. Landing in the south of France, he made his way to Paris, where he arrived with a large army of his old troops, who on the approach of their great commander had deserted to his standard. Louis XVIII.* fled before his old

---

* Louis, the son of Louis XVI., was known as Louis XVII., just as though he had actually reigned. His successor in the family, therefore was proclaimed Louis XVIII.

enemy. The news of Napoleon's return was the signal for a reassembling of the allies, by whom he was again defeated on the field of Waterloo, June 17, 1815. Exiled to the island of St. Helena, Napoleon ceased to be a factor in European politics. He died in 1821.

The "man of destiny" once safely out of the way, the rulers of Europe met in Vienna to decide upon the best plan for rearranging the continent. It is important to note that these monarchs, Francis I. of Austria, Alexander of Russia, Frederick William of Prussia, and others of less importance, were anxious, not to serve the people, but to look after the interests of the "bereaved princes," whose rights had been shamefully ignored by Napoleon.

The final arrangement reduced France to her boundaries of 1792, with Louis XVIII. as king. Austria received a large part of Northern Italy, and the Tyrol. Prussia regained her original territory, together with the Rhenish provinces, a large portion of Saxony, and other important additions. The thirty-nine German states were combined in a loose federation with Austria at its head. Russia had as her share the larger part of Poland. In Spain, Naples, the papal states, and other smaller countries, the old families were restored to power. After the Congress of Vienna the map of Europe looked very much as it did in 1789, but, as events finally proved, it was a very different Europe.

The czar, the Austrian emperor, and the Prussian king formed what they called the "Holy Alliance," and announced that they would rule their countries in accordance with the principles of Christianity. Fair promises were made, and there was talk of granting constitutions. A new era seemed about to dawn. There was much rejoicing, especially in Germany, where the war against Napoleon had aroused something very like a national spirit. But put to the test, the "divine right of kings" was the essential piety of the "Holy Alliance." Francis of Austria and his minister, Prince Metternich, became ardent advocates of the old order, and not only restored it in Vienna, but used all their influence against liberal tendencies in the German states, over which Austria exercised a sort of presidency.

Louis XVIII. granted a fairly liberal constitution in France, but unwisely accepted the counsel of emigrants who had deserted their country and aided her enemies during the revolution. As a result of unfair election laws, the legislature soon contained many friends of the old order of things, who tried to bring back in a measure the "good old times." This course was very unpopular, and the right to vote was extended to merchants and manufacturers, whose liberalizing influence was soon felt. Unfortunately, in 1820 a fanatic assassinated a strong conservative, the Duke of Berry. At once a cry was raised that dangerous republican notions were rife again, a reaction set in, severely conservative laws were passed, and the public school system was put into the hands of the Catholic clergy. The death of Louis in 1824 put upon the throne his brother, Charles X., who continued a reactionary policy until 1830, when a popular revolt drove him from power.

This protest of France against a return to the past caused excitement in all parts of Europe. The various German rulers under the influence of Austria had either refused constitutions, granted half measures, or withdrawn concessions. The universities and literary men had agitated earnestly for liberty, but met with severe repression.

The Paris revolution of 1830 was the signal for outbreaks in Saxony and the minor German states, by which the governments were in a measure brought to terms. The arranging of a "customs union," which with the exception of Austria included the principal German states, was a first step toward

German unity. In Spain and Naples the tyranny of the restored families had caused uprisings, which were put down by the aid of France and Austria. Greece had thrown off the Turkish yoke in 1827. In 1830 Belgium, joined to Holland against her will by the Congress of Vienna, revolted and set up an independent constitutional government.

In England the years from 1815 to 1832 saw the government policy gradually liberalized. The law which had long prevented Catholics from holding office was repealed, and the representation in Parliament which had been unjust in the extreme was vastly improved by the "reform bill" of 1832.

After the abdication of Charles X. in 1830, there was talk of another French republic, but at last Louis Phillippe, a cousin of Charles, was chosen king upon his expressly promising a liberal constitution. He liked to be styled "the citizen king," but the Bourbon blood ran in his veins. His reign was characterized by avarice and family ambition, gradually growing conservatism, a weak foreign policy, bad election laws, and industrial distress. The refusal in 1848 to grant certain popular demands brought on an important revolution.

This third French uprising had a most important influence on the rest of Europe. Even Austria felt the shock, and Metternich, the arch-conservative, was driven from Vienna. A national parliament was called, and fair promises made. Francis abdicated in favor of his son, Francis Joseph, the present emperor. Most of the revolts were easily suppressed, but Hungary, an unwilling part of the Austrian empire, was subdued only with the aid of Russia.

Prussia and other German states were the scenes of popular outbreaks, followed by concessions and constitutional reforms. Another attempt to unite Germany into a federation gave promise of success, but the time had not yet come. The rivalry between Austria, the old leader of Germany, and

Prussia, the new aspirant for that honor, became more and more apparent. Italy caught the spirit of the times. Revolutions occurred in almost every state. In the north there were demonstrations against the hated power of Austria, and attempts to establish a free and "united Italy." The king of Sardinia was especially active, but, defeated by Austria, he resigned his throne to his son, Victor Emanuel. France, meanwhile, in alleged defense of the pope, had occupied Rome.

The downfall of Louis Phillippe in France was followed by a republic, and for a time by a dictatorship. The socialistic ideas then current, the demoralizing influence of "government workshops"—a socialistic device for aiding the unemployed—and the general feeling of unrest and uncertainty, all made a demand for strong government. A republican constitution was set up, and Louis Napoleon, a nephew of Bonaparte, was chosen president by an overwhelming popular vote. Twice before, he had failed ridiculously in attempts to gain power, but this time his name and the career of his famous uncle worked in his favor. Louis Napoleon, though vain, was not so weak a man as he was generally supposed to be. Following the traditions of his family, he restored the empire by strategy, and was recognized in 1852 as Napoleon III. He declared that his sole aim would be to promote the welfare of France and the peace of Europe.

England since 1830 had seen important changes, chief of which was the repeal in 1844 of the "corn laws," measures which by unjustly taxing imported grain had cruelly oppressed the body of the nation. Other indefensible trade restrictions were also abolished. Poor laws, under which a premium had been put upon pauperism, were modified. Queen Victoria had ascended the throne in 1837. Large conquests had been made in India.

France and England found themselves allies in 1853-56 in the

Crimean War. Russia, always with an envious eye on Constantinople, found a pretext for war with Turkey. France and England aided Turkey to resist invasion, and saved the Ottoman Empire— "the sick man of Europe," whom the governmental doctors will not permit to die, only because they cannot agree upon a plan for dissecting him.

Napoleon next joined Victor Emanuel against Austria, and with such success that the union of Italy seemed virtually accomplished. But the French emperor made a separate peace with Austria by which the latter was to retain Venice. All the other countries except the papal states joined Victor Emanuel's government, and, in part at least, the ideal was realized.

The attention of Europe was now turned toward Germany, where Prussia and Austria only needed a pretext to join battle. Prussia under King William, Bismarck, the "iron chancellor," and General Von Moltke, had become powerful in affairs and in arms. An excuse for the conflict was found in a dispute over the control of a small district, Schleswig-Holstein. War was declared in 1866, and after a short, vigorous campaign ended in the complete triumph of Prussia and the formation of the North German Confederation, in which the government of

William I. had the predominant power, and the command of the united armies. Austria, as one of the articles of peace, ceded Venice to Italy, and thus another step was taken toward that union of the peninsula which was accomplished in 1871, when French interference in Rome was withdrawn.

Napoleon III. was chagrined by Prussia's sudden and brilliant victory. He had hoped to act as arbitrator in the dispute and to extend French territory on the east. The French people were dissatisfied with the empire at home and could be appeased only by victories abroad. Under pressure of necessity, Napoleon found excuse in certain fancied insults, for declaring war. France was aflame at once, and Germany responded enthusiastically to the call of Prussia. The poorly equipped and disciplined French soldiers were no match for the German troops. Napoleon surrendered at Sedan, September 1, 1870.

After a siege of four months Paris capitulated, January 18, 1871. Just before the close of the siege, the German princes assembled at Versailles and decided to establish a German empire. William of Prussia was crowned emperor, and within a short time the present government was founded. The German Empire is, strictly speaking, a federation of states, each of which conducts its own domestic affairs, surrendering the management of foreign relations, the army, and the navy, to the central imperial government. William I. was succeeded in 1888 by his son Frederick, who in a few months gave place to the present emperor, William II.

The Franco-Prussian War was at the time a severe blow to France. She not only lost Alsace and part of Lorraine, but was compelled to pay an enormous sum of money. Before all the German troops had retired, a civil war broke out in Paris between the provincial government and the wards or communes, which demanded an extremely democratic constitution. The city was given up to fire and pillage, during which many public buildings were destroyed. At last Thiers, president of the new republic, with the aid of Marshall MacMahon, restored order. In 1875 a new constitution providing for a president, ministers, and a legislature of two branches, was adopted, and is now in force. In 1880, after a hard struggle, the public school system was taken from the control of the clergy. The present republic has lasted much longer than its predecessors, and seems fairly stable. The French are naturally dissatisfied with the loss of territory and fame, and there are frequent, though generally idle, rumors of war.

Russia has grown in importance during the century. In

spite of the check received in the Crimean War, she again engaged Turkey in 1877, but the interposition of other powers robbed her of the best fruits of her victory. England, by the occupation of Egypt in 1882 and by "protecting" the country ever since, has guarded that important highway to India, the Suez Canal, and retained an indirect influence in Turkish affairs. Great Britain as well as other European powers, has gained territory in Africa and elsewhere, and extended an empire already vast. That the relations of dependencies like Canada to the imperial government present certain difficulties, has been shown by such cases as the fishery and sealing disputes with the United States.

One hundred years have seen great changes in Europe, not only in the rearrangement and consolidation of governments, but in social and political ideas. In most cases the forms of monarchy have been retained, but outside of Russia the theory of "divine right" goes begging. The democratic spirit is growing rapidly in Germany; England's royalty is hardly more than an historical and sentimental appendage to an essentially republican government; Italy's constitution is liberal; Austria, though still accounted conservative, is by no means Metternich's ideal state; Spain seems likely at almost any time to make another republican experiment; Belgium, Holland, Sweden, are far from oppressive kingdoms; and little Switzerland through all these stormy years has maintained with slight changes her sturdy republicanism.

CHAPTER XI.

GENERAL DIPLOMATIC RELATIONS WITH GREAT BRITAIN.

The young republic, in its infancy, was confronted with diplomatic problems quite as serious and perplexing as any that have since occupied the attention of its statesmen. The chief difficulties of Washington's administration were found in the preservation of peace with foreign powers, and the necessity of peace was never so urgent. The states were just recovering from the devastation and impoverishment of an eight years' war; they had no army and no navy; the revenues were meager, and the public debt was large. The populated portion of the country was but a narrow strip of land along the Atlantic coast, with harbors unprotected and nearly every city of commercial importance within range of the guns of a hostile fleet. Behind these settlements were tribes of savages in a continual state of irritation that was caused and increased to a large degree by foreign influences.

It may be said that throughout the entire world there was a general and genuine sympathy with the infant nation, England alone excepted, notwithstanding the fact that the success of popular government in America was a menace to the thrones of Europe. When Washington became President in 1789, six years after the close of the struggle for independence, eight treaties had been concluded with foreign powers. Embodied in these treaties was a policy whose broad statesmanship and ripe wisdom commanded the respect and admiration of the world, and furnished an example that has had a powerful and perpetual influence upon the diplomacy of all civilized nations. Benjamin Franklin, John Adams, and other patriots, by whom the treaties were negotiated, by their skill and candor not only succeeded in securing an acknowledgment of the rights of the republic, but the recognition of principles of international law more just and generous than had ever before been enunciated. More than thirty years afterwards, Lord Canning, the British secretary of state for foreign affairs, declared in the House of Commons that if a guide were needed for a system of neutrality it could be found in these documents.

But Washington had scarcely taken his seat as President when he found himself involved in the most serious complications with France, which had been our ally during the Revolution, as well as with Great Britain, which refused to comply with the terms of the treaty of peace. In this treaty, made in 1783, England agreed to abandon, without delay, all fortifications and military posts within the boundaries of the United States; but in 1789 her army still remained in possession of Detroit, Niagara, Oswego, Lake Champlain, Ogdensburg, Mackinaw, and other points which commanded the northern and western frontier of the country, as her fleets commanded the harbors on the Atlantic. At the same time England refused to pay the damages agreed upon for carrying off slaves at the close of the war, and forbade trade between the United States and her colonies in the West Indies, whence came our supplies of sugar, coffee, and other tropical products.

As an excuse for this England charged that the United States had neglected to restore the confiscated estates of citizens who had remained loyal to the crown during the Revolution, and prevented the collection of debts of American citizens contracted in London and other British cities before the war. She had refused to send a minister to this country, and by other means shown contempt for her former colonies.

For three weary years John Adams remained in London endeavoring to secure an adjustment of the difficulties, and then returned to the United States to assume the office of Vice President, to which he had been elected. Gouverneur Morris, who was residing in Paris, was sent to London to see what he could do, and succeeded in persuading the British government to send a minister to the United States, but he made no further progress, and in 1791 Thomas Pinckney was appointed as his successor. Under instructions from Mr. Jefferson, then secretary of state, Mr. Pinckney earnestly pressed the claims of the United States, demanding that the posts upon the frontier should be evacuated; that free navigation should be permitted upon the lakes and rivers that formed the boundary with Canada; that the fur trade in the Northwest should not be interrupted; that American seamen should not be impressed into the British service; and that other causes of complaint should be removed. But, although Mr. Jefferson wrote many long and convincing arguments, Mr. Pinckney was kept waiting in the anteroom of the foreign office at London, where he got few replies and no satisfaction.

Then came the troubles with France. In 1778, to secure her friendship and assistance, the American colonies, then in the midst of the Revolution, made a treaty of alliance with that government, under which they guaranteed to protect the French possessions in America. They also stipulated that French privateers should always have the right to seek refuge in our harbors to obtain provisions and other supplies; and to bring into them for sale or repair any vessels that they might capture at sea. This was a favorable treaty for the United States when we were at war with England, but when we were trying to preserve peace with her it was not; for France, being now in open hostilities with England, demanded the privileges which the treaty bestowed. If our government adhered to the terms of the treaty it meant another war with England; a violation of those terms threatened a war with France.

To make the situation more serious there was a bitter and determined struggle between the two political parties in the United States. The Democrats, or Republicans, for the same party was then known by both names, under the leadership of Jefferson, were outspoken in their hostility to England; and the Federalists, with Alexander Hamilton at their head, favored a conciliatory policy and a strict adherence to neutrality toward the European powers. Both leaders were members of Washington's cabinet and the struggle was carried to the desk of the President. Washington, in the midst of these perplexities, decided upon the policy advocated by Hamilton, and issued a proclamation warning all citizens of the United States against participation in the struggle between England and France, and forbidding them to give aid or comfort to either of the belligerents. At the same time Hamilton, who was secretary of the treasury, issued an order to collectors of customs directing them to prevent the entrance of French privateers to our ports, and to prohibit the sale of ammunition and supplies to foreign vessels. Whereupon Mr. Jefferson retired from the cabinet.

But in spite of the proclamation of the President and the order of the secretary of the treasury, public sympathy with France was so universal throughout the states, and the animosity toward England so bitter, that French privateers were hailed with a joyous welcome whenever they entered one of the harbors on the Atlantic, and they were not only able to secure all the supplies they needed, but were allowed to bring in captured vessels of Great Britain, and sell them and their cargoes to our citizens. Agents of the French government found no difficulty in purchasing arms and ammunition, and the French minister, M. Genet, who landed at Charleston in a privateer, was followed to the seat of government at Philadelphia by ovations which equaled those that greeted Washington on his journey to New York after he was elected President.

The followers of Jefferson in Congress, where sympathy with France was unconcealed, introduced a bill closing the ports of the United States to British commerce. The enactment of such a law would unquestionably have resulted in a war with England, and there was a very narrow escape, for it actually passed the House of Representatives, in spite of the remonstrances of Washington and Hamilton, and was defeated in the Senate only by the vote of John Adams, who as Vice President was presiding over that body.

To allay the excitement in England and counteract the effect of the hostile demonstrations among our people, the President decided to send as minister to London, Alexander Hamilton, who was born in the British West Indies, and whose cordial sentiments toward the British government were well understood on both sides of the Atlantic; but he reconsidered that determination when it was found that Hamilton's nomination would be rejected by the Senate. John Jay, afterwards chief justice of the Supreme Court, was therefore selected, and he, with the powerful influence of public sentiment in the United States, succeeded in bringing England to terms. He negotiated a treaty which provided:

(1) That the frontier posts should be evacuated by British troops within two years.

(2) That there should be free commercial intercourse across the border between the United States and the British possessions.

(3) That trade could be carried on between the United States and the British West Indies by vessels of both nations carrying only the products of either country.

(4) That foreign privateers should not be allowed to fit or arm in the ports of either country for war against their vessels.

(5) That criminals taking refuge in either country should be surrendered.

(6) That commissions should be appointed to survey the upper Mississippi River; to determine the boundary between the United States and Canada along the St. Croix River; to settle debts contracted by American citizens in England before the Revolution; and to assess damages sustained by American commerce from British privateers.

While this treaty was in fact a great triumph for American diplomacy, it was bitterly denounced by French sympathizers in the United States, and public meetings were held all over the country to condemn the action of our government. But it was finally ratified by the Senate, by a narrow majority, and public excitement subsided.

But the great defect in the treaty was the absence of any provision to prohibit the impressment of American seamen into the British service, and it was soon realized in a serious manner. Complaints of this character were frequent and they finally culminated in an attack upon the United States man-of-war *Chesapeake* by the British frigate *Leopard*, which demanded the right of search for some deserters from the British navy who were alleged to be serving on the former vessel. Taken by surprise, the *Chesapeake* surrendered after a brief engagement and four sailors were taken off. Our government demanded reparation and an apology, and a proclamation was issued ordering all British vessels to leave American waters. Mr. Monroe, who was minister to England, failing to secure satisfaction, left for home, and the British government issued a retaliatory decree prohibiting trade between the United States and countries that were then at war with England.

Lord Erskine, the British minister, proposed that this order should be withdrawn, and that reparation would be awarded for the *Chesapeake* incident, provided the United States would revoke its decree against British vessels. On his faith in this assurance the President withdrew the order, but the British government claimed that Erskine was not authorized to make the proposition, and refused to comply with its terms. All attempts to settle the difference by diplomatic negotiation having failed, the President, on the 19th of June, 1812, proclaimed war, and hostilities began.

In March, 1813, the emperor of Russia offered his services as mediator, and they were accepted by the United States but refused by Great Britain. The latter government, however, consented to meet on other neutral ground, and a commission, consisting of Albert Gallatin, James A. Bayard, John Quincy Adams, Henry Clay, and Jonathan Russell, was sent to the city of Ghent, Belgium, to meet Lord Gambier, Henry Goulburn, and William Adams, the representatives of Great Britain. The British demands, as originally made, were rejected, but being modified afterwards, a treaty of peace was concluded on the 24th of December, 1814.

Although, singularly enough, not one of the causes of the war was alluded to in this treaty, and the right of Great Britain to impress American seamen was not even discussed, the result was received with great favor in the United States, and the President in communicating the information to Congress declared that "it terminates with peculiar felicity a campaign signalized by the most brilliant successes."

This treaty provided for the cessation of hostilities, the restoration of prisoners taken, the suppression of the slave trade, and the establishment of the boundaries between the United States and the British possessions in America by a joint commission.

In 1815, John Quincy Adams, Mr. Clay, and Mr. Gallatin were appointed commissioners to negotiate a commercial treaty with Great Britain. This treaty provided for free commerce between the ports of the two countries, and with the British colonies in the East Indies, and left the conditions of trade with the West Indies as had been arranged by the treaty made by Mr. Jay in 1793. It also stipulated that all duties and port charges should be the same upon the vessels and products of both countries.

In 1818 another negotiation was made necessary by a difference of interpretation of the meaning of the previous treaties, and another attempt was made to secure our ships from the right of search for alleged British subjects, and to prevent the impressment of American citizens; but the only concession that could be obtained was an agreement that American vessels should not be interfered with while England was at peace. The same treaty provided that the naval forces upon the lakes should be limited to one vessel for each nation on Lake Ontario, two vessels on the upper lakes, and one on Lake Champlain; but none of them were to be of more than one hundred tons burden or carry more than one eighteen-pound cannon. It also provided that the citizens of the United States should have the right to fish only along certain uninhabited coasts of Newfoundland and Labrador, and that their vessels should only be permitted to enter the bays and harbors of the British possessions for shelter in time of storm, and for repairs, wood, and water. The 49th parallel of latitude was agreed upon as the boundary line from the Lake of the Woods to the Rocky (then called Stony) Mountains, and the English renounced their claim to the free navigation of the Mississippi River.

The emperor of Russia, who had been selected to settle a dispute as to the meaning of the first article of the treaty of 1814, decided that the United States was entitled to indemnification for slaves carried away by the British at the close of the Revolution; a commission was appointed to assess the damages, and in 1826 the sum of $1,204,960 was paid by England to settle all claims.

The discovery of the mouth of the Columbia River by an American vessel, and the exploration of its headwaters by Lewis and Clark, gave the United States the right of title to a large tract of territory in the Northwest, which was acknowledged by Great Britain by a treaty in 1827, but the boundary question was again under discussion in 1842 between Daniel Webster and Lord Ashburton. In the treaty arranged by them the line of partition between the two countries was minutely described from the easternmost frontier of Maine to the Rocky Mountains. The limits of the British possessions west of the mountains were determined by a treaty negotiated by James Buchanan and Lord Pakenham in 1846. The 49th parallel was accepted as the boundary to the point in the channel separating Vancouver Island from the mainland, and from that point to the ocean.

In the Webster-Ashburton treaty both governments agreed to unite in the suppression of the slave trade, and the list of crimes for which fugitives might be extradited was considerably enlarged.

During the Crimean War the British authorities attempted to secure recruits for its armies in the United States. Regular recruiting stations were not opened, but agencies were established in some of the larger cities where transportation was furnished to able-bodied men who would go to Canada for the purpose of enlistment. Our government complained that this was an evasion of the principle of neutrality and after some correspondence it was stopped.

The Civil War in the United States furnished many serious subjects for diplomatic controversy and negotiation with Great Britain. One grew out of the seizure of Messrs. Mason and Slidell, the ministers accredited by the Confederacy to England and France. These gentlemen, having reached Havana on a blockade runner, took passage for Southampton on the British mail steamer *Trent*, which was overhauled at sea by Captain Wilkes of the U. S. gunboat *Jacinto*. The British government, claiming that the arrest was an assault upon its flag, demanded the release of the prisoners and an appropriate apology. The prisoners were released, and Secretary

Seward admitted that Captain Wilkes had exceeded his instructions, holding that he should have conveyed the *Trent* to the nearest port where the arrests could be formally made under judicial authority. To this proposition Lord Russell dissented, and denied to the United States the right which the British government had always claimed, and by the exercise of which it brought on the War of 1812,—that is, the right to search a neutral vessel for belligerents.

During the war, the Confederate authorities succeeded in securing and fitting out at English ports several privateers, chief of which was the *Alabama*, and they committed many depredations upon the commerce of the United States. Our government held that this was in violation of the laws of neutrality and its treaties with the British government. The question was submitted to a joint commission, which met at Washington in 1871 and decided that the claims for damages by these cruisers should be settled by the arbitration * of a court to meet at Geneva, Switzerland. The same commission concluded what is known as the treaty of Washington, in which the rights and obligations of neutral nations were clearly defined:

(1) That they should prevent the equipment in their ports of vessels intended for war or for the destruction of commerce.

(2) That they should not permit their ports to be used as a base of supplies for such vessels.

(3) That they should use all possible vigilance to prevent the violation of these rules.

The same commission took under consideration the fisheries and other questions, and by the treaty recognized the equal reciprocal rights of the citizens of both countries to the fishing grounds in the waters of the United States and British

---

* The Geneva arbitration and the fisheries question are treated elsewhere (see Chapter XII).

North America. A commission was authorized to decide what compensation, if any, should be paid by the United States for this privilege; the navigation of the rivers, lakes, and canals between the United States and Canada was declared free; a plan was adopted for the shipment in bond through the United States and Canada of goods intended for the interior cities of both countries; and the disputed boundary along Puget Sound was left to the arbitration of the emperor of Germany.

When the revolt of the Irish subjects of Great Britain in America began in 1866, the British government suspended the *habeas corpus* with as much promptness as they had displayed in censuring the United States for the same act in 1861. In view of the crisis Mr. Seward, who was secretary of state, instructed Mr. Adams, our minister to London, that it was "by no means the purpose or policy of the United States to suffer their own laws to be violated or their honor and dignity to be compromised. It may be expected that some of our Irish-born naturalized citizens will be arrested on complaints of complicity in seditious proceedings. It may also be expected that some who will thus be accused will be innocent, while others will be guilty. Give a careful examination to each complaint, dealing at all times frankly with the British government and asking on their part strict justice in their proceedings where American citizens are concerned."

This line of policy was pursued during the Fenian disorders. Abroad the rights of American citizens were protected. At home the violation of the neutrality laws was resented. Three months later there was an attempt to invade Canada. On the 30th of May, 1867, numbers of so-called Fenians appeared at Buffalo, and it was rumored that others were proceeding toward Potsdam, N. Y., and toward St. Albans, Vermont, with the purpose of invading Canada. On the night of the

30th one thousand men passed over the Black Rock ferry at Buffalo, but they were intercepted and seven hundred were captured by the United States steamer *Michigan*. Two days after, the President issued a proclamation warning all citizens of the United States against taking part in the movement, and directing General Meade to employ the land and naval force of the United States and the militia of the several states to defeat the purposes of the conspirators.

The prompt action of the President had the effect of suppressing any further attempt at invasion from the United States. A number of those who had crossed over to Fort Erie, Canada, among whom were Colonel Robert B. Lynch and the Rev. Father McMahon, a Roman Catholic priest from Indiana, were captured by the Canadian forces. These prisoners were tried in Toronto for treason and condemned to death. Secretary Seward, in order to protect any rights that the prisoners might be entitled to as citizens of the United States, directed the consul to secure the services of counsel (Mr. Devlin) to defend them. Notwithstanding the efforts of Mr. Devlin, Mr. Lynch and Father McMahon were condemned to death. This severe penalty imposed upon two citizens who claimed to have had nothing whatever to do with the belligerent movement, aroused great interest throughout the country, and among others the legislature of Vermont and the council of Chicago petitioned for clemency. After repeated applications by the secretary of state, he was at last successful, and the sentence in both cases was commuted to imprisonment for life. The prisoners captured by the *Michigan* were held for trial before the United States district court at Buffalo, but all hostile demonstrations having ceased the cases were never prosecuted.

An interesting discussion between the two countries was awakened by the arrest in England of a man named Winslow, who had committed extensive forgeries in Massachusetts and fled from the country. The British government refused to surrender him unless the United States would agree that he should not be tried for any other offense than that for which his extradition was asked. This was refused and Winslow being released fled to the Argentine Republic, where he has since been residing.

During the presidential campaign of 1888, Sir Lionel Sackville-West, the British minister at Washington, received a letter from a man in California, who gave the name of Murchison, and claimed to be a naturalized Englishman. He asked the advice of the British legation as to which candidate for President he should support, as he desired to vote with the party whose success would most promote the interests of Great Britain in the United States. To this the British minister replied with great frankness, expressing his opinion and his preference. The letter was widely published as a campaign document by the opposing party, and President Cleveland asked the British government to recall Sackville-West because he had been guilty of unwarranted interference in the domestic affairs of the United States and was no longer a *persona grata*. Sir Lionel insisted that his letter to Murchison was a private and not an official communication, but the government of the United States refused to recognize him as a medium of correspondence between the two countries and he was recalled.

Three months having elapsed before the appointment of his successor, Secretary Bayard intimated that, unless the vacancy was filled, the United States would withdraw its minister from London. The British government, however, gave an assurance that no affront was intended, but the vacancy was continued until the retirement of President Cleveland and the inauguration of his successor.

CHAPTER XII.

DIPLOMATIC RELATIONS WITH GREAT BRITAIN—THE BERING SEA AND FISHERIES QUESTIONS.

THE people of the colonies which afterwards became the United States had enjoyed, during the period preceding the Revolution, in common with their fellow colonists of Nova Scotia and New Brunswick, the right of fishing all along the Atlantic from off New England, where the schools of cod and mackerel were met in the early spring, to the limits of their northward course in the Bay of Fundy or the Gulf of St. Lawrence, and the bays and inlets of the coasts. The claim was made by Great Britain during the negotiations at Paris in 1782 that resulted in the recognition of our independence, that the war of the Revolution had canceled that right, but the American commissioners would not agree to such a proposition.

Thus the matter stood down to the declaration of war in 1812, although the right of our fishermen to approach the shores of the British possessions was questioned in many cases, and there were many contentions and frequent collisions between the rival fishermen. After the two governments had agreed to consider terms for peace at Ghent in 1814, the commissioners for Great Britain insisted that, as the treaty of 1783 which recognized American fishing rights had fallen by the declaration of war, his majesty's government would not renew the privilege of fishing along the Newfoundland banks without some equivalent concession from the United States. It was claimed by them that the liberty enjoyed by the American fishermen was granted by the treaty and when the treaty fell the fishing right fell with it.

The American commissioners denied this, and held that the rights and liberties in the fisheries as acknowledged by the treaty of peace and independence in 1783 belonged permanently to the citizens of the United States, and were no more affected by the War of 1812 than were the boundaries of the country. Taken by surprise and having received no instructions from the President on this subject, but unwilling to give up their position, the Americans proposed to the English commissioners that the stipulation of the treaty of 1783 should be repeated or that the matter should be temporarily laid aside. The latter course was adopted, and so the treaty of Ghent was silent on the subject of the fisheries.

Negotiations were continued, however, and although it was not possible to come to an agreement when the commercial treaty of 1815 was signed, the treaty of 1818 defined the places where it was agreed that American citizens should forever have the right to take fish, naming also specific localities where they might land to cure them, and renouncing the liberty which they had claimed and enjoyed "to take, dry, or cure fish on or within three marine miles of any of the coasts, bays, creeks, or harbors of his Britannic majesty's dominions not included in the above mentioned limits. Provided, however, that the American fishermen shall be permitted to enter such bays or harbors for the purpose of shelter, of repairing damages therein, of purchasing wood, and obtaining water, and for no other purpose whatever."

But the meaning of the "four purposes" defined in the above quotation from the treaty, and what is known as the "headland theory," have given rise to continual correspondence and discussions, which, beginning soon after the adoption of the treaty of 1818, are still going on. The legislatures of the British colonies adopted many laws declared to be in accordance with the provisions of the agreement, but very much more stringent, and, under these, many American fishing vessels have been seized and sold for alleged violations of the treaty. The British have claimed that the three marine miles specified in the treaty should be computed as three miles from a straight line connecting one headland with another, and should include all the water within such a line even though the shore might be many leagues distant from it. The Americans have insisted that the three-mile limit should be measured by following the actual shore line and that beyond such a parallel three miles from the coast lies the open sea.

Neither side would admit the contention of the other; American vessels continued to be seized; and in 1852 a squadron was sent by the British government to the fishing waters to secure the enforcement of the British statutes; but a respite was secured in 1854 by the adoption of the reciprocity treaty, which, in return for the permission to import certain British-American products free of duty into the United States, granted to American fishermen "the liberty to take fish of every kind, except shellfish, on the seacoasts and shores, and in the bays, harbors, and creeks of Canada, New Brunswick, Nova Scotia, Prince Edward Island, and the several islands thereunto adjacent, without being restricted to any distance from the shore." Permission was also given to American citizens to land on the coasts in order to cure their fish and dry their nets.

This agreement brought with it a temporary cessation of the discussion, and the fishing fleets of the United States were no longer interfered with, until the denunciation of the treaty in 1866 by the United States. Then the legislatures of the British colonies enacted stringent laws to prevent the Americans from taking fish along their shores, and the troublesome question again occupied the time of the foreign departments of the two countries. Many protests and counter-protests were filed against the abuse of privileges by the fishermen and against the unwarranted exercise of authority by the officials.

With a view to settling these disputes, Sir Edward Thornton proposed to Secretary Fish, in January, 1871, that a joint high commission should take the matter into consideration. The proposition was accepted by the secretary on the condition that the claims of the United States for damages committed by the privateer *Alabama* during the War of the Rebellion should be submitted to the same commission for adjustment. This commission concluded what is known as the "treaty of Washington," in which it was agreed that for ten years or until either government should give two years' notice of a desire to terminate it, the inhabitants of both countries should have an equal right to engage in the sea fisheries on the Atlantic coast under the same conditions that were provided for in the reciprocity treaty of 1854 ; fish and fish oil were to be admitted free into each country from the other ; and commissioners were to be appointed to determine what amount of money, if any, should be paid to the British government for these privileges accorded to the American fishermen.

Thus again was temporary quiet secured, and the fishermen pursued their perilous calling unmolested by adverse legislation until the season of 1886. The commission which sat at Halifax to determine the amount due the British government for the privilege of fishing in the waters of their American dominion, awarded $5,500,000 as the sum to be paid by the United States. Although the amount was deemed exorbitant by the people of this country it was paid; but under the instructions of Congress the American minister at London informed the British government on Monday, July 2, 1883, that the fishery articles of the treaty of 1871 would terminate in two years.

The termination of the treaty taking place in the midst of the fishing season, it was agreed between Mr. Bayard, then secretary of state, and Sir Lionel West, the British minister at Washington, that its privileges should be enjoyed throughout the season of 1885. It was declared in the notice issued by Mr. Bayard, however, that this temporary postponement in no way affected the principles involved in the case and did not allow the exemption of fish and fish oil from customs duties.

The President in his annual message recommended the appointment of a joint commission to consider and settle upon a just, equitable, and honorable basis the entire question of the fishing rights of the citizens of the two governments, and Mr. Phelps, the American minister in London, presented his views to the British authorities in order to suggest a basis for negotiations. But the proposition of the President was not favorably acted upon.

When the season of 1886 opened, the New England fishermen followed the fish northward, as usual, and when they reached the Canadian coasts, there was a repetition of the previous troubles with the local authorities. These cases beginning with that of the *David J. Adams* in May, 1886, were brought to the attention of the British government by Mr. Phelps under the instruction of the secretary of state, and earnest remonstrance was made. But the seizures continued, and on March 3, 1887, Congress passed an act authorizing the President to retaliate by denying Canadian vessels access to the ports of the United States, and prohibiting the importation of their fish. This brought the matter to a crisis, and with a view to reaching an amicable settlement, a commission was appointed, consisting of Secretary Bayard, Judge Putnam of Maine, and President Angell of Michigan University, to meet Sir Lionel Sackville-West, Sir Joseph Chamberlain, and Sir William Tupper representing Great Britain. They concluded a treaty in February, 1888, which was submitted to the Senate of the United States for ratification, but rejected by that body. At the time the treaty was agreed to, the British commissioners presented what is known in diplomatic language as a "modus vivendi,"—that is, a temporary agreement to be in force until a definite and final arrangement could be concluded. By this *modus* the fishermen of the United States were allowed to take out licenses from the customs authorities of Canada, which would secure them from molestation.

Upon the rejection of this treaty by the Senate the President sent a message to Congress in which, after stating the history of the negotiations and the fact of the rejection of the measure proposed by mutual treaty concessions, he suggested that it would be necessary for the legislative power to provide some means to protect our fishermen from further molestation; but up to this writing no final action has been taken.

The Bering Sea Dispute.

Closely connected with the attempts of the government to secure the rights of the New England fishermen on the Atlantic coast, has been the protection of the seal fisheries on the coast of Alaska and the Aleutian Archipelago of the North Pacific Ocean. In 1823 Alexander I. of Russia issued a ukase, prohibiting foreign vessels, under the penalty of confiscation, from engaging in commerce, fishing, or sealing, or even sailing within one hundred miles of the coasts of Russian possessions in America. Mr. Adams, who was United States minister at St. Petersburg, protested, as did the representatives

MAP OF ALASKA,

Showing by the dotted lines the jurisdiction claimed by Russia and transferred, as our government asserts, to the United States, together with the territory of Alaska. Under this claim the part of the sea frequented by seals is not an "open sea," and cannot be entered without the permission of the United States.

of other nations, but the question did not assume any great degree of importance until the purchase of Alaska by the United States in 1867.

Soon after the transfer of the territory, Mr. Hayward Hutchinson of California, who had gone to Alaska with General Rousseau, the commissioner of the United States appointed to receive the property, made an arrangement with Prince Matsukoff, who had been governor of Alaska and was still in control of the Russian Fur Company, for the purchase of the property and the rights of that corporation. On his return to San Francisco, Mr. Hutchinson organized what was known as the Alaska Commercial Company, to which, on the 3d of August, 1870, were leased the Pribyloff group of islands, Saint Paul and Saint George, upon which the fur seals assemble in great multitudes during the breeding season. The lease was for twenty years and gave the company the exclusive right to take fur seals on those islands or to send vessels there. The number to be taken annually was limited to one hundred thousand, and the company agreed to pay the United States government a yearly rental of $55,000, $2.62 for every seal skin taken, and 55 cents per gallon for all seal oil sold.

To preserve the animals from extinction, it was made unlawful to kill them, except on the islands and in the adjacent waters; and there only from June 1 to October 31. The killing of female seals or males less than one year old was entirely prohibited.

Under this law and the other regulations seal fishing was confined almost entirely to the Commercial Company, who derived an immense profit from their privileges. No attempt to dispute their exclusive right to the fisheries seems to have been made until the season of 1886, when three Canadian schooners which were in pursuit of seals in Bering Sea were captured by the United States revenue cutter *Corwin*, and brought before the district court at Sitka, where their masters were fined and the vessels confiscated.

The orders under which the *Corwin* made the arrests were issued by the Treasury Department in pursuance of a section of the Revised Statutes, which provides: "that any person killing seals, etc., within the limits of Alaska Territory or in the waters thereof" shall be fined and imprisoned, and all vessels engaged in the violation of the law forfeited.

The British government protested against the capture and confiscation of these schooners, which were taken at sea, out of sight of land, while pursuing what they claimed to be a peaceful and lawful occupation. It denied that the United States had authority in the waters of the Bering Sea beyond the ordinary limit (three miles) of jurisdiction allowed under maritime international law, and the claim that vessels could be arrested seventy miles from land on the charge that they were violating the laws of the United States within the waters of Alaska Territory, was resisted as being an unwarranted assumption of authority.

By order of the President the proceedings against these vessels were discontinued, and they were restored to their owners. But the secretary of state at once commenced negotiations with Great Britain and other maritime powers to secure the adoption of general and uniform regulations to govern the seal fisheries, and to prevent the total destruction of those valuable animals, which have contributed so much to the wealth of this country and to the comfort of mankind.

The seals require both land and water for their existence, and during the breeding season are in the habit of leaving the coast of Alaska for the Pribyloff Islands, where in seclusion they produce and rear their young. In making the passage they must cross the Bering Sea more than three miles from the coast, a distance which is accepted by international law as the limit of national jurisdiction. For several years it has been the practice of Canadian vessels to intercept seals in the open sea, and shoot them in the water. Many are lost, and the skins of none are so good as when taken at other seasons of the year. This reckless and indiscriminate mode of killing male and female alike has greatly reduced their numbers, and if long continued will result in their complete extermination. The purpose of the United States, therefore, was to prevent that barbarous destruction by foreigners as well as by Americans which is forbidden by the laws of Congress.

It was proposed that Great Britain, Russia, and the United States should unite in regulations forbidding the killing of female and young seals at any time, and limiting the period during which full-grown male seals might be taken to the season when their skins are in the best marketable condition. Both the emperor of Russia and the British government very promptly consented to accept the terms of the agreement, admitting that such regulations would be of great benefit. A formal draft of a treaty embodying these provisions was prepared at Washington and submitted to both governments for their ratification, but, in the meantime, the Canadian authorities, having no interest in the preservation of the seal, protested against the action of the cabinet at London and succeeded in persuading Lord Salisbury to withdraw from the agreement.

Thereupon the British government began to oppose the proposition with as much earnestness as it had originally advocated it; and held that the United States had no right to forbid or attempt to regulate the killing of seals when they were taken in the open sea more than three miles from land.

This government, in its correspondence with Great Britain

on the subject, held that the place where the seals were taken by the Canadian vessels was not the open sea, but a part of the territory of the United States, bounded upon the east and north by Alaska, on the south by the Aleutian Islands, and on the north and west by the Russian possessions in Asia; that jurisdiction over these waters was conceded to Russia by Great Britain by treaty in 1824, and that such jurisdiction was conveyed to the United States when the latter purchased from Russia the territory which surrounds it. The United States also took the broad ground that the wanton destruction of useful animals even in neutral waters was unlawful because it was a violation of the laws of nature and of humanity, and an injury to the rights and the welfare of the public. While the fish and animals that live in the sea are common property, of which all people are entitled to their just share, no nation could be conceded the privilege of destroying them and thus preventing others from participating in the benefits. This is the unwritten law of civilization, which recognizes the common rights of all, but requires that they should be exercised with injury to none. At the same time our secretary maintained that the colony of seals which make their permanent home within the territory of the United States are the property of the United States, and do not lose their character as such when passing from one part of that territory to another, even across a neutral sea; particularly as such passing was a regular and periodical migration in obedience to the laws of nature, and a necessary feature of seal life.

The correspondence upon this subject was continued at great length and with considerable bitterness until February, 1892, when it was agreed between the two nations to submit the questions at issue to arbitration by a tribunal consisting of seven persons: two to be named by the President of the

United States, two by her Britannic majesty, one each by the president of the French Republic, the king of Italy, and the king of Norway and Sweden.

Scarcely was this treaty submitted to the respective governments for ratification when another and equally serious difficulty arose by reason of the refusal of Great Britain to consent to a suspension of seal fishing by Canadian vessels while the main question was under arbitration. Lord Salisbury suggested and insisted that the destruction of the seals should continue until a decision was reached, and then if the claims of the United States were sustained Great Britain would pay in cash the value of the seals taken in the meantime. If the claims of England were sustained there would be nothing to pay. But our government declined to concede this for the reason that the chief object of the United States was to prevent the extermination of the seals, and that their destruction by Canadian fishermen was so rapid that if it was allowed to continue until after the arbitration was completed there would be nothing left to arbitrate. The President gave notice at the same time that the United States would protect the seals by force, and warned all vessels from entering the Bering Sea for the purpose of killing them. England finally consented to a "modus vivendi," or temporary agreement, until the arbitration was concluded, and vessels from the United States Navy were sent to the fishing waters to see that the agreement was respected.

The Geneva Tribunal.

During the progress of the Civil War the commerce of the United States received almost incalculable damage from Confederate cruisers, many of which had been built, manned, or furnished with supplies and equipments in the ports of the British colonies or in Great Britain. It was also claimed that England's course in so quickly recognizing the belligerent rights of the Confederacy was an act unfriendly to the United States.

The losses which the government sustained from this cause together with those which individuals had met with from the ravages of the privateers, were brought to the attention of the British government by Mr. Seward soon after the war, and a demand was made for compensation. An arbitration to ascertain the amount due being proposed, Great Britain declined either to acknowledge the responsibility or to offer compensation for the losses sustained or to refer the question to arbitration.

During the first administration of General Grant, when the British minister proposed a commission to consider the questions arising out of the fisheries and other matters over which there was a serious conflict of views, the proposal was accepted by Mr. Fish with the proviso that the commission also take up the question of the *Alabama* claims. Accordingly there met in Washington in the early part of the year 1871, a joint high commission composed of twelve members, the United States representatives being Hamilton Fish, secretary of state, Robert C. Schenck, minister to Great Britain, Justice Samuel Nelson of the Supreme Court, E. R. Hoar of Massachusetts, and Geo. H. Williams of Oregon. The plenipotentiaries of her majesty were the Earl of Grey and Ripon, Sir Stafford Northcote, Sir Edward Thornton, Sir John Macdonald of Canada, and Montague Bernard, professor of international law at Oxford. The first meeting of the commissioners was held February 27, and on the 8th of May was signed the treaty known as the "treaty of Washington."

It consisted of forty-three articles, of which the first eleven related to the claims growing out of depredations by the Confederate cruisers and the alleged violations of neutrality by Great Britain. The *Alabama* claims were referred to a tribunal of arbitration which sat in Geneva, Switzerland, and was composed of five members, one named by the President, Charles Francis Adams; one by the queen, Chief Justice Cockburn; one by the king of Italy, Count Sclopis; one by the president of the Swiss Confederation, M. James Stämpli; and one by the emperor of Brazil, Viscount d' Itajubá.

The cruiser *Alabama*, whose depredations gave a name to these claims, was built on the Mersey in 1862, and left for the Azores under the British flag entirely unarmed and without any indication of a warlike purpose. She was met at sea, off Terceira, by two vessels, the *Agrippina* and *Bahama*, bringing all the necessary equipments, a complete armament, provisions, uniforms, coal, and her captain, Semmes, together with her other officers. As soon as the transhipment was completed the Confederate colors were displayed at the *Alabama's* masthead, and her career of devastation upon the commerce of the United States ended only near the close of the war with her destruction by the *Kearsarge*.

The claims presented by the United States before the tribunal were for recompense for: First, direct losses growing out of the destruction of vessels and cargoes by Confederate cruisers, equipped in Great Britain; second, the expense occasioned by the pursuit of such cruisers by naval vessels of the United States; third, the losses sustained by the transfer of the American commercial marine to the British flag; fourth, the enhanced premiums for insurance; fifth, the prolongation of the war, and the addition of a large sum to its cost.

The tribunal held that the last three classes of claims should be excluded from consideration; that the second class was not properly distinguishable from the general expenses of the war and no sum could be awarded under that head. Under the first class there was awarded for depredations committed by the *Alabama*, the *Florida*, and the *Shenandoah* and by their tenders, the sum of $15,500,000, which was paid to the United States by Great Britain and distributed by a court of adjudication, which sat from July 22, 1874, until December 29, 1876, and paid to claimants the sum of $9,316,120.25.

As there remained in the treasury a balance which had been increased to $10,089,004.96, by reason of accumulation of interest and premiums on the sale of certain bonds, Congress passed the act of June 5, 1882, re-establishing the court for the purpose of distributing this balance among those who, during the rebellion, had sustained losses resulting from damage done by Confederate cruisers on the high seas. These losses included vessels and cargoes attacked within four miles of the shore on the high seas, and also premiums for war risks whether paid to corporations, agents, or individuals, after the sailing of any cruiser. This court decided 4,643 claims favorably, and ended its labors December 31, 1885.

CHAPTER XIII.

DIPLOMATIC RELATIONS WITH FRANCE AND THE PURCHASE OF LOUISIANA.

THE history of the early diplomatic relations between France and the United States reads like a romance. Mysterious men and anonymous women passed in and out of the negotiations; mercantile houses were established under fictitious names to conceal purchases of arms and loans of money for the American patriots; official representatives were known by the letters "X," "Y," "Z," and other cabalistic signs, and intrigue followed intrigue at the corrupt and frivolous court, as in the novels of Dumas or Victor Hugo. But above all this conspiracy and mystery rises the serene and benevolent character of Benjamin Franklin, whose honesty of purpose could not be diverted, and whose profound patriotism could not be contaminated by any aid or obstacle with which they were associated. Following him as minister to France came Thomas Jefferson, a man of even simpler tastes, for whom the frivolities of court life had no fascinations, but whose affection and gratitude toward France, first inspired by her generous sympathy for the struggling colonies and the young republic, and strengthened by a long residence in Paris, could not be impaired by the fickleness of the people or the cruelties that stained their political history.

These two men, pre-eminent and peculiar, full of zeal and

patriotism, framed the fraternal relations that existed between France and the United States in the days of the Revolution and the first years of the republic, and, when Jefferson was recalled from Paris to take a place in the cabinet of Washington, there were no two nations in the universe whose friendship was more cordial or whose sympathy was more sincere.

Relying upon the aid she had furnished the colonies in their struggle for independence, France made, during the last ten years of the eighteenth century, demands of the most extravagant character upon the young republic for support against the allied nations of Europe. Had these requirements been complied with, the United States, even though sustained as they were by public sentiment this side of the Atlantic, would have been embroiled in a ruinous war with all the rest of Europe.

The complications arising from America's refusal to comply with the demands of France were made more serious by the imprudent conduct of M. Genet, who was commissioned by the French Directory as minister to the United States. He arrived at Charleston in April, 1793, and was received with great enthusiasm as the representative of a people who had given us aid and encouragement during the Revolution, and the envoy of a republic whose establishment the success of popular government in America had made possible. But the French minister, in defiance of Washington's proclamation of neutrality, made every effort to incite Americans to take the side of France, issuing military commissions to officers and men and granting licenses to privateers. His conduct was so outrageous that our government was compelled to ask for his recall.

The United States were powerless to aid France, and still more impotent to defend themselves against the combined forces of Europe, a resistance which would have been necessary had the terms of the treaty been fulfilled. There was no military force, no navy, no money, no credit, and, had a loan been attempted, the only source of financial assistance was Holland, already actively engaged in hostilities with France. The country was just beginning to recover from the effects of the Revolution, and the revenues of the government, even with the greatest economy, were barely sufficient to sustain its ordinary expenses. The deliberations of the administration on this subject were long and earnest, and, although public sentiment was strongly in favor of active co-operation with France, President Washington issued a proclamation announcing the policy of the United States to be that of strict neutrality and warning American citizens against any direct or indirect participation in the European war.

The demand for the recall of M. Genet, the French minister, was complied with but it was coupled with a condition that Gouverneur Morris, the American minister in Paris, should be replaced on the ground that by his protection of the adherents of the late king he had made himself odious to the republic. Washington consented to recall Morris, and appointed as his successor, James Monroe, although the latter was an active opponent of the administration and sympathized with France. Monroe received carefully drawn instructions setting forth at length the policy of the government toward the French republic, which was defined to be that of sincere friendship, although it was deemed inexpedient to comply with its demands.

The negotiation by Mr. Jay of a treaty of amity and commerce with England at this time created great indignation in France, and our minister was informed that the government of that republic intended to break off all relations with the United States, but by his skillful diplomacy and well-known friendship for the French people Mr. Monroe was able to avert such a crisis. When, a little later, Mr. Monroe was recalled, the

French republic refused to receive his successor, Mr. Pinckney, on the ground that our government had insulted France by making a friendly treaty with her enemy, England.

In 1797, when John Adams became President, he appointed a commission, consisting of three gentlemen of the greatest distinction, John Marshall, Elbridge Gerry, and C. C. Pinckney, to make an effort to effect a reconciliation with France, and re-establish commercial intercourse with that country. These emissaries, although not received officially by the French Directory, engaged for six months in a series of remarkable negotiations with Talleyrand, the minister of foreign affairs. The government of the Directory was notoriously corrupt. The Americans were treated as suppliants for favor and were asked not only to promise a large loan to France but to make a generous personal gift to the directors. These proposals were made through mysterious persons designated in the French correspondence as "X," "Y," and "Z," and "a lady." The commissioners of the United States refused the demands of Talleyrand, and finally, after exhausting every honorable means for an amicable arrangement, withdrew to the Netherlands.

In the United States the conduct of M. Adet, who had succeeded Genet as minister, was quite as extraordinary as the latter's had been. He indulged in frequent tirades against the government and Washington for their ingratitude to France. Like his predecessor he endeavored in various ways to stir up a rebellion among the French sympathizers in the United States, and used every possible means to defeat the ratification of the treaty Mr. Jay had made with Great Britain, but Washington treated him with the greatest forbearance. He returned to France in 1796, and there was no French minister in the United States until after the treaty of 1800.

The conduct of the French minister, and the discourteous

treatment which the commissioners from the United States received in Paris, together with the frequent attacks made by French privateers upon American shipping, awakened a resentment in this country which was quite as vigorous and determined as the sympathy for that republic had formerly been. Congress passed several laws in retaliation; all treaties with France were declared abrogated; and active preparations for war were begun. Washington was appointed Lieutenant General and Commander in Chief of the Armies, and Hamilton second in command. A Navy Department was organized; money was voted to purchase and equip vessels of war and to construct fortifications in the several harbors along the Atlantic coast; and the enlistment of an army of ten thousand men was ordered. In fact, so serious was the situation that the courts were afterwards called upon to decide whether there was actual war between the two countries in 1799 or not. The effect of the judicial decision was that although several engagements actually took place between armed vessels belonging to the respective countries, hostilities were never formally declared on either side, and that no war existed.

At this time a curious incident occurred, which created great excitement. After the return of the commissioners from France, with tales of their extraordinary experience, a benevolent Quaker of Philadelphia by the name of George Logan, without the authority or the knowledge of the government, but upon his own responsibility, and solely because of his philanthropic desire to prevent a war between the two young republics, proceeded to Paris, and undertook negotiations with Talleyrand with a view to the restoration of cordial relations. The only papers he carried with him were a certificate of citizenship in the United States and an open letter from Mr. Jefferson testifying to his good character; but Mr. Logan succeeded in obtaining repeated interviews with the members of the French Directory, explaining to them the condition of affairs and the public sentiment in the United States, and the determination of the ruling faction of the government to punish the insults of France by war. Nor is it unlikely that his representations had a profound effect, because the French authorities were laboring under the delusion that the people of the United States still retained their patriotic gratitude and sympathy toward France, and would not sustain the Executive in any hostile demonstrations. It was something more than a coincidence that the temper of the French Directory was considerably modified thereafter; but the sentimental interference of the Quaker was not grateful to the officials on this side of the Atlantic, and when the facts became known to Congress, an act, known as "the Logan law" was passed, punishing with $5,000 fine and three years' imprisonment any citizen who "should carry on any verbal or written correspondence with any foreign government, or any officer or agent thereof, with interest to influence the measures or conduct of such government, or any officer or agent thereof, in relation to any disputes or controversies with the United States."

But notwithstanding the official criticism of his conduct, and the prohibition of such interference in the future, Mr. Logan's endeavors to promote peace were warmly commended by the public, and true to the professions of his faith he made a similar but futile attempt eleven years later in 1810 to prevent war between the United States and Great Britain.

A change had occurred in the composition of the French Directory, which, with other circumstances that have been suggested, had a softening effect upon the relations between the two countries. Mr. Murray, our minister to Holland, was approached by the representative of France at The Hague with an assurance that his government had no desire for war with the United States, and profoundly regretted that anything had occurred to disturb the friendship that had always existed. He intimated that Talleyrand would be glad to confer with Mr. Murray if the latter could find it convenient to visit Paris.

About the time Mr. Murray's report of this incident reached Philadelphia Mr. Gerry received letters from Talleyrand expressing a desire for peace and promising that the French Directory would respond promptly to any overtures for the restoration of intercourse that might be made by the United States. He repudiated the demand for a loan, and insisted that the suggestion that personal gifts must be made to the Directory was unauthorized. He declared the willingness of the French republic to enter into a commercial treaty with the United States, and to concede all that this government had asked for. Mr. Gerry also received a copy of an order that had been issued to the commander of the French fleet in the West Indies to prevent all interference with American commerce; and a curious statement to show that the French Directory had treated nearly every other nation with even greater insolence than had been shown toward the United States, for, inflated with the victories of Napoleon Bonaparte, it had expelled thirteen foreign ambassadors from Paris, imprisoned one in the common jail, and another in the chambers in his own house. In comparison Mr. Gerry thought the commissioners from the United States had been treated with considerable hospitality.

In opposition to a majority of his cabinet, and in violence to the sentiments of the people, which from the warmest sympathy had changed to the bitterest hatred for France, Mr. Adams decided to renew relations with that republic, and on the 17th of February, 1799, nominated as plenipotentiary to Paris William Vans Murray, who had been minister to The

Hague for some years. There was earnest opposition even among the closest adherents of President Adams, and in the Federalist party generally, to what was considered a humiliating surrender to the insolence of the French government, which ought at least to offer an apology and apply more directly for a restoration of intercourse.

It was finally agreed, in the nature of a compromise, that no regular and permanent legation should be established at Paris, but that the dignity of this government would not be impaired if a temporary commission were sent there to receive whatever assurances and concessions the Directory might desire to make, to negotiate a treaty for commercial intercourse, and to demand reparation for damages committed by French privateers. Chief Justice Ellsworth of Connecticut and Patrick Henry were selected to co-operate with Mr. Murray, but Mr. Henry declined on account of his advanced age and ill health, and ex-Governor Davie was appointed in his stead.

The commissioners, only after official assurance that they would be properly received, proceeded to Paris, and March 20, 1800, were presented to Napoleon, the First Consul, who welcomed them cordially. Their instructions required them to assume that all previous treaties with France had been revoked by the action of Congress two years before, and were not to be revived; especially the treaty of alliance made in 1778. They were to demand a recognition of the right of the United States to make treaties of friendship and commerce with other foreign powers even though these might at the time be hostile to France; to adhere to the laws of neutrality, and to forbid the admission to our ports of privateers and vessels captured by them. They were to demand indemnity for losses sustained by American commerce from French privateers, and the appointment of a commission to ascertain the amount of damages. There was to be no guarantee for the protection of French possessions in America, as was provided for by the treaty of 1778; no financial aid, no gifts or bribes, no loans, and no entangling alliance, and the treaty was to last twelve years.

The French government immediately insisted that the old treaties were still in force, and that an arrangement having been entered into by two governments could not be abrogated by one without due notice and the consent of the other; that if the United States had done this it was a violation of friendly relations between the two governments and equivalent to a declaration of war. Therefore no indemnity could be claimed for damages done to commerce after the abrogation of the treaties by the United States, as the two nations were technically engaged in hostilities and had the right to attack the shipping of each other.

The American commissioners were confronted by a perplexing dilemma. If they denied the existence of the treaties they could claim no damages; if they admitted their existence they must acknowledge that the United States had been in the wrong. They decided to accept the first alternative, admit that the treaties had been revoked, abandon the claim for damages, and begin anew the relations between the two governments.

The result was a long treaty of twenty-seven articles, which in itself contained little or nothing of practical utility, but delivered the United States from the perils of war, and made it possible to acquire possession of Louisiana.

The war between Napoleon, now emperor of the French, and the rest of Europe brought into existence a series of decrees* and orders in council by the British government,

---

* Consult page 139.

which had the effect of shutting up the ports of Great Britain to American vessels. The so-called Berlin, Milan, and Rambouillet decrees of Napoleon made every American vessel bound for ports in Great Britain or her colonies subject to seizure and condemnation. The United States were practically the only neutral power on the seas, and upon American vessels fell the heavy pressure of this general war. Diplomatic representations were unavailing; the seizures increased until the United States as a measure of precaution sought to withdraw her commerce from the ocean by a general embargo. This was a great sacrifice and the results were looked for with grave apprehension. Any hope that it would produce an amelioration in the decrees of the belligerents was doomed to disappointment.

Instead of that, by the Bayonne decree, under the pretext that as the embargo made it unlawful for any American ship to be abroad, those vessels which happened to be in the French ports claiming to be American as well as any which might arrive should be seized as British property. Still later the Rambouillet decree directed that all vessels which entered any French port after March 20, 1809, under the United States flag, should be seized and sold.

Vigorous but unavailing protests were made by General Armstrong, the American minister at Paris, and matters continued in the same unsatisfactory condition until upon notification of the passage of the act of May 1, 1810, suspending the nonintercourse act, M. de Champagny, the French minister, informed Mr. Armstrong that the decrees would cease after November 1, 1810, adding: " It being understood, that in consequence of this declaration the English shall revoke their orders in council, and renounce their new principles of blockade, which they have wished to establish, or that the United States, conformably to the act you have just communicated, shall cause their rights to be respected by England." This communication was not received by England as evidence of the repeal, though it was so accepted by the United States and on the 2d of November the President issued a proclamation restoring intercourse with French armed vessels. Although after this no vessels were condemned under the decrees, the seizures calling forth protests from the American minister still occurred under various pretexts.

The overthrow of Napoleon and the restoration of the Bourbons were followed by efforts on the part of the American ministers to secure a commercial convention which would place our vessels on an equality with the French in the carrying of the products of the United States to France. Propositions were submitted on the basis of the convention of 1815 with England, but the French government having imposed an extra duty on cotton brought in American ships her ministers were not anxious to surrender these benefits. They were supported in this course by commercial bodies of various cities, which viewed with delight the rapidly increasing tonnage of their vessels employed in the transatlantic trade. This situation was very exasperating to the people of the United States. Whereupon Congress passed a law imposing a tonnage tax upon French vessels which deprived them of the immense advantages and profits they were enjoying. The effect of this action was to cause a speedy agreement providing for the equal interchange of products in the ships of both countries,—an arrangement which was immediately felt in the increase of American tonnage employed in the French trade.

An obstacle to the arrangement of the difficulties between the two countries arose from the interpretation the French ministry insisted upon giving to the eighth article of the treaty ceding Louisiana. This provided that after the expiration of twelve years the ships of France were to be treated upon the same footing as those of the most favored nation. A treaty had been made with England under which British vessels were admitted into American ports, and American vessels into British ports on equal terms, and by this compact British vessels had greater advantages than those of the French. The United States government contended that England had given us a valuable consideration for this privilege, which France could enjoy on the same terms. The French minister and John Quincy Adams, who was secretary of state, argued the case at great length, and on June 24, 1822, signed a treaty which fixed a discriminating duty of twenty francs (about $3.85), on each ton of merchandise exported from the United States to France in American vessels, and a discriminating duty of $3.75 on each ton of merchandise imported from France into the United States in French vessels. This was a large reduction from the taxes formerly levied by the two nations on the commerce of each other.

In 1831 the questions of claims were settled by the consent of France to give twenty-five millions of francs to those whose property had been destroyed or damaged by French cruisers; and the United States agreed to pay one million and a half of francs to satisfy certain claims which had been made against the government by French citizens. It was agreed also that the duty on cotton imported into France should be reduced. The Congress of the United States promptly passed the laws necessary to carry this treaty into effect, but the French Chamber of Deputies refused to make the necessary appropriations and in 1836 Mr. Livingston, our minister to Paris, having failed to induce the French government to carry out this agreement, was directed by President Jackson to ask for his passport, and return to the United States. The French minister was shortly afterwards recalled from Washington, and for a time it seemed as if there would be war between the two countries. In the House of Representatives there was a violent debate, after which the President was directed to use the entire power of the government, and, if necessary, resort to force, to compel France to carry out this agreement, but no declaration of war was made on either side. In 1836 the British government offered its services as mediator, but before this offer had been accepted the French government made known its purpose to pay the promised indemnity, and, after being suspended for nearly two years, the cordial relations between the two nations were thus restored.

In 1853 there was concluded a consular convention, the former one of 1788 having expired by limitation. A provision of this treaty, that consuls should never be compelled to appear before the courts as witnesses, occasioned in 1854 a serious complication. The Mexican consul at San Francisco being on trial for an offense against the United States laws, the prosecuting officer sought to obtain the evidence of the French consul, who, claiming the privilege under the treaty, refused to appear. But the accused, resting his right under the sixth amendment to the Constitution, to have compulsory process for obtaining witnesses in his favor, sought and obtained the process. Secretary Marcy agreed as a reparation for the violation of the treaty that when a French ship or squadron should appear in the harbor of San Francisco, the United States authorities should greet the French flag with a national salute, which should be returned by the ship or squadron. This salute was accordingly given in 1854.

The declaration of war between France and the North German Confederation in July, 1870, brought the diplomatic transactions of the legation of the United States at Paris into great prominence. The German minister at Washington, having requested of the secretary of state that the United States legation at Paris during the war should have permission to protect from molestation German subjects who were noncombatants, Mr. Washburn, our representative, was instructed to apply to the French authorities for such permission, which was duly accorded him. Therefore during the continuance of the war the American minister was occupied in securing freedom from arrest, and alleviating the condition of the German-born residents of Paris. The legation was also used as a medium of communication between France and Prussia. Remonstrances for alleged illegal acts, and notifications of a varied character were made to the American minister in London by the German ambassador to England. These communications were thereupon forwarded by the dispatch pouch to Mr. Washburn to be presented to the appropriate French authority. During the siege of Paris the dispatch pouch of the United States legation was the only communication permitted by the besieging force to pass to and from the city. The American minister, while keeping up relations of entire good will with the French during the war, rendered important services to all foreigners and his dispatches to the department form a graphic picture of the march of events during the struggle with Germany and the terrible scenes of the commune.*

In 1881, the formation of the French Company under De Lesseps for the construction of a canal across the Isthmus of Panama, brought again into prominence the treaty of 1846 with New Granada, by which the United States guaranteed the neutrality of transit across the isthmus. It was suggested that, in view of the possibility of the ultimate construction of the canal, other countries should be asked by Colombia

---

* Consult page 146 and page 147.

to join in the recognition of neutrality. In order to prevent any misapprehension as to the views and position of the administration on this question the secretary of state issued a circular of instruction to the American minister in France and other capitals, in which, while disclaiming any purpose to interfere with the commercial enterprise of the citizens of France or of other nations or to seek exclusive privilege for American vessels, it was insisted that the United States would exercise her right to take all needful precautions against the possibility of the isthmus transit being in any event used offensively against her interests upon the land or upon the sea. Any attempt to supersede the guarantee already made by the United States by an agreement between European powers, it was stated, would be regarded as an indication of unfriendly feeling.

The various decrees of the French government restricting and suspending, on alleged sanitary grounds, the importation of that very important class of American commodities, pork products, has furnished the theme for continuous diplomatic correspondence for twenty years, during which time a suggested reprisal of an extra duty on French wines has met with considerable favor. Upon the passage of an act by Congress providing for a thorough inspection of all meats intended for exportation, the American minister, Mr. Whitelaw Reid, was enabled in 1891 to secure the repeal of the prohibition.

The French Spoliation Claims.

The so-called French "spoliation" claims have had continued prominence in both the diplomatic and domestic history of this country longer than any other matter of diplomacy. They grew out of the depredations committed by French cruisers upon American shipping, commencing in 1793. When, as has been recited, the war between England and France began, the latter nation called upon the United

States to comply with the terms of the treaty of alliance made in 1778, when our fathers were seeking aid to carry on the Revolution. Under this treaty the United States bound itself to render military aid to France when required; to permit French privateers and vessels of war the same privilege in their harbors that were given to their own shipping; and to protect the French possessions in America. The reasons why the provisions of the treaty could not be complied with have been explained, but the failure of the United States to comply with the expectations of France exasperated that nation to such a degree that retaliation was resorted to. Vessels belonging to citizens of the United States to the number of one hundred and three were forcibly detained in the harbor of Bordeaux; many other vessels were overtaken at sea by French privateers and were captured or destroyed with their cargoes; supplies were forcibly taken in the ports of the United States by French men-of-war, and payment was refused for those that had been contracted for and delivered.

The ministers and commissioners who went to Paris from 1793 to 1800, vainly endeavored to persuade the French government to prevent these depredations, and to pay the damages they had caused, but it was not until the latter year that the privateering was stopped, nor was it until 1803 that France would admit that any indemnity was due for the losses suffered. When Louisiana was bought, the United States were permitted to deduct 2,000,000 francs (about $400,000) from the purchase money, and to use it in the settlement of such claims; but after that date the plundering continued, and the effect upon American commerce was disastrous. Again claims for damages were made by America. After much discussion the French government finally agreed in 1815 to pay an indemnity of 25,000,000 francs ($5,000,000), while the United States were to be released from all French claims by the payment of 1,500,000 francs ($300,000); but the legislative chamber failed to make the necessary appropriations. The continued delay of France was complained of by the United States until at last in 1835 matters took a serious turn and diplomatic relations were severed. When the French government realized that this country would brook no further hesitation, the appropriations were passed.

Thus the diplomatic history of the spoliation claims ended. Not so the domestic, for though the bills that have been introduced in Congress authorizing the President to pay the claims have received no less than forty-three favorable reports against three that were adverse, it was not until the act of January 20, 1885, that provision was made for settlement. This act referred the petitioners to the Court of Claims, and in May, 1886, Judge John Davis delivered an elaborate judgment in favor of the claimants and reviewed the entire history of the affair. The first appropriation on account of the claims was made in the deficiency act of March 3, 1891, and the money is now being distributed among the heirs of those who owned the vessels that were destroyed.

The Purchase of Louisiana.

When in 1800 the United States government learned of the secret treaty by which Spain had agreed to return to France her vast Louisiana territory, there was a general feeling of apprehension. The power controlling the Mississippi River was a natural enemy to our government. Spain as a comparatively weak nation was not greatly to be dreaded, but France, an old friend, would be a formidable rival. Then again the possession of Canada by England, the enemy of France, would in case of war make the northwestern part of the United States a battle ground. Probably, however, the conviction that the best interests of this government were imperiled by the presence on American soil of any foreign power was the fundamental idea of the American people.

Mr. Robert Livingston, who was minister to France, presented to the authorities of the French republic a proposition for the purchase of New Orleans. It was received with so much favor that Mr. Monroe was sent to Paris in March, 1803, bearing instructions to carry out that project if possible. The original plan was to purchase only that part of the French possessions lying east of the Mississippi River, but Talleyrand suggested the cession of the whole French domain in North America, and asked how much would be given for it. Mr. Livingston intimated that twenty millions of francs might be a fair price, but Napoleon Bonaparte said this was too low, and named one hundred and twenty-five millions of francs. In a very short time however, after negotiations began between Mr. Livingston and Talleyrand, the American commissioners agreed to pay eighty millions of francs for the vast territory along and beyond the Mississippi River. This act, although unauthorized and unexpected, was agreed to by the President, Congress was at once summoned to consider the proposition, and on the 20th of the following December the province of Louisiana was officially surrendered to Governor Claiborne of Mississippi and General Wilkinson of the United States Army, who were empowered to take charge and assume command. It was afterwards disclosed that the territory could have been obtained for fifty millions of francs had our commissioners insisted upon that sum, for the instructions of Napoleon to his agents fixed that as the lowest limit. The transfer took place on the 30th of November in the council chamber at New Orleans, where M. Laussat, the plenipotentiary of the French republic, who twenty days before had received the transfer of authority from the Spanish government, handed Governor Claiborne the keys of the city and at the same time hauled down the flag of France, which had floated from the mast on the building. The American flag was then raised to its full height and the agents of the two governments in the transaction exchanged congratulations. The transfer of upper Louisiana to the United States took place at St. Louis on the 8th and 10th of March, 1804.

The actual cost of the Louisiana purchase was $27,267,621.98, of which $15,000,000 was the purchase money, $8,529,353 represented the interest upon that amount to the redemption of the bonds that were issued to cover it, and $3,738,268.98 the French spoliation claims which were paid by the United States under the treaty.

For this money 1,182,755 square miles were obtained.

CHAPTER XIV.

DIPLOMATIC RELATIONS WITH SPAIN AND THE PURCHASE OF FLORIDA.

The administration of Washington inherited from the Continental Congress a perplexing legacy in the form of a dispute over the navigation of the Mississippi River. Therefore, one of the first acts of Mr. Jefferson, when he became secretary of state, was to demand of Spain the right of free navigation for the purpose of commercial intercourse. That government, however, declined to discuss the question, and in the following year a commission was appointed to visit Madrid to determine the question of boundaries between the United States and the Spanish possessions in America; as well as to secure the navigation of the river. These commissioners were instructed to insist that the boundaries acknowledged by England in the treaty of peace should be recognized by Spain so far as they touched her possessions; and that the citizens of the United States must have the right to navigate the Mississippi from its source to its mouth without hindrances or obstructions or the payment of tolls. They were also to insist that this be acknowledged as a right, and not as a concession or grant from Spain. The Spanish government had little respect for the power of the United States, and was, moreover, secretly influenced by France to resist our claims, so that the negotiations came to nothing.

The change in the political relations of Europe caused by the conclusion of peace between France and Spain at Basle in July, 1795, led Great Britain to consider plans for attacking Spain. Upon the commencement of hostilities his Catholic majesty's ministers became more inclined to view favorably the requests of the United States for an agreement on the points at issue. In the meantime, complaint having been made by Spain that the United States had not hitherto sent to that country an envoy of the rank due to her position, and able to deal properly with such delicate and important affairs, Washington in December, 1794, commissioned General Thos. Pinckney as minister plenipotentiary to Madrid with full powers to negotiate a treaty or convention concerning the navigation of the river Mississippi; and such other matters relative to the territories of the respective countries as required to be adjusted and regulated, and in reference to their mutual commerce. Pinckney was also empowered to secure, if possible, compensation for the damages and losses sustained by American citizens from the acts of Spain or her subjects.

After General Pinckney had set out for his post, but before he reached Madrid the Spanish minister sent a note to Mr. Randolph, the secretary of state, informing him that the king was ready to enter into negotiations; to fix the boundaries agreeable to the United States as far as they might be compatible with the treaties made with the Indians, and to consider the navigation of the Mississippi River, expecting in return a substantial treaty of alliance and a reciprocal guarantee of the possessions of both countries. It was also hoped that the questions of trade might be arranged on a footing of reciprocity.

Notwithstanding the assurances that the Spanish government had given of its readiness to treat on these points, General Pinckney encountered the usual delay, until, believing that it was useless to make any further endeavors to reach an agreement, on the 24th of October, 1795, he demanded his passports.

This decided step induced Prince Godoy, the prime minister, to act promptly and within three days he and Pinckney signed a treaty of friendship, limits, and navigation.

By this treaty Spain agreed to the southern boundary of the United States as it had been settled in the treaty with Great Britain, and consented to the appointment of a commission to fix the limits. It was agreed also that the navigation of the Mississippi River from its sources to the ocean should be free "only to his subjects and to the citizens of the United States, unless he should extend the privilege to other powers by special convention." Places of deposit for merchandise in transit for export were established at New Orleans or at some other convenient place on the bank of the Mississippi. The provisions concerning navigation were similar to those in the treaties previously negotiated with other countries. In respect to the claims against Spain a commission was authorized to sit in Philadelphia, and "impartially to examine and decide the claims in question, according to the merits of the several cases, and to justice, equity, and the laws of nations."

Although speedily ratified by both countries, disputes constantly arose as to alleged infringements and protests were made for the failure of Spain to comply with its engagements. In violation of the express agreement Spanish troops were not withdrawn finally until almost the time of the cession of France; and what was of much greater importance the Spanish intendant of New Orleans in contravention of Article 22, suspended the right of deposit for American merchandise at that city without designating "an equivalent establishment" on another part of the bank of the Mississippi.

When the Jay treaty (see page 154) with England took effect the Spanish authorities complained that the United States had no right to accord to Great Britain the liberty to navigate the Mississippi River, claiming that it was prejudicial to Spanish interests. Chevalier de Yrujo, the Spanish minister in the United States in 1797, made an elaborate protest against the treaty and the explanatory article, declaring that no subsequent treaty had impaired the right to free communication. Secretary Pickering met the arguments with a long reply, but the difficulties remained unsettled, and another treaty was found necessary, though it was over twenty years before an agreement was reached. In the course of the contentions respecting the boundary, the French prime minister, to whom both parties appealed as to the true interpretation of the specified limits, exerted every influence in his power against the claims set up by the United States.

The incidents of D'Yrujo's career formed a striking episode in the diplomatic history of the country. Having protested strongly against the Jay treaty, he redoubled his exertions as soon as the cession of Louisiana to France by Spain was made public. He fairly outdid the French minister Genet in his outrageous attacks on the United States government, going so far as to have his strictures printed in certain Philadelphia newspapers. Mr. Madison naturally requested the recall of this obnoxious envoy but the home government attempted to support the untenable position of D'Yrujo. After an animated correspondence, in the course of which each government demanded damages for the conduct of the other, the Spanish court yielded and changed its representative.

Disputes having arisen on account of the revocation of the right of deposit at New Orleans granted under the treaty of 1795, demand was made upon Spain for satisfaction and payment. To these claims were added those for spoliation committed on the sea before the peace of Amiens (1802). An agreement was reached between Cevallos, the Spanish secretary of state, and Charles Pinckney, the American minister, referring certain of the claims to a commission, and the convention was signed August 11, 1802. After some discussion it was ratified by the Senate in 1804, but the king of Spain having protested against the establishing of a customs district at Mobile, refused to ratify the agreement unless the act was repealed or a declaration made recognizing the sovereignty of Spain over Mobile Bay. Consequently the treaty was not finally promulgated until 1819, and was really never put into effect.

Meanwhile negotiations were carried on for an adjustment of the boundaries and for a settlement of all other pending questions. The wars in Europe, with the dethronement of Ferdinand VII. of Spain, interrupted the negotiations, which after the restoration in 1814 were resumed through Mr. Irving, the United States minister at Madrid, while the secretary of state made propositions to Don Luis de Onis, the minister at Washington. The propositions submitted by the United States were: First, that Spain should cede all the territory east of the Mississippi; second, that her eastern boundary should be marked by the Colorado River; third, that claims for indemnities for spoliation committed either by the Spanish or French within the waters of Spain, and for the losses occasioned by the abrogation of the right of deposit, should be settled by a commission; fourth, that the lands from

East Florida to the Louisiana boundary should be held as security for the payment of these claims, and that no alleged grant of land by Spain in this territory subsequent to the date of the treaty of 1802 should be held as valid; fifth, and that in consideration of this transfer Spain should be released from the claims urged by the United States.

Many troublesome incidents occurred during the course of this long discussion, which tended still further to increase the irritation existing between the two countries. In 1806, a Venezuelan patriot by the name of Miranda,* who had served with Lafayette in the Army of Washington, made a revolutionary invasion of Spanish America, and claiming that the administration of Jefferson was friendly to the movement, enlisted a number of prominent men in the scheme. As a consequence the Spanish government forbade all trade between the United States and her American possessions, and though her fleet was insignificant, she declared a great extent of coast to be in blockade, and harassed the commerce of the Gulf of Mexico and the Caribbean Sea so that heavy losses were sustained by the American shipping.

While the negotiations for the purchase of Florida were gradually reaching a conclusion, the Spanish king made several grants of immense tracts of land in that territory, which he was proposing to cede to the United States, and had it not been for the firm position maintained by the American government there would have been only a very small part of the land to transfer. Indeed the draft submitted by the Spanish minister a few months preceding the treaty was to cede the provinces of East and West Florida, and provided that "the donations or sales of lands made by the government of his majesty or by legal authorities until this time, are nevertheless to be recognized as valid."

---

* For an account of this expedition, see page 37.

The treaty was concluded on the 22d of February, 1819, which purported to settle all the difficulties and pretensions of the two countries, and to designate with precision the limits of their bordering territories. John Forsyth of Georgia was appointed minister plenipotentiary in February, 1819, and he was made the bearer of the treaty to the court of Spain. The United States ship *Hornet* was placed at his disposal, and he received instructions to procure the ratification by the king at the earliest practicable moment. The *Hornet* was ordered to wait for the treaty and bring it back. But the king sent word that in view of the great importance of the treaty it was indispensable that he should examine it with the greatest caution and deliberation.

While Forsyth was protesting at Madrid against the delay in formally ratifying the treaty, the Spanish king sent General Vives to Washington to inform the American government that if measures would be taken to prevent alleged piratical excursions from ports in the United States; if further aid to the invasion of his Catholic majesty's possessions in North America would be stopped; and if assurance would be given that no relations would be formed with the revolted provinces of Spain, then the treaty would be ratified. This proposition was received with surprise and indignation, and a carefully drawn reply was made by the secretary of state, in which he firmly refused to consider the terms of the treaty as open to question. After a delay of precisely two years, upon the adoption of a constitution to which the king was compelled to take an oath of allegiance, the treaty by the advice of the Cortes was finally ratified. Incorporated with the ratification of the king was a specific declaration that the three grants to the Duke of Alagor, the Count of Puñonrostro, and Don Pedro de Vargas, which had been made secretly during the progress of these negotiations, were invalid and null.

The treaty ceded all of the Floridas to the United States, and marked the western boundary of the United States by the Sabine River, the Red River to 100° of west longitude, the Arkansas River to latitude 42° north, and thence to the Pacific Ocean. Surveys were provided for; religious freedom was secured; previous Spanish grants were recognized and confirmed; mutual claims upon the two continents were renounced, and the United States undertook to satisfy the demands of their citizens against Spain, to the extent of five millions of dollars. Provision was made for a commission of three to examine and decide upon the amount and validity of these claims. As a proof of the friendly sentiments toward Spain, the United States agreed to permit vessels laden with Spanish products from her ports or colonies, to enter St. Augustine and Pensacola without paying other duties than those imposed upon American vessels. This exemption was to be exclusively enjoyed by Spanish vessels, and was to last for twelve years.

The general revolt against the Spanish crown in the countries of South America led to many depredations upon the commerce of the United States by privateers sailing under commissions from the Spanish authorities. Upon the capture of some of these vessels by the armed ships of the United States, the Spanish minister, Señor de Anduaga, sharply assailed the authorities for this necessary retaliation. Mr. Adams replied asserting the entire friendship of the United States, but insisting on the right to protect trade from the incursions of the so-called privateers. Matters grew so bad that the President asked the authority of Congress to construct additional vessels and recommended the pursuit of the offenders even after they had landed, and if that were not successful, he urged the making of reprisals on the property of the inhabitants and the blockade of the ports from which the pirates came or in which they found shelter.

The losses suffered by the owners of American vessels and cargoes were the subject of protracted discussion between the two governments, resulting in the "claims convention" of 1834, by the terms of which Spain acknowledged her liability and agreed to pay to the United States twelve millions of *reals vellon* bearing interest at five per cent per annum payable in Paris; the government of the United States was to make the distribution to the claimants.

The kingdom of Spain was at this time so disturbed with insurrections and civil wars that it became practically impossible for her to meet the payment of this interest and finally, Mr. Buchanan, when secretary of state, accepted the payment of $30,000 annually at Havana as the interest on the debt.

The location of Cuba and its remaining a colony of Spain, instead of joining in the column of the republics which had thrown off the Spanish rule, led to many delicate questions between the United States and the home government. In 1840 it was gravely suspected that agents of Great Britain who were determined to put an end to the traffic in negro slaves were intriguing with malcontents in Cuba to arouse a rebellion against the government. So deep was the conviction that the President sent a special message to the consul general at Havana informing him that this government having learned, from what appeared to be a reliable source, of a probable uprising, it was important that exact and detailed information should be communicated at once. At the same time the minister at Madrid was directed to inform the Spanish government that the United States, having so great an interest in the condition of the island, would never permit it to be occupied by British agents or forces under any pretext whatever, and in the event of any attempt by any European power to disturb Spain's sovereignty the United States would lend its whole naval and military resources to aid in preserving or restoring it.

Such assurances were repeatedly conveyed to the Spanish ministry, and at various times propositions have been broached to purchase the island. These however have been declined as the pride of the country would not permit the disposal of the territory in that manner. Nevertheless the American ministers at Madrid have been constantly instructed to advise the Department of State, should there appear to be a disposition at any time to consider the question.

In 1851 when England undertook to assist Spain in preserving the island of Cuba from suspected invasion by parties organized in the United States, it was plainly intimated that such a course would not be permitted by this government, as it would involve the act of searching American merchant vessels to ascertain whether they contained alleged invaders.

The relations between the United States and Cuba suffer from the same inconvenience that has been experienced with Canada. Both being dependencies of European powers there are no diplomatic officers in either colony with whom the authorities at Washington can communicate. Every question which arises is subjected to a roundabout and triangular course of correspondence. The home government must be approached, and before a reply can be made, a report is generally required from the governing power of the dependency. When it was proposed that the United States should unite with England and France, in guaranteeing the Spanish dominion of Cuba and mutually disclaim forever all intention to obtain possession of the island, President Fillmore promptly declined to become a party to such an agreement, yet at the same time the powers were informed that the United States had no designs of acquisition.

In 1869, the disaffection against the Spanish rule which had existed so long among the native Cubans broke out in active rebellion. A republic was proclaimed at Yara; an army was raised to secure independence and a desultory warfare lasting for nearly ten years ensued. The interests of the United States were deeply affected, owing to the large amount of capital from this country invested in the sugar plantations and coffee estates throughout the island. In August, 1869, the Spanish authorities in Cuba issued a decree seizing the estates of all persons who were suspected of sympathy with the revolutionists. Under this decree the property of many American citizens valued at millions of dollars was confiscated. The protests made by General Sickles at Madrid resulted in a decree releasing such estates as were owned by Americans, but the authorities on the island paid little heed to this action, and it was not until a voluminous correspondence had taken place that any measure of relief was afforded. Meanwhile it was agreed that the claims for damages should be referred to a commission of arbitration which met in Washington.

On the 31st of October, 1873, the steamship *Virginius*, sailing under the United States flag, was captured by the Spanish man-of-war *Tornado*, and on the afternoon of the 1st of November carried into the port of Santiago de Cuba. In spite of the protests of the United States consular officer, Gen. Burriel, the commandant of the city, convened a court martial, which met at nine in the morning and before four had concluded its bloody work. As the result of its labors General W. A. C. Ryan, who had been connected with the Irish revolutionary movement, and three others were shot to death on the 4th. Four days later twelve more of the passengers were executed, and on the 13th Captain Fry and thirty-six of his crew met the same fate. General Sickles at Madrid so vigorously protested against the action of the Cuban officials that the relations of the United States were on the point of being broken off. Upon failing after repeated efforts to obtain any promise of reparation for the insult to the flag, our minister asked for his passports. But through the Spanish envoy at Washington an agreement was reached, whereby the *Virginius*, with those of her passengers and crew who had escaped the fate of their companions, should be surrendered to an American naval vessel. It was also agreed that, if the *Virginius* should be found to have the right to sail under United States papers, the flag should be duly saluted at Santiago de Cuba. The ship and passengers were surrendered but, the attorney general having decided that the *Virginius* was not entitled to be considered an American ship, the salute was not demanded. In the meantime, the Spanish government officially disclaimed any intent of indignity to the flag of the United States.

After more than a year of persistent pressure Spain paid to the United States as a reparation for the killing of passengers and crew of the *Virginius* the sum of $80,000, which was distributed to the heirs of the victims. Earnest efforts to secure the punishment of General Burriel for his butchery were unavailing, although a thorough investigation by a military tribunal was promised. Far from being punished, he was promoted to be a field marshal.

Other and frequent questions between the two countries have arisen from the peculiar provisions of Spanish customs laws, which, imposing heavy fines for even unintentional infractions, have led to a constant series of complaints. In 1891, under the provisions of the tariff act of October 1, 1890, an arrangement was effected whereby special reductions were made in the duties on certain American products imported into Cuba and Puerto Rico.

The Purchase of Florida.

When Mr. Jefferson opened negotiations with Napoleon

Bonaparte for the purchase of New Orleans he intended only to secure control of the navigation of the Mississippi and the mouth of that river. By the treaty of peace in 1782, by which the independence of the American colonies was acknowledged by Great Britain, the southern boundary of the United States, as recognized by that government and Spain, was a line running from the mouth of the Yazoo River to the Appalachicola. The Spanish colony of Florida was thus separated from that of Mexico, and as the former was principally settled by Englishmen, whose interests were allied to those of the United States, Spain realized that she was destined to lose control by revolution sooner or later, and the revolt of her colonies in South America made the situation more perilous. In fact as early as 1810 a revolutionary party in Florida declared for independence and established a provisional government. They asked admission to the United States, and a loan of money to maintain themselves against the authority of Spain. President Madison declined to grant their requests, but sent a commission to negotiate for the purchase of the Florida territory. Spain refused. In 1812 General Matthews of Georgia was sent to Florida to receive the province if the Spanish authorities would surrender it peacefully. They again refused, and with the concurrence of the Georgia legislature he co-operated with the revolutionists, and defied the Spanish commander. Troubles with the Seminole Indians again broke out, and in 1814 General Andrew Jackson was ordered to undertake their suppression. The Spanish government remonstrated against the occupation of Florida by United States troops, but Mr. Monroe, who had become President, in reply proposed the cession of Florida in lieu of the payment of claims of American citizens against Spain. In 1818 General Jackson took possession of the Spanish forts at Pensacola, and drove out the governor and his garrison.

Spain protested, but the United States justified his action on the ground of military necessity as the Spaniards were accused of giving aid to the Indians.

Negotiations for the purchase of the territory were then resumed, and finally ended in a treaty made by Señor Onis, the Spanish ambassador, and John Quincy Adams, who was secretary of state, signed at Washington, February 22, 1819. The Florida purchase cost the United States $6,489,768, and added to the national domain 59,268 square miles including all of the territory east of the Mississippi River.

CHAPTER XV.

RELATIONS WITH RUSSIA AND THE PURCHASE OF ALASKA.

THE archives of the State Department at Washington show that there has been uninterrupted cordiality between the empire of Russia and the United States since the beginning of our history, and it may be said that the czar is the only ruler among the great powers of Europe with whom there has not been at one time or another some little friction. Nor have we ever had trouble with a foreign government without receiving from Russia the cordial proffer of her good offices in settling the difficulties. She offered her mediation to terminate the War of 1812, and under her arbitration the difficulties that grew out of the treaty of Ghent were settled in 1822. During the war of the Rebellion we felt more than ever her friendly sentiments, and her solicitude for the preservation of the Union was frequently and sincerely expressed. She furnished no hospitality to rebel cruisers, and no agent of the Confederacy was ever encouraged or permitted to live at St. Petersburg; while on the other hand the ports of Russia were always open to the United States cruisers, which were permitted not only to seek shelter and supplies but to carry there the prizes captured at sea.

In 1861 the two governments agreed to co-operate for the establishment of a telegraph service between San Francisco and St. Petersburg across Bering Strait. The Russian fleet visited the United States in 1863 as a friendly demonstration to affect the attitude of foreign powers toward this country during our war.

In 1864 the Archduke Constantine received a formal invitation to visit the United States in order that the government might by its courtesies to him, the brother of the emperor, show its gratitude and good will. In 1866, when the emperor of Russia narrowly escaped assassination, Congress, by solemn resolution, conveyed its sympathies and its gratitude to Almighty God for his preservation, and Mr. Fox, at that time the assistant secretary of the navy, was appointed to bear the resolution in person to the emperor, as an additional evidence of the friendly sentiments of this country. He was conveyed to Cronstadt in the monitor Miantonomoh, the most formidable vessel in our navy, and thus a ship of war became a messenger of peace.

The Purchase of Alaska.

Few treaties have ever been negotiated and concluded in so simple a manner as that by which Alaska became a part of the United States. Two brief notes only passed between the governments of Russia and the United States. The first was written by Mr. Seward on the 25th of March, 1867, renewing in formal terms and in a letter of not more than one hundred and fifty words the proposition that had previously been made in conversation for the purchase of the territory. The other communication was even more brief, which it is well to note:

WASHINGTON, March 29, 1867.

Mr. Secretary of State:—

I have the honor to inform you that by a telegram dated 28th of this month from St. Petersburg, Prince Gortchakoff informs me that his majesty, the emperor of all the Russias, gives his consent to the cession of the Russian possessions on the American continent to the United States for the stipulated sum of $7,200,000 in gold, and that his majesty, the emperor, invests me with full power to negotiate and sign the treaty. Please

accept, Mr. Secretary of State, the assurances of my high consideration.
STOECKL.

To the Honorable *William H. Seward*,
Secretary of State of the United States.

Alaska was the last portion of the American continent to be discovered, and Russia held the title to the territory by the right of discovery and occupation. Peter the Great, in 1725, was curious to know if Asia and America were separated by the sea or if they were twin continents attached by ties of land. To obtain this information he ordered an expedition to be equipped, but he died before the preparations were completed. His widow, Catherine I., did not permit the enterprise to be abandoned, and made Vitus Bering, a Danish navigator of experience, the commander of the party. Taking with him seventy sailors and some shipbuilders, Bering left St. Petersburg on the 5th of February, 1725, and crossed Siberia and northern Asia to the coast of Kamchatka. It took him more than three years to make the journey. When he reached the coast he built a small vessel and cruised along until he reached the frozen sea. Then he returned to his starting place and crossed overland to St. Petersburg, where he arrived in March, 1730, after an absence of a little more than five years. He was created commodore, and in 1741 repeated the expedition with a larger force and better equipments. On this journey he discovered and named Mount St. Elias, in honor of the saint on whose anniversary he saw it first. On the return Bering suffered desperate hardships, and his party were at last wrecked upon a desert island without a name, where, sheltered in a ditch and covered with sand to protect him from cold, he died on the 8th of December, 1841. Shortly after, Spanish and French voyagers visited the coast, but the Russians soon established military posts and colonies there, and their title to the country was recognized by the rest of the world.

The first proposition to purchase Russian America was made during the administration of President Polk, but it was not seriously considered. When Mr. Buchanan was President he authorized Senator Gwin of California, afterwards created duke of Sonora by Emperor Maximilian, to confer with the Russian minister at Washington on the subject, and $5,000,000 was offered as purchase money. The Russian minister replied that while the offer was not what might have been expected, it deserved mature reflection, and stated that the minister of finance had been instructed to make an investigation as to the value of the territory. Meanwhile the rebellion having begun and ended, attention was again directed to the Russian possessions, which by that time had become familiar to the fishermen on the Pacific coast and to the whalers and seal catchers that went all the way around from Gloucester and Newburyport, Mass. The matter was first brought officially to the attention of the government through a memorial presented by the legislature of Washington Territory in the winter of 1866, asking that the President would secure for the fishermen of the United States full privileges from Russia for the use of its fishing grounds. This memorial was forwarded to the Russian minister at Washington, Mr. Stoeckl, and as he was about to leave for St. Petersburg on a vacation he promised to bring the matter to the attention of his government and secure the most favorable terms. Archduke Constantine, brother and chief advisor of the late czar of Russia, was selected to confer with Mr. Stoeckl, and as a result the latter was authorized to treat with the United States for the purchase of the territory. He arrived in Washington early in March, had several conferences with Mr. Seward, and arranged with him the terms which were expressed briefly in the letter before mentioned.

When the purchase of Russian America became known to

the public it evoked a storm of protests and ridicule. It was declared to be a barren, worthless region, whose only products were icebergs and polar bears, where the ground was frozen six feet deep from year to year and all the streams were glaciers. It was called "Seward's Polar Bear Garden," and the administration was abused without limit for the alleged folly of paying $7,200,000 for an iceberg. Mr. Sumner, who had taken a great interest in the matter, made a speech in the Senate, which was one of the most remarkable ever delivered in that body. From the moment he decided to give his support to the treaty he commenced to study the condition and resources of Alaska and read everything that had previously been published concerning the Russian possessions in America. The treaty was ratified by a vote of 37 yeas to 2 nays, the latter being cast by Mr. Fessenden, of Maine, and Mr. Morrill, of Vermont.

A public proclamation of the treaty was made in the following June, and in August Major General Rousseau of the United States Army was appointed officially to receive Alaska from the Russian government. Although the funds had not been appropriated by Congress, Russia imposed perfect confidence in the good faith of the United States, and the delivery was made without waiting for the payment of the purchase money. Embarking from San Francisco on a man-of-war, General Rousseau, with General Jefferson C. Davis and about 250 troops, went to Sitka, where the Russian garrison received them with military honors. The two battalions exchanged flags, and then alternate salutes were fired from the American and the Russian batteries. The troops were then brought to "present arms," and the Russian banner was lowered from the flagstaff on the top of the garrison. The Russian representative then said:

"General Rousseau:—By authority of his majesty, the

emperor of all the Russias, I transfer to the United States all right and title to the territory of Alaska."

General Rousseau replied :— " By authority of the President of the United States I accept the transfer."

The United States flag was then hoisted above the barracks, and the ceremonies ended by a banquet on board one of the men-of-war.

Until its purchase by the United States the country had always been known upon the maps and in published volumes as Russian America, and while the treaty was pending in the Senate there were frequent discussions among the members of the cabinet and the officials of the State Department as to the name that should be bestowed upon the new territory. Several were suggested as appropriate, but Mr. Seward, with whom the decision rested, preferred Alaska, which was the title of the long strip of land that extends from the main territory into the Bering Sea. At the next session of Congress a bill was introduced to appropriate the money for the payment provided by the treaty, and on the 27th of July, 1868, it was finally passed, whereupon the secretary of state handed a draft for $7,200,000 in gold to the Russian minister.

CHAPTER XVI.

RELATIONS WITH ITALY.

THERE have been few diplomatic incidents in the relations between the United States and Italy. The first treaty with any of the Italian nations was made with the kingdom of the Two Sicilies in 1832; the next with the kingdom of Sardinia in 1838; another with the Two Sicilies in 1845; a third in 1854; a fourth in 1855; a treaty of friendship, commerce, and extradition with the consolidated kingdom in 1868, and another in 1871. The first minister was sent from the United States to the Two Sicilies in 1816; one was sent to the kingdom of Sardinia in 1840, and to the States of the Church in 1846.

During the years 1809 to 1812, when Prince Murat was king of the Two Sicilies, the commerce of the United States suffered much damage from the privateers that infested the Mediterranean, and at the close of the War of 1812 our government demanded reparation and indemnity for the losses sustained. William Pinckney was sent to the capital as a commissioner to conduct the negotiations, but he failed to accomplish any results and was recalled. The claims continued to be the subject of correspondence until 1832, when John Nelson succeeded in making a treaty under which the government of the Two Sicilies agreed to pay the sum of 2,115,000 ducats as indemnity for the destruction of vessels and cargoes. This money was afterwards distributed by a commission among those who suffered loss. Similar claims were afterwards made against the kingdom of Naples and were collected in a similar manner.

Several attempts were made to involve the United States in the struggle between the papal church and the kingdom of Italy, but Mr. Fish, who was secretary of state under President Grant, succeeded in preserving a strict neutrality, and, since the abolition of the civil authority of the pope, this government has had no official intercourse with the Vatican.

The most serious controversy that has ever occurred between the United States and the Italian government was that which arose over the New Orleans massacre in 1890.

On the night of October 15, 1890, David C. Hennessey, chief of police in the city of New Orleans, was murdered in the streets of that city. On the 13th of December following, a score of Italians were indicted for direct or indirect complicity in the crime. About the middle of February, 1891, they were arraigned for trial. Nine of them were tried separately. On the 13th of March three of the prisoners were found not guilty and in the cases of three others the jury failed to agree. The verdict was universally condemned in New Orleans as unjust and a meeting was called for the 15th of March to consider means for the vindication of the law. At the appointed hour a large crowd assembled and, proceeding to the parish prison, forced an entrance and shot the accused. In all eleven were killed, the six who had been tried and five of those awaiting trial.

On the 4th of December the secretary of state requested the attorney general to ascertain whether the persons indicted for the Hennessey murder were citizens of Italy or of the United States. On the 20th of that month the United States district attorney at New Orleans reported that of the persons indicted a majority were naturalized citizens of the United States.

On the 15th of March, 1891, Baron Fava, the Italian minister at Washington, informed our government that the eleven prisoners had been murdered by a mob, and he submitted a dispatch from the Marquis di Rudini, Italian minister of foreign affairs at Rome, demanding in the name of justice and civilization that the federal administration interfere for the protection of the living prisoners and the other members of the Italian colony in New Orleans. Italy demanded also that the mob and those who inspired it be speedily brought to justice.

The secretary of state at once telegraphed to the governor of Louisiana deploring the massacre and expressing the hope of the President that the subjects of a friendly power would be furnished adequate protection, and that the leaders of the mob would be promptly brought to justice. At the same time a telegram was sent to the United States minister at Rome instructing him to convey to the Italian government the profound horror and regret of the President and to give assurance that every possible effort would be made to protect Italian subjects. Several dispatches of a similar character passed between Washington and Rome on the following dates:

Governor Nichols on the 16th of March informed the secretary of state that there was no reason to apprehend further trouble, and that the action of the mob was directed against individuals and not against their race or nationality. Copies of the correspondence were telegraphed to Rome.

On the 18th of March Baron Fava handed the secretary of state a long statement of the massacre and the incidents that preceded it, and complained that the local authorities at New Orleans had been guilty of neglect of their duty. He also submitted a cablegram from the Marquis di Rudini directing him to apply for indemnity, as a declaration of regret on the part of the United States could not be accepted as reparation.

On the 21st of March Baron Fava repeated the demand and submitted a cablegram from Rudini insisting upon an official assurance from the government of the United States that the persons guilty of the massacre had been brought to justice. He also insisted upon immediate indemnity. On the same date Mr. Blaine called upon Baron Fava for the names and condition of the Italian subjects murdered in New Orleans.

On the 24th of March Baron Fava handed Mr. Blaine a cablegram from Rudini insisting that the demand of the Italian government for the punishment of the mob, and indemnity for their victims must be complied with or he would be under the painful necessity of recalling the Italian minister from a country where he was unable to obtain justice. On the following day Rudini telegraphed: "I cannot admit further delay." On the same day Baron Fava submitted a statement from the consul at New Orleans showing that three of the persons murdered were citizens of Italy, and that six had only declared their intention to be naturalized. On the 26th of March Baron Fava sent a note to Mr. Blaine by his secretary requesting an immediate answer to the demand of Rudini. In the meantime Mr. Blaine instructed the United States minister at Rome to explain to the Italian government the dual character of the government of the United States and the necessity of a thorough investigation of the circumstances of the massacre before a proper answer could be made to the demands of Marquis di Rudini.

On the 31st of March Baron Fava again called the attention of Mr. Blaine to the demands of the Italian government, and insisted upon the assurance (1) that the guilty parties should be punished and (2) that the principle that indemnities were due to the families of the victims should be recognized by the United States. As the secretary of state had in an interview declined to give this assurance, Baron Fava announced his withdrawal from Washington under the instructions of his government. On the following day Mr. Blaine replied to this communication, expressing regret at the departure of Baron Fava for which he was unable to see "adequate reasons."

Several diplomatic communications followed, in which the Italian minister reiterated the demands of his government and charged the United States with not showing proper vigor in investigating and punishing the crime under discussion, while our secretary of state replied at length claiming that everything possible had been done, but asserting a doubt about Italy's right to demand indemnity. These documents were characterized on both sides by courteous phrases, which, however, sometimes bordered on acrimony, and for a time there was much idle talk of war between the two countries. The fact that the Italian parliament met soon after the New Orleans affair, probably induced the ministry to make a show of aggressiveness and vigor not quite necessary. When it seemed clear that the matter could not be immediately adjusted, this government, following the example of Italy, granted a vacation to Minister Porter. Thus diplomatic relations, except the ordinary routine business, were suspended.

Early in 1892 an intimation was given the Italian government that the United States would voluntarily offer some indemnity for the massacre of its subjects at New Orleans, and the suggestion was received with the greatest cordiality by Signor Rudini. After a brief and very friendly correspondence Mr. Blaine paid $25,000 out of the fund appropriated for the expense of conducting diplomatic negotiations to be divided among the families of those who had been killed. The Italian government expressed its satisfaction, and its legation at Washington, which had been left vacant since the peremptory recall of Baron Fava, was again filled by his reappointment as minister to the United States. Ex-Governor Porter, of Indiana, who had been minister to Italy, but had been recalled when Baron Fava retired from Washington, was sent back to his post at Rome and the friendly relation between the two governments was entirely restored.

CHAPTER XVII.

RELATIONS WITH OTHER EUROPEAN POWERS.

Germany.

PRUSSIA was the fourth power to conclude a treaty with the United States, yet her relations with this country extend to the very beginning of the war of the Revolution. The king of Prussia, Frederick the Great, was in his old age. When he had at last established his kingdom on a firm basis, he exerted himself to serve, rather than to rule his subjects. Austria and Kaunitz were against him; his Russian alliance seemed transitory and he had not the real friendship of any power in Europe. Old and childless, he must keep up until the end his struggles to make Prussia a permanent political force. On him alone fell the burden of maintaining Protestant freedom and preserving the independence of Prussia. Frederick's ideas of government were very liberal. "The most perfect government," he said, "is a well administered monarchy. But then, kingdoms are subjected to the caprice of a single man whose successors will have no common character. A good-for-nothing prince succeeds an ambitious one; then follows a devotee; then a warrior; then a scholar; then, maybe, a voluptuary; and the genius of a nation, diverted by the variety of objects, assumes no common character. But republics fulfill more promptly the design of their institution, and hold out better—for good kings die, wise laws are immortal." When he held such views as these, it is with little surprise that one hears him say: "The treatment of the American colonies appears to me to be the first step toward despotism. It is hard to proclaim as rebels free subjects who only defend their privileges against the despotism of a ministry." But although he looked with favor upon the revolt of the colonies in America, the future of Prussia demanded that during the war of the Revolution he should observe the strictest neutrality. If the new government was to be recognized, some other continental government must take the initiative. A copy of the Declaration of Independence was sent to Frederick by the American commissioners at Paris. The king strongly approved of the manifesto and, while he refused to open negotiations with the United States, he gave express commands to his minister at London "to do nothing which could offend or wound the American people."

Arthur Lee, one of the commissioners, went to Berlin in 1777 but no notice was taken of him officially. During Lee's stay all of his papers were stolen by a servant and turned over to the British minister, who returned them the next day apparently unopened. There was evidence, however, to show that they had been examined. When Frederick heard of the outrage he refused to receive the British minister and wrote to his representative at London: "The English should blush for shame in sending such ministers to foreign courts."

Lee desired that, if a treaty of alliance could not be effected, at least the port of Emden on the German Ocean might be opened to American privateers. This Frederick refused for the reason that Prussia was not a maritime nation and could not protect her interests against the British. "But," he wrote, "if the American colonies maintain their independence, a direct commerce will, of course, follow." Although Emden was not opened, Frederick finally allowed Dantzig to be used as an asylum for our cruisers. When he had done this, he became more open in his admiration for America. He attempted to dissuade the German princes from furnishing mercenaries to the British and refused to allow such troops from Hesse to pass through his domains. Following this refusal, he gave the American commissioners the greatest facilities for purchasing arms and ammunition in Prussia, and thus opened a direct way for a treaty. His minister wrote in January, 1778, to the commissioners: "The king will not hesitate to recognize your independence when France shall have given the example."

Two months later the treaty with France was made public. The commissioners who expected to follow up their French success with a similar victory in Prussia, were disappointed, for Frederick, menaced on every side and threatened by the English navy, hesitated. He continued, however, to express his cordiality toward the new power, and, when peace with England had been declared, he negotiated a treaty similar to those existing between France and Holland and the United States. The American negotiators were Franklin, Adams, and Jefferson. The arrangement was an admirable conclusion to the work of Franklin, who then ended his European career.

This treaty, which was called at the time an "admirable abstraction," is remarkable for its provisions; all blockades were to be abolished, contrabands were not to be subject to confiscation, and privateering was condemned. This instrument expired by its own limitation in 1796 and a new treaty was concluded in 1799 (thirteen years after Frederick's death), in which the provisions just noticed were omitted.

Other German states following the example set by Prussia made treaties with the United States. In 1828 a treaty was proclaimed by the Hanseatic Republics, headed by Hamburg and Bremen. From that time until the formation of the

North Confederation in 1868, treaties were made with nearly all the petty German states. In 1868 George Bancroft arranged a naturalization treaty with the Confederation. He was also the signer of the convention which relates to the duties of consuls, between the United States and the German Empire in 1871, soon after the establishment of that government.

The conflict in Samoa in 1888 between the revolutionist Tamasese and the reigning king Malietoa, and the connection of Great Britain, Germany, and the United States with the affair caused a sharp correspondence. Germany had for several years evinced a strong desire to annex the Samoan Islands and for that end she was ready to aid the revolutionists. In 1884 she had drawn up a treaty with Samoa which virtually gave Germany possession of the islands. This treaty was disallowed by Great Britain and the United States and was repudiated by Malietoa as having been extorted by threats. The treaty with the United States was explicit in its terms, one of which is as follows: "If unhappily any difference should have arisen or shall hereafter arise, between the Samoan government and any other government in amity with the United States, the government of the latter will employ its good offices for the purpose of adjusting these differences upon a satisfactory and a solid foundation."

When the Germans took sides with Tamasese the American consul, in conformity as he thought with the clause of the treaty quoted above, raised the American flag in protection of the Samoan government, in order that a conference might adjust the difficulty. Before this conference could be held the secretary of state repudiated the action of the consul.

Germany continued her policy and forced Malietoa to abdicate. He was taken as a prisoner on board a German man-of-war and late in 1888 he was carried to Berlin. Soon after, Germany announced to the United States that she had declared war on Samoa. Mr. Bayard replied that she had no right to do this. Bismarck rejoined that he regretted that the state of affairs in a far-off island should disturb the friendly relations which had ever existed between the United States and the German Empire. At last a conference composed of representatives from the three powers was appointed to attempt pacific adjustment of the Samoan difficulty. As a result, a general act was agreed to, which guaranteed the neutrality of the Samoan Islands and settled matters of minor importance.

In 1883 the Germans laid an embargo upon American pork. A long diplomatic correspondence on this subject followed until in 1891, largely through the exertions of our minister at Berlin, Mr. William Walter Phelps, the embargo was raised and American meats were admitted into the empire subject to certain inspection which the German government considered necessary.

The same year a reciprocity treaty was negotiated with Germany under which all food products and many manufactured articles of the United States are admitted into German ports at a rate of duty less than is imposed upon the same articles from other countries. In return for this concession the United States admits free into her ports the beet root sugar of Germany.

Austria.

Commercial intercourse between the United States and Austria was insignificant during the early years of this century, and the Napoleonic wars discouraged any attempt to arrange a treaty. By the year 1829, however, trade had increased to such an extent that a treaty of commerce and navigation was arranged. It went into effect in 1831 and has been twice extended.

In 1853 there was an incident in which the United States and Austria were interested, that occasioned wide discussion at the time and has since been regarded as one of the most remarkable cases in international law. An Austrian subject, Martin Koszta, emigrated to the United States and declared his intention of becoming a citizen of this country. He had been implicated in the unsuccessful revolution of 1848 but managed to escape from Austria to Turkey. Here he was arrested and confined but he was finally liberated upon his promise to leave Turkish territory. From Turkey he went to the United States, where he resided until 1853. Then, before the term of years necessary for his naturalization had expired, he went to Smyrna. Here the American consul granted him a traveling pass which entitled him to the protection of the United States. While at Smyrna, he was seized by several men in the employ of the Austrian consul, and carried out into the harbor, where an Austrian man-of-war was anchored. His captors threw him overboard. He was rescued by the sailors of the man-of-war, taken on board that vessel, and placed in confinement.

The American consul at Smyrna immediately entered a protest against this action and reported the matter to the American minister at Constantinople, who directed a United States steamer to proceed to Smyrna, demand the release of Koszta, and, if necessary, follow up the demand with a resort to force. In order to avoid a conflict and all that might ensue, the French consul at Smyrna offered his mediation, and Koszta was given over to him until the case could be decided.

After a diplomatic warfare, jurisdiction over Koszta was surrendered by Austria and he returned to the United States, with the understanding that, should he ever again be on Turkish territory, Austria could proceed against him. The reasons for the decision in favor of the United States were:

First, that the acts of the Austrian officials on Turkish territory were an insult to the sovereignty of the latter country; and, second, that, if the pass granted by the American consul was correct, he was entitled to the protection which is accorded all American citizens in Turkey. If Koszta was not entitled to the pass, Turkey, and not Austria was the power to complain. The resort to force to gain possession of Koszta was contrary to the principles of international law but the action was justified as it indicated the sovereignty of Turkey.

In 1870 the United States and Austria concluded a naturalization treaty and two years later a correspondence ensued over the citizenship of one François Heinrich, who was born in New York of parents who were Austrian subjects and only temporarily resident in this country. The treaty of 1870 required that a five years' residence was necessary for naturalization. Heinrich's parents did not fulfill this stipulation as they returned to Austria before the allotted time had elapsed. The laws of the two countries conflict on the subject; the United States holding that a man is a citizen if born within its territory; Austria, on the contrary, determines a man's nationality by that of his parents.

Heinrich returned to Austria with his parents and performed none of the duties of an Austrian citizen, but accepted an Austrian passport. In 1872 he was notified that he must perform service in the Austrian army. He refused to comply with the demand and asked the interference of the United States in his behalf. Our government finally refused to aid him as he had shown by his long residence in Austria that he intended to reside there permanently and his allegiance to the Austrian government was shown by his willingness to travel under one of its passports.

Besides the treaties of commerce and of naturalization,

there have been proclaimed by the two countries, two treaties, on extradition (1856), and on the rights of consuls (1870), besides a convention relative to trade-marks.

Holland.

The diplomatic relations between the United States and Holland began in 1782 with a treaty of amity and commerce, entered into by "Their High Mightinesses, the States General of the United Netherlands and the United States of America." While the United States were British colonies, all European countries were denied the right of trade with them. When the bonds of the mother country had been thrown off, the continental powers were eager to share American commerce. The readiness of France and Holland to enter into diplomatic relations with the young country was apparent. In 1778 France had negotiated a treaty with Franklin, Deane, and Lee for the States. In this treaty, however, France instead of securing a monopoly, obtained merely the right of trade without exclusive advantages. The same general idea was carried out four years later in the treaty between the United States and the Netherlands. Citizens of the United States were to have the same privileges in the United Netherlands as had those of the most favored nation; and liberty of conscience was secured to the citizens of each country in the other's dominions. This last clause, though omitted in the French treaty, occurs in treaties with Sweden and Prussia.

Although the Dutch treaty was proclaimed four years later than that with France, negotiations had begun only eight months after the declaration of the latter. In September, 1778, the American commissioners at Paris were notified that as soon as the United States were recognized by the English, the Burgomasters of Amsterdam were willing to treat " concerning the most extensive reciprocal advantages in relation to the commerce of the two powers." It was suggested that the treaty recently concluded between the United States and France be used as a basis, "changing only those provisions which cannot be applicable to the republic of the United Netherlands."

In spite of emphatic protests on the part of England, John Adams conducted the negotiations to a successful issue. The cumbersome constitution of the Netherlands required that the treaty should receive the approval of each of the legislative bodies of the seven provinces, and it was not until late in April that Mr. Adams was officially received as a minister. Three months afterwards the treaty was signed and a loan to the United States of five million guilders ($2,000,000) secured.

The French revolution and empire so disturbed the governments of Europe that after the Congress of Vienna, by which the Netherlands were established as a constitutional monarchy, that country claimed the right to abrogate all former treaties. The United States demurred at first but finally acquiesced and from time to time the usual treaties and conventions regarding commerce, the rights and privileges of consuls, the extradition of criminals and the like have been concluded.

Belgium.

Our regular diplomatic relations with Belgium began in 1845, at which time was negotiated a treaty to be in force for ten years. In this treaty freedom of commerce and navigation was secured to vessels of the United States, and Belgium agreed to make a restitution of the Scheldt dues, which were levied by the Netherlands on all shipping which passed up that river. As there was some delay in the exchange of ratifications, and as it was to hold for one year in addition to the ten years' limitation, the treaty did not expire until late in

1857. On the twentieth of August in that year, the secretary of state, Lewis Cass, was notified officially that the Belgium government wished to terminate it, the next year a new convention was negotiated, with approximately the same provisions, which was to hold for another ten years.

But the dues which Holland levied upon commerce on the Scheldt were obnoxious and out of conformity with the practices of most nations, so that in 1863 a treaty was entered into by the United States and Belgium for the capitalization of the dues, and later in the same year they were abolished. Since that time eight treaties have been ratified between the United States and Belgium, on the subjects of naturalization, trade-marks, consuls, etc., and in 1875 a new treaty of commerce and navigation was drawn up and ratified, which is still in force.

Within the last few years, however, the two countries have been brought more closely together on account of the connection of each power with the Congo Free State, whose sovereign is the king of the Belgians, and the discoverer of whose territory was an American, Henry M. Stanley. This relation is described fully in Chapter XXII.

Sweden.

In 1782, the Swedish minister at Paris, by the direction of his sovereign, Gustavus III., called on Benjamin Franklin to inquire about the desirability of a treaty between the two countries. In the course of conversation the minister remarked that it was a pleasure to him to think, and he hoped it would be remembered, "that Sweden was the first power in Europe which had voluntarily and without solicitation offered its friendship to the United States." Dr. Franklin informed Congress of the application by Sweden and he was empowered to agree on a treaty, which he did, April 3, 1783. The provisions of this instrument resembled closely those of the

Dutch treaty of the previous year and its validity was limited to fifteen years. The relations between the two countries have ever been the friendliest. In 1810 certain claims against Sweden, concerning the spoliation of American property, were adjusted privately. After the union of Sweden and Norway a new treaty was effected (1827); since then there have been two treaties, for extradition (1860) and for naturalization (1869).

Denmark.

The United States has had diplomatic intercourse with Denmark since 1779, but it was not until fifty years after the Declaration of Independence that regular diplomatic relations began and ministers were accredited from one country to the other. In 1779 Benjamin Franklin remonstrated to the Danish minister of foreign affairs at Copenhagen against the seizure of American vessels within the jurisdiction of Denmark. The remonstrance received no attention at the time, but when later troubles of a similar nature arose, the Danish government paid indemnities.

In 1783 the minister of foreign affairs wrote to a friend who was about to travel in France, "I cannot omit recommending to you to endeavor during your stay in Paris to gain, as much as possible, the confidence and esteem of Mr. Franklin. We are persuaded that it will be for the general interests of the two states to form, as soon as possible, reciprocal connections of friendship and commerce. Nothing would be more agreeable to us than to learn by your letters that you find the same disposition in Mr. Franklin."

De Waltensdorf, to whom this letter was written, had several conversations with Franklin, and they agreed that a treaty of amity and commerce would be very desirable for both countries. Congress was informed of the negotiations and was asked to give Franklin the necessary power to conclude a treaty, using that with the Netherlands (concluded the year before) as a model. But as Denmark, under pressure from England, had seized three American vessels off the coast of Norway, Congress brought the negotiations to a close and the matter was dropped.

The Napoleonic wars brought the United States into collision with Denmark as well as with almost all the other European nations. During 1809 and 1810 one hundred and sixty American vessels were seized by Denmark and many of this number were confiscated on the ground that they were really English sailing under false colors. After the usual diplomatic contest our government succeeded in securing an indemnity of $1,750,000, which in view of Denmark's diminished resources was deemed a substantial victory.

The favorable settlement of these claims, which has ever since been considered a masterpiece of diplomacy, was no sooner accomplished than the United States set about securing the abolition of a tax, which Denmark, from time immemorial, had placed upon all shipping passing through the Sound connecting the Baltic and the North Sea.

These taxes, called "Sound dues," are mentioned as early as the thirteenth century and they were tacitly admitted as just by all of the maritime powers of Europe. The treaty of Christianople regulated them in 1645 and they were again fixed in 1701 and continued at the rate agreed upon at that time until the early part of this century. Denmark claimed that the dues were levied for the purpose of raising money to maintain lights and buoys as aids to navigation but more probably they are based historically on a quasi feudal privilege of the king of Denmark, to which the tolls levied by the mediæval German barons might be compared. The Sound dues formed a large part of the income of the Danish monarch, and in 1830 American vessels contributed one hundred thousand dollars to this fund. The first notice taken by the United States of the imposition occurs in the treaty of 1826, between this country and Denmark, a clause of which stipulated that American vessels, passing through the Sound were not to pay higher dues than those paid by the ships of other powers. This clause shows clearly that the United States recognized Denmark's right to levy the tolls and this view continued to be taken by the United States until 1843, during the secretaryship of Mr. Upshur, who, in a communication to President Tyler, stated, that "Denmark continues to this day, without any legal title, to levy exceedingly strange duties on all goods passing through the Sound. She cannot lay claims to these duties upon any principle, either of nature, of the law of nations, or from any other reason than that of antiquated custom. . . . For the United States the time has come when they can appropriately take decisive steps to free their Baltic trade of this pressure."

In 1845 the United States offered to give Denmark $250,000 if she would forever exempt American vessels from Sound dues; the sum to be regarded not as the payment of a claim, but as remuneration for the maintenance of lights and buoys. Denmark at first looked favorably at the proposition but hostilities with Germany caused a suspension of the negotiations. Eight years later our government withdrew its offer and declared that the United States were no longer willing to recognize a claim based upon a mediæval custom, and announced the abrogation of the treaty of 1826. Denmark realizing that her ancient privilege was in peril, proposed a plan to all nations by which each country should pay her a sum proportionate to the amount of merchandise passing through the Sound. The European states accepted the proposition, which took the form of a treaty in 1857. Soon after, the United States made a similar but separate arrangement by which the payment of about four hundred thousand dollars secured the exemption of American shipping from the obnoxious dues.

The negotiations between the United States and Denmark over the cession of the island of St. Thomas by the latter have been fully described in Chapter IX.

Portugal.

Early in Washington's administration, proposals were made for a treaty with Portugal, in order to gain a common cause with that power against the piratical Barbary States, with whom she, as well as the United States, was at war. Before these transactions took place, however, Benjamin Franklin had written to Congress, in 1783, that "the conclusion of the Portuguese treaty waits only for the commission and instructions of Congress." Three years later an understanding was reached between the two powers, but no definite treaty was decided upon.

Beginning in 1791, regular diplomatic relations were sustained with Portugal, with resident ministers accredited from each country to the other. In 1801, however, the ministers were recalled, owing to the general disturbance in continental affairs, and no regular minister was sent from the United States to Lisbon until 1822.

While the War of 1812 was in progress, a conflict took place in the harbor of Fayal, in the Azores Islands, between a British man-of-war and an American privateer, in which the latter was destroyed. The United States immediately claimed damages from Portugal as being responsible for the violation of the neutrality of the port. Portugal refused to award damages for the reason that the American vessel had gone into battle without having asked the protection of the port.

The incident gave rise to a correspondence between the two powers, which lasted from 1814 until 1851, when it was agreed to refer the matter for settlement to some foreign ruler. Accordingly, the president of the French republic (afterwards Napoleon III.) was selected as a referee and the case was decided in favor of Portugal. The conclusion of the decision reads: "The government of his most faithful majesty cannot be held responsible for the results of the collision which took place in contempt of the rights of sovereignty, in violation of the neutrality of her territory, and without the local officers having been required in proper time to grant aid and protection to those having a right to the same. Therefore, we have decided that the claim of the United States has no foundation and no indemnity is due from Portugal."

This is the only controversy of importance which has ever occurred between the two countries. Two treaties have been concluded and proclaimed; one of commerce and of navigation in 1840, which gave reciprocal rights of commerce, regulated consulates, and decided upon the proper disposition of deserters. The other treaty was ratified in 1851. By this instrument, the claims of the United States against Portugal, as described above, were referred to a foreign arbitrator, and certain claims of American citizens against the Portuguese government were settled.

The government of Portugal, however, showed its good will toward the United States by surrendering without an extradition treaty the person of William M. Tweed, the notorious politician of New York, who fled to Lisbon when his rascalities were discovered. He sought an asylum in Portugal, knowing that there was no extradition treaty between that government and the United States, but when his presence there was discovered, he was arrested and the authorities offered no objection to his removal to this country.

CHAPTER XVIII.

RELATIONS WITH EASTERN AND MEDITERRANEAN POWERS.

Turkey.

DURING the early years of this century American commerce in the Eastern Mediterranean was under the protection of what was known as the English Levant Company and no attempt was made to arrange commercial relations with Turkey on a treaty basis until 1817. From that time until 1830 various propositions were suggested for a treaty between the United States and the Ottoman Porte, but without success. In 1830, however, President Jackson appointed a commission for that purpose. This commission consisted of Commodore Biddle, who was stationed in the Mediterranean, David Offley, the consul at Smyrna, and Charles Rhind, who was directly from the United States. In order to keep the negotiations secret, Rhind proceeded alone to Constantinople, and drew up a treaty. When this had been done, his colleagues joined him.

This treaty gave privileges of trade equal to those of the most favored nations, allowed American ships passage through the Dardanelles, and agreed upon the establishment of consulates in both countries.

In addition to these provisions, the original draft, prepared by Rhind, contained a separate and secret article, which provided for the purchase of timber by Turkey in the United

States and for the building of ships in this country by the former. Biddle and Offley, on arriving at Constantinople, disapproved of this secret article, but they signed the treaty and forwarded it, with their reasons for ratifying, to the secretary of state. The Senate ratified the treaty, but rejected the separate article.

The original draft of the treaty was in Turkish and, as the commissioners were ignorant of the language, complications arose as to its real contents and stipulations. There were four different translations sent to America; and it was found that the one considered in the Senate, and subsequently ratified by that body, was not that signed by the commission.

The Turkish government complained to David Porter, who had been sent to exchange the ratifications at Constantinople, that the original translation was not the one acted upon by the Senate. Porter thereupon signed a paper, which was in Turkish, pledging that the United States would abide by the stipulations of the Turkish original, should complications arise.

However, no trouble occurred until 1868, when Turkish officers arrested and imprisoned two American citizens for alleged offenses against that government. The United States complained that such actions were directly contrary to the provisions of the fourth article of the treaty of 1830; the last part of which reads, in the Senate version: "Citizens of the United States of America, when they may have committed some offense, shall not be arrested and put in prison by the local authorities, but shall be tried by their ministers or consuls and punished according to their offenses, following, in this respect, the usage observed toward other Franks."

The Turkish minister for foreign affairs replied to our minister that this clause was incorrect and did not occur in the original Turkish document. The American minister then requested several officers in the Russian and French legations to make translations from the original draft, and none of these new translations contained any phrase corresponding to that in the copy sent to the Senate.

The discussion, in regard to the true meaning of the Turkish text, raised at that time, is still unsettled; but this one clause seems to be the only discrepancy between the two versions.

Six years before the case referred to occurred, a new treaty of commerce was negotiated, which, however, did not abrogate that of 1830, but only changed some of its minor provisions and said nothing concerning the extraterritorial jurisdiction of American consuls.

The treaty of 1862 was to be valid for twenty-eight years, subject to termination by a notice to be given one year before the expiration of fourteen or twenty-one years.

In 1874 the United States was informed that the Turkish government intended to terminate the treaty. The reply was made that this government could not receive, in advance of more than one year, notice of such a desire. When the proper time arrived for the notice to the government, Turkey neglected to send it.

The matter was left in abeyance and the treaty held until March 12, 1883, when notice was again given that Turkey desired to abrogate the existing convention the following year.

The United States replied that such a notice would not be in order until June 5, 1883. The Turkish government acted again as it had done in 1874, and the proper time passed without any further action being taken. According to the stipulation of the treaty, if notice was not given one year in advance of the expiration of the twenty-first year, the treaty was to be binding until the twenty-eighth year.

Turkey refused to agree with the United States that a proper notice had not been given and has considered the treaty of 1862 as abrogated ever since June 5, 1884.

To show, however, the good feeling of that government toward the United States, she has given a standing invitation to negotiate a new treaty, but as yet the offer has not been accepted. Nevertheless, American commerce has ever been treated most favorably by the Turkish government and the cordial relations between the two powers are proverbial.

Persia.

Mohammed, the father of the present shah of Persia, Nasr-ed-Din, was a prince possessing enlightened views, and he desired to improve the condition of his country. England and Russia, now so opposed in their Eastern policy, concurred in securing him the throne, and England exerted a strong influence over his policy throughout his whole reign from 1834 to 1848. Once, in the war with Afghanistan (1836–38), he proceeded contrary to the wishes of the British government, but in this campaign, and particularly in the siege of Herat, the Persians were totally unsuccessful. From the end of this war until the shah's death, England and France attempted to negotiate commercial treaties. England succeeded in doing so, but the French mission was for a long time unsuccessful.

Acting upon English success, and observing the increasing trade between the United States and Persia, Secretary of State Marcy instructed our minister to Turkey, Carroll Spence, to arrange with Persia a treaty of friendship and commerce, which he did, December 13, 1856. The ratifications were exchanged at Constantinople and the treaty was proclaimed in August, 1857. Of all the treaties arranged with Eastern powers, the one with Persia exhibits the most Oriental character in its opening sentences; it is contracted by "The President of the United States of America and His Majesty as exalted as the Planet Saturn; the sovereign to whom the sun serves as a standard; whose splendor and magnificence are equal to that of the skies, the Sublime Sovereign, the Monarch whose armies are as numerous as the stars."

Following the negotiations of the treaty, Secretary Marcy sent a communication to Congress requesting an appropriation for the maintenance of the legation at Teheran. The House voted a specified amount for the yearly salary of the minister and corresponding sums for the other officers. The relations between the two countries have always been cordial and no complications of any importance have ever arisen.

The Barbary States.

During the early part of this century what were called the Barbary States—Morocco, Algeria, and Tripoli—lying along the north coast of Africa, made a business of piracy, and were known as the "piratical nations." They had a fleet of swift-sailing ships, commanded and manned by cutthroats, who watched the straits of Gibraltar to seize, plunder, and burn merchant vessels, and hold their crews for ransom or sell them for slaves. They often pursued vessels even into the Atlantic. Navigation upon the Mediterranean in those days was therefore attended with the greatest perils. The great French dramatist Regnard was once captured and served for seven years as a slave in Algiers; Jacob Leisler, afterwards governor of New York, served four years as a slave in Morocco; and Cervantes, the Spanish author of Don Quixote, was held for five years as a captive before he was ransomed.

Some of the European nations, in order to protect their commerce, paid large sums annually to the dey of Morocco and the dey of Algiers in the form of a bounty. France, by a formal treaty in 1788, agreed to pay $200,000 each year for ten years, besides giving presents to the principal officials of the two countries, and in ten years, from 1790 to 1800, Spain is variously estimated to have paid from three to five millions of dollars in blackmail for the same purpose. England paid an annual tribute of $280,000; while other countries were in the habit of keeping agents at Tunis and other places for the purpose of securing the release of any of their subjects that might be captured by the payment of ransom at so much per capita. From 1786 to 1790 the price of ransom ranged from $1,200 to $3,000 per man; and from 1790 to 1800 it ranged from $500 to $3,000.

Before the war of the Revolution the United States had

a large commerce with the ports of the Mediterranean, employing about one thousand vessels and twelve thousand seamen. The vessels were protected by Great Britain as long as the states were colonies of that government, but at the close of the war, in 1783, when trade began to revive, the rulers of the Barbary powers began a concerted and determined attack upon shipping that carried the flag of a new nation that paid them no tribute. Several ships were captured and burned, and the masters and men sold into slavery. Mr. Jefferson, who was then minister to France, was instructed to make an investigation and endeavor to secure their release. He succeeded in rescuing the crew of one vessel through the good offices of the Spanish government, but in his report to the President said: "It rests with Congress to decide between war, tribute, or ransom as the means of re-establishing our Mediterranean commerce."

In 1784 Congress authorized Dr. Franklin, John Adams, and Mr. Jefferson to make a treaty with the Barbary States, and they carried on negotiations with an agent who was sent to Paris to confer with them. But he demanded about $1,500,000 as blackmail for his sovereign and $50,000 for himself, which the commissioners refused to pay. Thomas Barclay was then sent to Morocco to deal directly with the dey, and made a treaty with him, under which he agreed to let American ships alone if the United States would give him a hundred cannon. These were sent and cost but $9,000. But the treaty was very soon terminated by the death of the dey, whose son and successor refused to renew it without the payment of tribute.

John Lamb, who was sent to Algiers on a similar mission, failed entirely in his negotiations and, very shortly after, Richard O'Brien was dispatched to see what he could accomplish. Of this remarkable, but appropriate diplomatist,

Mr. Adams wrote: "O'Brien is an old Irishman, who was once consul general at Algiers chiefly because he had been for nine or ten years a slave there. He was the master of a vessel, and is an exact copy of one of Smollett's novel sailors. His discourse is patched up entirely of sea phrases, and he prides himself upon nothing so much as his language."

The dey of Algiers received O'Brien politely, told him he had heard of General Washington, and wanted a full length portrait of him to hang in his palace, but this admiration did not diminish his desire for money, as he demanded $6,000 ransom for each sea captain captured, $4,000 each for mates, and $1,400 each for ordinary seamen, with eleven per cent bonus on the total amount. This proposition was rejected, and O'Brien returned to Paris.

Mr. Jefferson then appealed to the Holy Order of St. Mathurin at Paris, a religious society organized in 1199 for the purpose of rescuing Christians captured by the infidels. The captain general of this order offered to undertake the rescue of the Americans then held in captivity, but required that the utmost secrecy should be observed in order that the Algerians should not know that the society was acting in behalf of the United States government. He had ransomed only one person, however, when the French revolution occurred, and all religious orders in France were abolished.

Paul Jones, the famous sailor, was authorized by Congress to undertake the work of rescue, but he died before he had accomplished his mission. David Humphreys, the American minister at Lisbon, was next selected to perform the delicate duty, and $800,000 was placed at his disposition, but he failed, and during the next few months ten more vessels were captured by the Algerian pirates and one hundred and fifteen American sailors were sold as slaves.

Congress then passed an act authorizing the President to employ a sufficient naval force to protect the commerce of the United States on the Mediterranean, and orders were given for the construction of six frigates and ten smaller vessels of war. But before they were completed an arrangement was entered into with a firm of Jewish bankers in Paris, who assisted in securing a treaty with Algiers under which the protection of American commerce was guaranteed. It cost $992,463.25 to fulfill this treaty. The sum of $642,500 was paid in cash to the dey of Algiers; he was presented with a frigate of thirty-six guns; the United States agreed to furnish him $21,600 annually in naval stores, besides $20,000 annually in cash, and $17,000 annually in presents to his officials. In 1798, the government having failed to pay the annuities, four armed vessels were presented to the dey instead.

A similar treaty was made with the bashaw of Tripoli by Joel Barlow, the poet; and he made another with the bey of Tunis, which cost $107,000, and a quantity of jewelry as presents. The whole cost of purchasing protection for American ships in this form of blackmail was over $2,000,000; and it amounted to nothing as within two years the bashaw of Tripoli became dissatisfied because he had not been paid as much as the dey of Algiers, and declared war against the United States. A fleet of ships under the command of Commodore Decatur was sent to Tripoli, and active hostilities were carried on until Tobias Lear, who had been private secretary to Washington, negotiated a treaty of peace and paid a bounty of $60,000 as ransom for American captives.

There was immediate trouble with Algiers, also, which continued through the War of 1812, until it was terminated by the very prompt action of Commodore Decatur, who declined to pay blackmail in any form, and threatened to bombard the capital unless the American captives were released. The dey asked three hours to consider, but Commodore Decatur replied: "Not one minute." Through the mediation of the Swedish consul the captives were released, and a treaty was signed under which tribute was abolished, and it was agreed that American sailors should not be made slaves.

Decatur then proceeded to Tunis and instead of offering ransom demanded an indemnity of $46,000 for two vessels that had been captured. The dey looked at the commodore's fleet through the windows of his palace, combed his beard for a few moments with a tortoise-shell comb heavily set with diamonds, and saying "I know this admiral," ordered the money to be paid at once.

A similar scene occurred shortly after at Tripoli, when the bashaw, in response to Decatur's demands, paid $25,000 as indemnity for two American ships, and released the prisoners.

The summary action of Commodore Decatur and its result attracted the attention of all Europe, and the several nations which had been paying tribute soon after united to suppress the Barbary pirates. The United States was the first government to defy them, and set the example for Europe, but the expenditures in tributes alone, not including the cost of the naval operations, reached a total of $2,650,709 before these bandits were taught to observe the principles of civilization.

The Egyptian Mixed Tribunals.

The methods of judicial procedure in the Oriental countries differing so widely from that in use in the United States, this government in its first treaty negotiations with those countries obtained their consent to vest American ministers and consuls with power to act in controversies affecting the property rights of our citizens. The criminal jurisdiction was also obtained, as the punishments inflicted by the laws of those countries were not in harmony with our own, bastinadoing and excessive fines being quite common penalties.

In 1860 a law was passed conferring judicial powers upon the ministers and consuls in China, Japan, Siam, Persia, and Turkey. This law remained in force in respect to Egypt until the organization of the Mixed Tribunals of Alexandria and Cairo. There were so many foreigners residing in Egypt, brought thither by the work on the Suez Canal and the extended commerce growing out of its navigation, that innumerable questions requiring settlement by lawsuits arose. Different nationalities being often represented in these controversies, resort was had to their respective consuls and great confusion naturally ensued.

The khedive, desiring that his government should be recognized as among the civilized countries, submitted plans for the settlement of these suits, and in 1873 there were established at Alexandria a Court of Appeals, and three inferior tribunals of first instance at Alexandria, Cairo, and Zagazig. These courts were composed of foreign and native judges, and were so arranged that the foreigners should have a majority in each court.

To these courts all questions in civil and commercial matters affecting our citizens residing in Egypt come for trial, whether the controversies are between them and natives or with citizens of other countries. Upon receipt of the notification that these courts were organized the President issued, October 29, 1874, a proclamation suspending the consular functions in these matters, being authorized so to do by the act of March 23, of the same year.

There is an American judge in both courts of first instance at Cairo and Alexandria, and one on the bench of the Court of Appeals in Alexandria. These judges are appointed by the khedive upon the nomination of the President of the United States and receive salaries of about $5,000 a year. The proceedings before these courts are of a very novel nature owing to the variety of nationalities represented. The judgments are delivered in French, but the testimony is given in almost every language in the world, while the pleadings and arguments depend upon the nationality of the counsel employed.

The government has not been willing to relinquish its jurisdiction over our citizens accused of crimes in Egypt, and it is still the duty of our consular officers to make the necessary investigations and punish offenders.

CHAPTER XIX.

RELATIONS WITH CHINA.

IN the sixteenth century China claimed Malacca as a vassal state. In the year 1510 it was attacked by some Portuguese pirates, who carried away a great booty. This was the first experience of the Chinese with the maritime powers of the West. From Malacca, Raphael Perestralo sailed to visit the coast of China, of which he had heard. A few years later another Portuguese, Ferdinand Andrada, found his way with his ship to Canton, and sent an envoy, Thomas Perez, to the emperor at Peking. He was well received, accorded the privilege to trade, and returned to Canton. But another Portuguese piratical squadron appeared off the coast and committed depredations which led to the execution of Andrada and Perez, in 1523. Such was the beginning of foreign intercourse with China.

The Russians and the Dutch established resident embassies at Peking as early as 1656. The latter were specially permitted to bring "tribute" and to send a trading ship to China once in eight years. This restriction upon trade was due to the generous consideration of the emperor, who feared that the boisterous winds might wreck the Dutch ships and cause him great sorrow, if he allowed them to come more frequently.

Since that time ambassadors from different European courts

have visited Peking with various experiences, but it is a question even to-day whether there is not, among the Chinese officials, beneath all the elaborate courtesies of formal diplomatic intercourse, a feeling of the infinite superiority of China over all other nations in greatness, power, and culture, and a disposition to regard or to represent to the people all foreign ministers as bearers of tribute to the Dragon throne.

The history of the relations between China and the nations of the Western world is full of strange incidents inexplicable even to-day. It is impossible for one of us to think as a Chinese thinks, or spontaneously to follow the strange course of reasoning which frequently leads him to most unexpected and astonishing conclusions. We should clearly recognize the fact that it was in response to a demand enforced by the conquest of allied armies, that the great empire was eventually opened to foreign trade and official intercourse, in entire disregard of the traditions and prejudices of the people and their rulers. The difficulties to be overcome were extraordinary. But China was too rich and productive a country to be neglected. Foreigners had already enjoyed the fruits of profitable trade at Canton for more than a century, but under conditions of ignominy and restraint which could not be indefinitely tolerated. So long as the Chinese had to deal with private traders alone, they could enforce such rules and restrictions as they pleased; but with the expiration of the charter of the great East India Company, in 1834, the traders became no longer members of a chartered company, but subjects of foreign powers, which was a very different matter.

But the Chinese government had always held itself high and mighty over all other powers. This was not a mere conceit, to be eradicated by an appeal to force and a crushing defeat of its brave but inefficient armies. It was, and still is, an inborn element of national faith, a belief fostered by centuries of intercourse and war with the uncivilized and far inferior peoples with whom the Chinese came into relations from time to time, a part of the education of every child from the cradle. It is, therefore, not unnatural that the educated people, the high officials of the land, owing to the limitations of their knowledge and their inadequate conceptions of the outer world and its inhabitants, should assume an arrogance and supremacy toward all foreign nations, and erect barriers of exclusiveness which required to be broken down before business could be permanently established, or the safety of foreign life and property assured.

In the early days of foreign trade all business was transacted at Canton with certain Hong merchants, who alone were permitted to deal with foreigners. There was no communication between the foreigners and the local or government officials except through the Hong merchants, and even after the appointment of foreign consular officers the Canton officials gave but little heed to their presence or representations.

The American flag first appeared at Canton in 1784 on the ship *Empress of China*. Trade with the Portuguese had then been maintained for nearly three centuries, since they had established themselves at Macao. The Dutch formed a settlement on Formosa in 1624. British trade at Canton dates from about 1637.

In the year 1790, President George Washington appointed Samuel Shaw as consul of the United States at Canton. Our interests in China were then considerable, but as an illustration of the disregard of foreign representatives manifested by the Chinese officials in those days, the following instance may be cited: An American sailor was accused of the murder of a Chinese woman. Doubtless he was guilty, but the consul was unable to secure him a proper trial. He was tried by a court from which the consul was excluded, and finally executed by the viceroy's order.

To break down the barriers of Chinese arrogance and exclusiveness doubtless required sooner or later an appeal to arms; but we may well deplore that such unjust and inadequate causes as led to the opium war, conducted by England in behalf of merchants engaged in an illegal trade, should have been the active means of introducing to China the civilization and morality of the West. The emperor Keen Lung, one of the truly great and wise rulers of the present dynasty, prohibited the importation of opium. In 1796 and 1800 more stringent laws were passed to stop the trade. But it was worth a million of pounds sterling a year to British traders! Two Chinese convicted of dealing in it were executed in front of the British factories, as an earnest of the determination of the authorities to stop the trade. But it was of no avail. The trade was illegal, every pound of opium was smuggled into the country in direct violation of the laws of the empire, yet the authorities were powerless to stop it.

In 1839 the imperial commissioner Lin was sent to Canton with full authority to stop the trade as best he could. He demanded that all opium in the hands of foreign merchants should be delivered to him, and enforced this demand by stopping all trade until it was done. More than 20,000 chests were delivered into his hands. The entire quantity was destroyed. An American merchant who witnessed the destruction was astonished "that while Christian governments were growing and farming this deleterious drug, this pagan monarch should nobly disdain to enrich his treasury with a sale which could not fall short of $20,000,000."

After this, trade was resumed and opium smuggling went on as before. In 1840 the English were declared to be outlaws, and their trade was stopped. The English then, regardless of a strong protest from the United States consul, declared a blockade of the river and port of Canton on the 28th of January, 1840. This was the beginning of active hostilities against the Chinese. The city of Canton was bombarded and captured. This glorious feat of arms was unnecessary and of no practical benefit; unless it be regarded, as one British author has declared it, as retribution for the destruction of the opium. As a result of this great conquest of British arms over matchlocks and culverins, the treaty of Nanking was signed, which accorded privileges of residence to British subjects at Canton, Amoy, Shanghai, Foochow, and Ningpo, ceded the island of Hong-Kong to the crown, and bound the Chinese government to pay an enormous indemnity for the opium so justly destroyed—opium which was contraband and liable to confiscation under the laws of all civilized countries. This treaty led to the opening of diplomatic relations between China and the United States. President Tyler alluded to its provisions in his message to Congress in December, 1842, and at the same time referred to the importance of our commercial relations with China. They require, he said, "at the present moment, a degree of attention and vigilance such as there is no agent of this government on the spot to bestow." He recommended the appointment of a commissioner to exercise watchful care over the concerns of American citizens, the protection of their persons and property, empowered to hold intercourse with local authorities and also with the emperor, through high government officers.

Mr. Caleb Cushing was soon after appointed commissioner and envoy extraordinary and minister plenipotentiary to China. He arrived at Macao in the U. S. steamer *Brandywine* in February, 1844, with the intention of proceeding directly to Peking to present his letters to the emperor. But the newly appointed Chinese commissioner at Canton, Tsiyeng, or Keying, strongly deprecated any thought of a journey to the capital, or even to Tientsin, saying that the appearance of the American ships on the coast would give rise to much anxiety and excitement among the people, and offering many arguments against the propriety of the undertaking. Mr. Cushing finally yielded to these protestations, which was doubtless the wisest policy at the time.

Mr. Cushing succeeded in negotiating a treaty, known as the treaty of Wang Hiya, which was signed July 3, 1844. By this treaty five ports were opened to American trade, privileges of residence granted to citizens of the United States, port regulations established, and two very important concessions secured, the first involving the right of foreigners to be tried by their own consular or other government authorities, the second according to the United States all privileges and advantages which China might concede to any other nation. These two provisions, known as exterritoriality and the favored nation clause, have been, and still are, of the greatest importance to foreigners in China and also in Japan.

A feature of the agreement is the privilege of direct correspondence between the United States government and the court, such correspondence to be transmitted through certain designated officers at the open ports.

The successful and prompt negotiation of this treaty was no doubt due to the fact that the Chinese commissioner became fully convinced that the United States did not desire to take possession of Chinese territory or to extort money or to offend the national pride or dignity.

The selection of Caleb Cushing as the first diplomatic representative of this country was most fortunate and wise. Looking over the correspondence conducted by him with the Chinese officials in the light of later years of experience in dealing with those personages, one can but feel impressed with his keen insight into their strange character and motives. Ever excessively courteous, in conformity with the customs of the East, he was firm in maintaining the dignity and power of the United States. The treaty which he negotiated was the result of the wisest diplomacy, through which we secured greater prestige and even more honorable concessions than British arrogance had enforced at the cannon's mouth. It was British trade which opened China with powder and ball and the sacrifice of thousands of lives and the payment of an enormous indemnity. But it was the United States which first secured the right of diplomatic correspondence with Peking. Although our minister was finally induced to desist from his avowed purpose to visit Peking and present his letter to the emperor in person, we can be sure now, that it was far better that he should have acquiesced in this, than to have made the journey under the same conditions as the earlier embassies of Lord Macartney and Lord Amherst, who knowingly traveled, at least by tacit acquiescence, as bearers of tribute.

In the year 1857 Mr. William B. Reed was appointed envoy and minister of the United States. Experience had already shown the necessity of a revision of the treaty and of a more rigid enforcement of its provisions. The British and French were united in their demands upon China and desired the assistance of the United States in armed co-operation. This, however, was refused. Our policy was to gain everything necessary by peaceful means and friendly overtures alone; a course also most consistently followed by the Russian minister, Count Pontiatine. Mr. Reed was particularly instructed to say to the Chinese that we were not parties to the existing hostilities—the second opium war, as it may justly be termed, having begun—but our people desired only to engage in trade under suitable guarantees for their protection, and that the United States government did not wish to legalize the opium trade, in violation of the laws of China.

The correspondence between the Chinese Commissioner Yeh, at Canton, and Mr. Reed is curiously illustrative of the skill and elegance of composition so typical of a learned Chinese diplomat. Mr. Reed says that citizens of the United States "have suffered many wrongs from the rulers and people of China." Yeh says: "But allow me to observe, that since the merchants and citizens of the United States have come to China to trade, they have ever been treated with courtesy and kindness, and therefore can have no wrongs to redress." When Mr. Reed expressed his regret that the commissioner was unable to meet him for a personal interview, the commissioner replied: "From this it is plainly to be perceived that your excellency well understands the position of things, and the heartfelt regrets which you express have greatly tranquilized my feelings"—which means that a personal interview is not necessary, and indeed it was not accorded. In fact, the tranquil and extremely arrogant Yeh could not be made to acknowledge that there was anything wrong or inoperative about the old treaty. "Our two countries," he said, "are like two good friends," and since making the treaty "are still in every respect on the best of terms."

The scene of action now changes. Finding satisfactory negotiation at Canton impossible, Mr. Reed determined to proceed to Peking. The British and French fleets were about to sail for the mouth of the Peiho, there to demand satisfaction for their wrongs, if necessary by an armed demonstration at Peking. Mr. Reed accompanied them, and was an observer of all that took place at Taku, but not a participant in any of the warlike operations. All his influence was exerted to prevent hostilities, but in vain. The allies captured the Taku forts and sailed up the tortuous channel to Tientsin, where new treaties were drawn up by all the powers represented and duly signed. It was agreed that ratifications should be exchanged the next year.

The treaty negotiated by Mr. Reed, signed June 18, 1858, gave to the United States the right of direct correspondence with the privy council at the capital. Under certain limitations the United States minister was to be allowed to visit Peking annually, but permanent residence was not granted. The ports Niuchwang, Tangchow (Chefoo), Swatow, Taiwan, Tamsui, and Kiungchow were opened to foreign trade at this time.

When this treaty was signed, and for several years before and afterwards, the country was in the midst of a disastrous civil war, which threatened the dynasty with extinction and the restoration of the Mings. This was the famous Taiping insurrection. We can only allude to its origin and progress. The emperor, Tao Kuang, died on the

26th of February, 1850. "At the hour *mao* in the morning, his celestial majesty transmitted the imperial dignity to his fourth son, and in the evening at the hour of *hai*, he set off for the abode of the gods." The new emperor was a young man of nineteen, who assumed the title of Hienfung. One of his first acts was to dismiss and degrade two of the best and highest officers in the court, and appoint in their stead persons most fanatically opposed to the foreign barbarians, as the Europeans were designated.

There was an old prophecy current in China that about this time, 1851, the former dynasty of the Mings would be re-established. This gave a sort of prophetic promise of victory to the rebellion, which just then broke out in Kiangsi and soon assumed such threatening proportions as seriously to endanger the government. It was originally a religious movement, inspired without any doubt by the teachings of the Christian missionaries, although by no means conducted in the interest, or with any clear conception, of the Christian religion. In 1852 the pretender occupied a throne at Nanking and issued edicts dated "the first year of Taiping of the dynasty of the late Mings."

This great rebellion, which for ten long years desolated the country, was finally suppressed with foreign aid. The British general, Gordon, has worn all the fame and laurels for the result, but the true victor was the one who organized and led the Ever Victorious Army. We read of him in English books as "an American adventurer named Ward." He may have been an adventurer and he certainly was an American named Frederick Ward; but he fell at the head of his men in 1862, at a time when General Gordon had only to reap the honors for the completion of a work already nearly done. Whatever may be said on the other side as to the relative merits of the two men, the one a mere "adventurer," if you like, the other an officer in the British army, one fact remains to testify how the Chinese recognized the services of our countryman. Only two foreigners have ever been awarded posthumous honors by the emperor of China. One of these is Frederick Ward and the other Anson Burlingame.

Mr. Reed departed from China in December, 1858, leaving Mr. S. W. Williams *chargé d' affaires*. He was succeeded by Mr. John E. Ward, who brought the treaty over for ratification. Arriving at Shanghai he was met by commissioners from Peking, who endeavored to have the ratifications exchanged there. But Mr. Ward was instructed to go to Peking, and, although no place was designated in the treaty for the exchange of ratifications, he proposed that it should be done at Peking. The British treaty, however, mentioned Peking particularly, and the British and French plenipotentiaries were determined to carry out the agreement. But unexpected obstacles were in the way. The very reasons which Mr. Ward urged for prompt action, in order that the treaty should be ratified on or before the 18th of June, the date specified, were ingeniously made an excuse for delay by the commissioners. They twisted the words about in this way: "But, as in our view the exchange of the ratifications of the treaty is a matter of high importance to both countries, it is undesirable that it be hastily done."

It soon became obvious that the commissioners were determined to delay the exchange of ratifications beyond the date appointed and also that they designed to prevent the foreign envoys from reaching Peking. The latter decided to lose no more time, so they left Shanghai and in a few days were again at anchor in the Gulf of Pechili. Greatly to their surprise they found the entrance to the Peiho closed by barricades, and the forts at Taku repaired and strengthened. The indications were that the approach of the foreigners to Peking would be met with resistance. The British admiral demanded the removal of the obstructions, adding that if not removed by the morning of the 25th of July he would order them blown up. Mr. Ward, however, determined to make an attempt to reach Peking in advance. Accordingly he crossed the bar early on Friday morning in a small steamer, but when about half a mile from the forts the steamer grounded and he had to remain there until the evening tide enabled him to return to the *Powhatan*. About midnight the British began removing the barriers and the forts opened fire on the ships. The next day the battle began in earnest, and the British suffered an ignominious defeat. This broke off all negotiations on the part of the English and French, who forthwith returned to Shanghai.

Mr. Ward, however, opened correspondence with the governor of Chihli and expressed his desire to visit Peking in accordance with the provisions of the treaty. In reply the governor stated that he would be conducted to Peking from Pehtang, a port a few miles north of Taku, and that carts, horses, and coolies would be provided for the journey by the provincial treasury. Accordingly Mr. Ward and his suite went to Peking; but during their brief sojourn there they were subjected to such restrictions that they were unable to see much of the city.

When Mr. Ward proposed the exchange of ratifications, he was told that before any business could be transacted in the city he must be received by the emperor. This was accompanied with the intimation that he must kneel before his majesty, but as such a ceremony could not be arranged, the audience was given up. Since without it the business could not be conducted at the capital, ratifications were finally exchanged at Pehtang on the 16th of August, 1859.

The next year the British and French returned to the Peiho

with a powerful fleet and army. They again captured the forts at Taku and marched to Peking. Their treaties were ratified in the Hall of Ceremonies and the British embassy was then established in the city.

We now pass over a few years not devoid of interest, because their events do not require especial attention here. Mr. Anson Burlingame became United States minister in 1863. He was the first of our representatives to reside in Peking. His policy, which he described as "an effort to substitute fair diplomatic action in China for force," was eminently successful, and made him popular at the Chinese court. In 1867 he left the diplomatic service of the United States, and was chosen by the Chinese as their representative to all the foreign powers with which they had treaty relations. His mission as the envoy of China to America and Europe did much to open the minds of the people to the fact that the Chinese had made great progress in literature and arts. But his death before he could return to Peking prevented the full results of his labors from being felt in China. The so-called Burlingame treaty, negotiated by him in behalf of China in 1868, contains the following declaration, which is of interest now because of its bearing upon the later action of the United States concerning Chinese immigration: "The United States and the emperor of China cordially recognize the inherent and inalienable right of man to change his home and his allegiance, and also the mutual advantages of the free migration and immigration of their citizens and subjects respectively from the one country to the other for the purposes of curiosity, trade, or as permanent residents."

This treaty was made after we had experienced the results of twenty years of Chinese immigration. Mr. Burlingame had encouraged it in 1866 by saying that a million Chinese would find employment on the Pacific coast. Then was the time when the people of California welcomed the Chinese. The development of the vast resources of that state was rendered possible by their presence. Even up to the year 1881 it was scarcely possible for the farmers of California to find laborers enough to carry on their work, and the cry was heard that only high wages would bring the Chinese over!

But the Chinese immigration had become an element in local politics, and the most unfounded and impossible assertions were made against them. When there were about 75,000 of them in California, and less than 94,000 in the whole country, it was declared "a well-known fact" that there were more than 150,000 of them in California, and the absurd prediction was made that "the Chinese population will, in the near future, exceed the population of Americans and all other races combined." This was in face of the fact that the Chinese population here was actually decreasing, and when there was even a smaller number of Chinese in the state of California than there were colored people in the District of Columbia. In considering the course of our legislation upon this subject, it should not be forgotten that the Chinese came here originally at our own solicitation, that they were an important element in the development of the state of California, that the Burlingame treaty guarantees "every privilege and complete protection to Americans in China," and "equal rights to Chinamen in the United States."

The so-called Angell treaty of November 17, 1880, was the first step in a course of restriction of immigration and exclusion. In this treaty it is agreed that "the government of the United States may regulate, limit, or suspend" the coming or residence of Chinese laborers, "but may not absolutely prohibit it," and that "the limitation or suspension shall be reasonable." Taking full advantage of the privileges thus granted, an act of Congress was passed May 6, 1882, suspending the coming of Chinese laborers for ten years and requiring that Chinese persons not laborers who desire to enter the United States, shall provide themselves with certificates from their government. It also provided for the issue of certificates to Chinese residents in this country who desired to go home and return. At a later period the certificates thus issued and accepted in good faith by the Chinese were arbitrarily repudiated, and our customs officers at San Francisco no longer recognized their validity.

The act of 1882 was amended in July, 1884, increasing the stringency of its provisions and extending the time of its operation two years—until 1894.

Both these acts, while purporting to admit persons not laborers, require that such persons shall exhibit certificates from the Chinese government attesting the fact. It is practically impossible to obtain such certificates, as the framers of the bill doubtless knew very well.

The climax of injustice was reached by the passage of the Scott act, October 1, 1888. This absolutely prohibits the return of Chinese laborers to the United States and declares all certificates hitherto issued in pursuance of law, void and of no effect. Since the opening of China the foreign powers, through their ministers at Peking, have been incessantly demanding that China should observe her treaties. A more conspicuous disregard of treaty obligations than is involved in the passage of the Scott act by the Congress of the United States cannot be found. It is absolute exclusion not only of laborers who come intending to remain in the country but, as at one time construed by the Treasury Department, prohibition even of travelers in transit. To make the matter still more discreditable to the United States, at the time when this act was passed, a treaty, which involved a prohibition of the immigration of Chinese laborers and which originated with the Chinese government, had been considered by the Senate, amended in minor details, and, the amendments having been accepted as satisfactory by the Chinese minister at Washington, had been sent to Peking for ratification. This treaty gave to us all we could possibly demand. In the preamble it reads as follows:

"Whereas the government of China, in view of the antagonism and much deprecated and serious disorders to which the presence of Chinese laborers has given rise in certain parts of the United States, desires to prohibit the emigration of such laborers from China to the United States," etc.

Article I. as amended reads: "For a period of twenty years the coming . . . of Chinese laborers to the United States shall be absolutely prohibited and this prohibition shall extend to the return of Chinese laborers who are not now in the United States, whether holding return certificates under existing laws or not."

There was no reason at the time to apprehend that the treaty would not be ratified. The Chinese did not recognize that there was any necessity for special haste about it and they had some further propositions to submit for consideration. But the demand was made through our minister, Mr. Denby, for immediate ratification. This met with no reply and it was therefore considered that ratification of their own treaty was refused.

The Scott act therefore received the President's signature and became a law. As regards the action of Congress in this matter it was "the first time," as Mr. Evarts declared, "in the diplomatic history of this country of an intervention by legislative action while there was a treaty negotiated by this government in all its constitutional forms pending for adoption by a foreign nation." Mr. Sherman declared that if Great Britain were to act thus toward the American people, he "would without hesitation vote for a declaration of non-intercourse or war."

The Chinese always maintained that they did not refuse to ratify the treaty. This is true enough, and at the time when the Scott act was passed there was no reason to doubt that they would sign the treaty. But later disclosures indicate that already they had begun to realize that the treaty proposed by themselves was a mistake—that it was a serious matter thus to sign away a nation's rights and privileges. That such an act was possible shows how lightly the high officers of the government at Peking esteem the privileges of their people abroad, but more clearly still how ignorant they are of their material interests in foreign lands. Before the time for the ratification of that treaty arrived, the action of one of the Australian colonies together with the representations of the Chinese minister at London, served to open the eyes of the Peking officials, and it is doubtful whether the treaty would ever have been ratified.

Coming down to the present time, a number of bills were introduced in the Fifty-second Congress to regulate or stop the immigration of Chinese, two of which, the Geary bill and the one drawn up at the Treasury Department and introduced by Mr. Sherman, were intended absolutely to close our ports to all Chinese except government officials. The less said about these bills, and the sooner they drop into oblivion, the better. The former passed the House by a vote of 179 in the affirmative. It may yet rise to confront us as an example of the utter disregard of our legislators of the highest obligations of this nation.

As one of the Chinese ministers wrote concerning the Scott act, he "was not prepared to learn . . . that there was a way recognized in the law and practice of your country, whereby your government could release itself from treaty obligations without consultation with or the consent of the other party."

Although the Geary bill was too harsh a measure to receive the support of the Senate, the practical effect of the bill which was passed and which became a law on the 5th of May, 1892, is scarcely less unjust and oppressive. This law continues in force all existing laws relative to Chinese immigration for ten years from the passage of the act. It also requires all Chinese laborers in the country who are legally entitled to remain, to obtain certificates of residence within one year.

The Chinese minister has made a strong protest against the passage of this bill. His ground of complaint is that it renews the Scott law of 1888, denies the right of bail to Chinese in *habeas corpus* cases, and requires registration under conditions which in most instances are practically impossible to fulfill. The last is the most serious consideration because it affects every Chinese laborer in the country. Owing to the regulations enforced during the last ten years, by far the greater number of Chinese laborers now here arrived before the exclusion act of 1882. Since that time up to June 30, 1890, 56,263 Chinese have arrived with certificates of previous residence, and of new arrivals, presumably not laborers, there have been only 10,242. Now, the total Chinese population in the United States does not exceed 110,000—a ridiculously small number to cause a great nation to break its faith. It may be said that practically every one of these who is a laborer, is now obliged to establish his right to remain in the country by the evidence of at least one white witness, who must have known him ten years ago, or before the law of 1882 was passed. The utter impossibility of securing such witnesses is obvious. The law therefore is not only one to exclude Chinese immigrants but it will have the effect of sending away thousands of industrious, frugal, and inoffensive laborers, who have both a moral and a legal right to remain here. And the question must arise in the minds of all who study this subject, whether the makers of the laws of this great nation are bound by any considerations of national honor. If not, if treaties are to be disregarded and abrogated without warning or just cause, other nations than China will begin to ask concerning the value of such engagements with this country.

This chapter is already so long as to preclude any discussion of the condition and influences of the Chinese population in the United States. So far as the writer's personal observation and inquiries on the Pacific coast extend, and considering also the weight of the published testimony concerning the Chinese, it would appear that most of the charges brought against them are either gross exaggerations or utterly false. But it is impossible to refute them here. If the opinion of an individual who has a knowledge of the Chinese in their native land is of any value, it may be said that they are a far more desirable class of immigrant laborers than a large proportion of the half million who annually come from Europe to increase our population and influence our politics.

It is impossible to foresee what the relations between the United States and China will be in the near future. Whether the Chinese will resent the recent action of Congress by withdrawing their legation from Washington, and also by adopting measures to expel Americans from China, is uncertain; but it cannot be doubted that the interests of American citizens in China have been jeopardized, and perhaps irretrievably ruined; not merely our present interests in the trade with China or the present business and employments of our countrymen in China, but opportunities which the near future is opening there to foreign enterprise greater than ever before, but now, doubtless, closed to the people of this nation. These opportunities have never been fairly presented to the people of the United States. There are few persons sufficiently familiar with the enormous resources of China and with the policy which, arrogant, conservative, suspicious as it is, is still tending toward their development, to foresee and take full advantage of the future course of events in that country.

There is still one important feature about the foreign relations of China which can only be briefly referred to here—the conditions under which foreign ministers are received by the emperor. Although the ports of China were opened to trade by foreign demands enforced by powder and ball, not one foreign envoy has for two hundred years been received by the emperor on terms recognizing the equality of the nation he represented. Imperial audiences have been very few it is true; but they have been frequently demanded. There was one in 1873, which was a mistake on the part of the foreign ministers, for which they were severely criticised at the time. But so subtle are the ways of Chinese diplomacy that the errors of 1873 were repeated in 1891. The explanations of the diplomatic corps at Peking are very specious and plausible, but the fact remains that the audience was another victory for Chinese diplomacy, and the high ministers of the empire must have enjoyed it keenly and indulged by themselves in that "smile which is childlike and bland" over the discomfiture of the foreign envoys.

At the time of the last audience the present writer penned in China the following lines: "The audience question in China is not yet settled. It is not much to the credit of foreign diplomats that it has so long remained open. A just and firm policy, coupled with an intelligent understanding of Chinese affairs and Chinese character, would have accomplished long ago what years of diplomatic intercourse without a defined policy or purpose have not done. The audience was granted: but has the persistent barrier of Chinese self-assumed superiority and supremacy been broken? Do we, or does any nation on the face of the earth, stand on an equality in Chinese eyes with the Chinese themselves? Certainly not. If we are not tribute bearers in fact, we are an inferior and unworthy people. The recent audience may be, for aught we know, represented to, and actually regarded by the Chinese nation, as a mere formality, not in any sense, as it should be, an acknowledgment of equality in rank or power. . . . . Future audiences are to be held in a special hall to be erected for the purpose. But may not this be another trap set for the unwary ministers by Chinese diplomacy? It is doubtful if the emperor would even now grant an audience to a foreign envoy in the imperial palace without the ceremony of the *kotow*. This fact may prove of greater significance in future than it now appears." Subsequent events and experiences have fully sustained the views then expressed.

The more one studies and reasons and attempts to fathom the peculiarities of the Chinese, the more he becomes conscious of the vast gulf which separates us from participation in the culture and thoughts and motives of that people. We cannot understand them, but we are forced to acknowledge their high culture, and to recognize that it is this which lies at the foundation of a great and successful empire. We learn to respect it for its permanence and antiquity, as well as for what it has led up to in industry and arts. And if ever we would boast of our own superior attainments in literature or science, let us not forget how very recently all this has come to us. What was there of our civilization in the thirteenth century? At that time China was at the height of her prosperity, with a civilization which extended back for many centuries and a written language which can be traced back, perhaps, to the time of the ancient Assyrians, long before the ancestors of the Chinese began their eastward march and founded an empire on the shores of the Yellow Sea. They used the magnetic needle in the fourth century, and printed books in the tenth century, five hundred years before that art was known in Europe.

CHAPTER XX.

RELATIONS WITH JAPAN.

THE empire of Japan was founded 660 years before the advent of Christ and was an absolute monarchy until 1889, when the despotism was abolished and a constitution adopted. It consists of four islands lying east of China, with an area of 147,655 square miles, or nearly as large as the state of California, and a population of 40,000,000, or a little more than that of France. The army consists of 80,000 men with 326 guns, and all its firearms, ordnance, and ammunition are made in Japanese arsenals. The navy is composed of seventeen steel and iron vessels, five composite and three wooden vessels, of 37,600 aggregate tonnage, and 11,463 officers and men. The imports in 1890 amounted to $80,000,000, about $7,000,000 of which was bought from the United States. The exports for the same year amounted to $55,000,000, of which $20,000,000 was sold to the United States.

The first intercourse of Japan with Europeans resulted from a visit of a Portuguese company to Nagasaki in 1545, with whom commercial relations were established. They were followed by the Dutch in 1600 and the British East India Company in 1613, with whom similar commerce was opened. Owing, however, to the intrigues and political intermeddling of Catholic missionaries, a decree of the government expelling foreigners from the country was enforced in 1639 against all aliens except a few Dutch traders, who were permitted, under severe restrictions, to remain within certain limits of the country.

This rigorous isolation from the other nations of the world was carefully maintained for nearly three centuries. But it must not be inferred that the Japanese were ignorant of all that happened during these many years, in Europe and Asia, since one of the conditions imposed upon the few Dutch residents remaining in the empire was that they were to collect and report to the government all important or interesting information relating to other nations. This information, studiously concealed from the people, was regularly communicated to the emperor and his advisers. Thus they had constant and accurate knowledge of the progress of European commerce and the British and Russian encroachments into Asia. They gave the closest study to the march of these events. They saw that the intrusions of Western civilization were inevitable and that, in the near future, they too would have to face the problem. Hence they were prepared, however unwillingly, to break down the barriers that had been so long and successfully maintained and, by virtue of necessity, to enter into relations with the outer world.

At this auspicious period, Commodore Perry of the American navy, specially commissioned by his government, entered the bay of Yedo. Although accompanied by an armament sufficient to have enforced any demand, he seems to have depended alone, for the success of his plans, upon the impressive moral effect that would result from such a display of force; and his conduct toward the Japanese authorities was marked by a scrupulous regard for their government and a punctilious respect for their people. After a few days of pleasant intercourse and the interchange of courteous civilities with the natives, he communicated to them the object of his mission and confided to their care dispatches to be conveyed to the emperor. Then he weighed anchor and, without waiting for any reply from the government, put to sea. This strange species of diplomacy, so fully in line with Japanese ideas of propriety, had a happy effect; for, contrasting this conduct of the Americans with that of the British and Russians toward Eastern countries, the people were deeply impressed with the delicate sense of honor displayed by the Americans; and, conscious of their inability longer to avert foreign intercourse, they were now prepared to entertain our advances favorably.

Under these circumstances, Commodore Perry again entered the Japanese waters in 1854, one year from the date of his first visit. This long period of time had afforded the Japanese an opportunity for careful deliberation; and, in view of the necessity of opening the country to foreign intercourse and because of the apprehension that they might soon have to experience some of the peculiar tactics of European diplomacy, they decided to respond to the advances of the United States government. Thus it happened that the visit of Commodore Perry was most opportune, and that officer, who had carefully acquainted himself with the circumstances, at once addressed himself to the successful accomplishment of his delicate task. His various steps in the process of negotiation were taken with caution, and his gracious and courteous conduct so completely dispelled suspicion that he was regarded as the representative of a friendly power with whom Japan might safely treat. Thenceforth his overtures, couched in deferential terms and free from every species of dictation and assumption, were respectfully and favorably considered by the Japanese government; so that, after some short delays incident to the arrangement of such matters, a treaty between Japan and the United States was signed. This treaty, the first one entered into by Japan, has resulted in the opening of the country to the world and, supplemented as it has been by our just conduct toward that people, has given to the United States a prestige and influence in Japan that no other nation so fully enjoys.

In 1855, Mr. Townsend Harris was appointed consul general of the United States to Japan by President Buchanan and, proceeding there, established his residence at Shimoda on the bay of Yedo, a port opened to our commerce under the treaty negotiated by Commodore Perry. From the beginning of his official career, this remarkable person exercised great influence in Japanese affairs. Although trained to mercantile pursuits, and without any previous experience in diplomacy, he seems to have understood intuitively the character of the Japanese and to have perfectly comprehended the complicated situation that had resulted from the opening of the country to foreign intercourse. And it should be recorded to his honor and to the credit of the government he so ably represented, that the great influence wielded by him was always exerted in a spirit of liberality toward Japan and with unswerving fidelity to the interests of his country. Soon after his arrival there evidences of a popular revolution were manifested. The opening of the country to foreigners, accepted as inevitable by the state, was resisted by the people, who were not yet willing to receive the western barbarians. The ruler was considered as a usurper and conspiracies were formed for his overthrow. Many of the powerful territorial nobles were in revolt. The country was in a state of chronic disorder and, amidst it all, those foreign nations that had followed the United States in making treaties with Japan, were holding the government to the strictest responsibility, in spite of the fact that it was doing everything in its power faithfully to comply with the treaties. Mr. Harris alone seemed to comprehend the real situation and to extend his sympathy and aid to the government. While carefully guarding the interests of his own country, he refused to lend his sanction to any harsh or oppressive measures and, by his prudent course, succeeded in obtaining from Japan all those concessions that are the bases of existing treaties. In 1857 he made a treaty enlarging the privileges granted to us in the Perry treaty and secured, among other advantages, the opening of the port of Nagasaki as well as the right of permanent residence for Americans at the ports of Shimoda and Hakodate. But his greatest diplomatic triumph was in the successful conclusion of the treaty of 1858, when, alone and unattended, he was the first foreign representative to be received in private audience at Yedo by the shogun, where, without any show of force or compulsion, he persuaded the government to enter into another treaty that revolutionized the relations of Japan with foreign nations. It is to his credit that, notwithstanding his great prestige and influence, he insisted upon no unjust exactions, but negotiated in the true American spirit of justice and tolerance; and there is little doubt but that, if the then tottering government could have had the co-operation of other powers in enforcing the terms of that treaty, Japan would have no reason to complain of the restrictions of succeeding treaties nor would foreign powers have to contend with the irritating obstacles that now hamper their intercourse with Japan.

The visit of Mr. Harris to Yedo, as special ambassador of the United States, deserves some special notice, on account of the careful and minute instructions of the government in reference to the manner of his conveyance to, and reception at, the capital. The governor of Shimoda, where Mr. Harris lived, was ordered to accompany him with his staff and the inspector of roads was commanded to provide relays of men and horses and to take care that the roads and bridges on the way, as well as the lodging places, should be placed in good order. Householders were required to keep the road in front of their houses cleanly swept and the people were forbidden to gather in crowds in front of shops or at the windows to gaze at the procession of Mr. Harris. The executive officers of the Tycoon were directed to make all needful preparations to facilitate his visit and for his accommodation at the capital, as well as for his visit to the palace and his audience with the Tycoon and council. His route upon entering the capital, his visit to the castle, and his way to the palace of Prince Hotta, where he should lodge, were all dictated by special order of the government. The preliminaries and formalities of his audience, and the dress of the officials to be in attendance at the reception were particularly prescribed. A special memorandum was arranged of the places to be visited and the streets to be traversed by the American ambassador during his stay at the capital, and, in short, every detail and ceremony that could add to the dignity of his mission and emphasize the sincere friendship and consideration of the Japanese for Mr. Harris, were carefully studied and minutely carried out. It is a gratifying fact that these high honors were first extended to our representative and that he himself was so worthy of this attention and esteem.

Mr. Harris was succeeded as United States minister by Mr. Pruyn, and, during the service of the latter in Japan, arose the difficulties between the shogun and the powerful nobles who had espoused the cause of the mikado. These troubles culminated in the attempt, by the daimio of Nogato, to close the straits of Simoneseki, and, in the execution of his purpose, he fired upon the merchant vessels of foreign powers. The conduct of this rebel against the legitimate government of Japan led to the expedition of the allied fleet to those waters, participated in by the vessels of the United States,

Great Britain, France, and the Netherlands, the result of which was that, after bombarding Simoneseki and otherwise punishing the rebel daimio, these foreign powers exacted from Japan an indemnity of $3,000,000. The foreign representatives, under the leadership of the British minister, attempted to use two thirds of this sum as a corruption fund to extort from the shogun further concessions, but he resisted their overtures and assumed its payment. Unhappily, however, for Japan, he yielded far enough to agree to the tariff of 1866, to which the United States, through Mr. Portman, *chargé d' affaires*, was a party, by the terms of which Japan was bound to levy a rate of duty on foreign merchandise not exceeding five per cent during the pleasure of the treaty powers, and although the treaty provided for the revision of this tariff within a specified period, yet it has been so far impossible for Japan to gain the consent of these powers with the exception of the United States.

Our government fully manifested its appreciation of the injustice done to a friendly nation by providing, in the treaty of 1871, that Japan should arrange her tariff in such manner that the owners and cultivators of her soil might be in a measure relieved from the heavy taxes imposed upon them by the deficit in her revenues. The United States Congress, also, in 1883, gave to Japan a further evidence of their good will and sense of justice by returning to that government our share of the Simoneseki indemnity fund of $3,000,000, at least two thirds of which has been popularly regarded as shameless extortion. Another proof of friendship and fairness was indicated in the apology of this government for the action of Commander Selfridge, who violated the sovereignty of Japan by firing at a target on her shores; and an additional act of justice was done in voting a satisfactory indemnity for the killing and wounding of several of her citizens, who, unacquainted with the character of the unexploded shells fired by the commander, suffered death or injury while trying to strip the copper from one of these missiles. Again, in the postal convention of 1873, the United States manifested anew the respect and confidence due to the Japanese by surrendering to their government the control of her own postal affairs. This sensible and proper recognition of the right and ability of Japan to manage her own mail system was fiercely assailed by European governments, but the wisdom of the step was fully justified by similar favorable action on the part of those governments. Indeed, the kind and liberal spirit that the United States have invariably manifested toward the Japanese has won their confidence and friendship to a degree not enjoyed by any other nation or people.

The brilliant reception extended by the government and people of Japan to General Grant during his visit there excited, in America, general admiration and grateful appreciation. The occasion afforded to the Japanese a favorable opportunity to demonstrate their high regard for America and Americans, and it was improved by them to the fullest extent. General Grant was received with royal honors and every day of his sojourn was distinguished by fresh manifestations of the high respect and gracious hospitality of the entire nation. His journeys through the country assumed the semblance of triumphal processions, his sojourns in the cities were characterized by splendid banquets and brilliant fêtes, and his voyages, as he sailed along the shores, were replete with spontaneous and splendid welcomes amid the roar of cannon, the blaze of fireworks, the waving of banners, and the deafening plaudits of a rejoicing people. Upon his arrival at Tokio, the capital of Japan, where the most elaborate preparations had been made for his reception, he was escorted in regal state to Euriokwan, one of the private palaces of the emperor, which had been designated as his quarters during his stay in the capital. There, attended by a numerous retinue of the royal officials and servants and surrounded by all the refinements of Japanese art and luxury, he was entertained with such a rare and splendid Oriental hospitality as has never been extended to royalty. There he was visited by the emperor himself, who, in a private interview, discussed with him the policies of state and asked his friendly counsel in the various matters relating to the welfare of his subjects and to the prosperity and progress of his country.

The question that at present overshadows all others in the empire of Japan is the revision and reformation of her treaties with foreign powers. If, upon the opening of the country to foreigners, the government had carefully pursued the prudent policy counseled by the American representative, it would have been spared many of the evils that now afflict the nation; but, in view of the threatening attitude of European diplomatists and the misfortunes that had overwhelmed China, it sought to temporize in the face of apprehended dangers and yielded step by step to the insidious demands that were preferred by England, Germany, and Holland. Thus it granted the right of extraterritoriality, under which foreigners are not amenable to Japanese law and by virtue of which the consular officers of various nations, notoriously uninstructed in legal matters and, in many cases, otherwise unfitted for the administration of justice, have set up miniature courts upon the soil of Japan to shield their subjects from merited punishment, to involve the natives in technical violations of their edicts and afterwards to speculate upon their misfortunes and trade upon their fears. They have resisted the payment of land taxes, of tonnage and lighthouse dues, and tolls upon bridges; they have quite monopolized the coastwise trade to the exclusion of Japanese vessels, and, in a notable instance, when the government had discovered smuggling and was adopting proper means to prevent it, the minister of Great Britain threatened to land troops to assist his countrymen in violation of Japanese regulations.

The tariff concessions also, extorted from the government in the same manner, have involved the country in financial distress. Under their provisions little more than four per cent can be collected by Japan upon imports from Europe, but the representative of Great Britain still clamored for reductions and finally succeeded in securing the promise of further rebates. By threats and importunities his suggestions and demands have from time to time been acceded to until it appeared that the government, to avoid loss in the collection of its scanty revenues, would be obliged to close its custom houses and declare its ports free to the world. The natural result of this foreign interference with the tariff has been to destroy a legitimate source of revenue and to burden the agricultural interests with taxes that they are unable to pay. Under these circumstances the government is fettered and prevented from adopting adequate measures for the relief of the people, who, groaning under taxes and indignant at the wrongs imposed upon them by foreigners, are beginning to evince those feelings of detestation for the government and disdain for Europeans that may, when least expected, overwhelm the country with terrible internal disorders.

CHAPTER XXI.

RELATIONS WITH KOREA, SAMOA, AND SIAM.

The Kingdom of Korea.

THE kingdom of Korea is situated in the northwestern part of Asia on the Pacific Ocean. It has an area of 82,000 square miles (about that of the state of Kansas), and is a peninsula like Florida, with a population variously estimated at from eight to sixteen millions. The religion of the country is Buddhist and the Chinese language is spoken. Until within recent years, Korea has been closed to the world. The policy of the government, like that long practiced by China and Japan, was to exclude all foreigners from the country and to prevent its citizens from going abroad; hence it has remained for ages in a state of seclusion and until lately very little was known of it by the people of the West.

The United States was the first nation to attempt relations with Korea, and this was due to a curious series of circumstances. An American citizen named Frederick Jenkins, who had for some time served as interpreter at the United States consulate general at Shanghai, formed a small band of conspirators of various nationalities in China, chartered an American schooner, the *General Sherman*, and sailed for Korea early in 1868 for the purpose of robbing the tombs of the deceased sovereigns of that country and holding their remains for ransom. Having sailed up a river some distance into the interior, the party cast anchor and several of the crew went ashore, when, after offering some indignities to the people, they were arrested. Afterwards reinforcements from the *Sherman* came to their assistance, rescued them, and took them on board. This conduct, however, inflamed the people to such a degree that they attacked the party, killed eight of them, carried the others ashore, and destroyed the vessel. The leader, Jenkins, escaped and returned to China.

In March, 1868, shortly after this event, the United States ship *Shenandoah*, then in Chinese waters, visited Korea. Upon her return, in May, 1868, the commander reported that although he had slight intercourse with some of the natives on the coast, he had failed to learn anything in reference to the destruction of the *Sherman* and the fate of the persons captured on board that vessel.

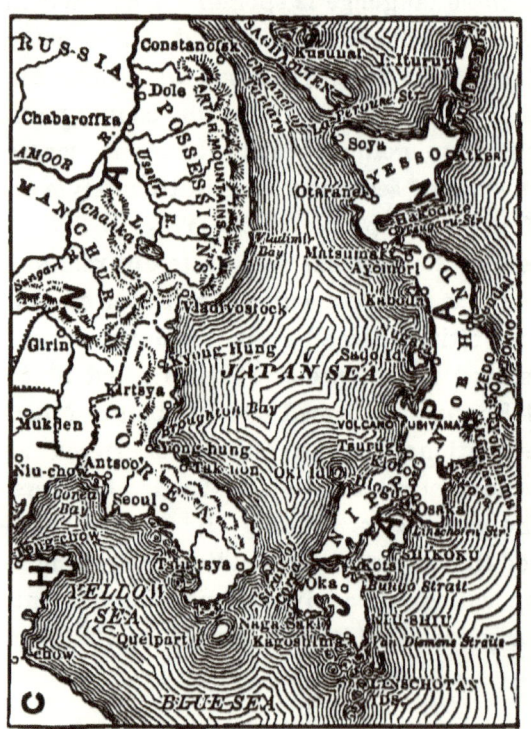

In April following, commissioners from Korea were sent to Shanghai with the object of learning the state of feeling with reference to the destruction of the *Sherman* and the killing of the persons on board that vessel, and to consult with the United States consul general as to the propriety of sending an embassy to Washington to explain the circumstances connected with the affair. They also represented that their government was considering the question of proposing the adoption of a treaty of friendship and commerce between the two nations. Mr. Seward, becoming interested in the subject, communicated some suggestions to the Department of State in reference to the propriety of making such a treaty and the correspondence was continued for some time. Meanwhile Admiral Rogers of the United States Navy, then in Chinese waters, also addressed our government upon the same subject and urged the negotiation of a treaty for the protection of shipwrecked seamen.

After prolonged consideration the secretary of state instructed Mr. Frederick F. Low, our minister to China, to confer with the Chinese government in reference to the conclusion of a treaty with Korea. This course was adopted for the reason that Korea was, in some respects, tributary to China and it was therefore deemed proper and advisable to secure first the good will and, if practicable, the good offices of that government. The Chinese minister of foreign relations, with characteristic eastern diplomacy, had little to say upon the subject that might involve him in any responsibility, but took occasion to inform Mr. Low that their relations with Korea were not such as to prevent the latter country from making such a treaty.

The preliminaries having been as far as possible arranged, the American commissioners, Mr. Low, Admiral Rogers, and Mr. Seward, with a squadron consisting of the United States vessels *Colorado, Alaska, Benicia, Monocacy,* and *Palos,* sailed from China, and arrived, May 30, 1871, off the coast of Korea at the mouth of the Salée River, fifty miles from Séoul, the capital of the country. Some of the natives, after the display of their customary caution and reserve, were induced, by the friendly demonstrations of the Americans, to come on board, where they were entertained with kindness and attention and informed of the object of the visit. They were also advised that it was the intention of the admiral to send a surveying party up the river on the following day for the purpose of marking out the channel, to which he hoped no objections would be made ; and he requested that the natives might be informed of their object and that, as their mission was peaceful, no hostile demonstrations might be made toward them. The natives replied that there would be no trouble about the survey, but that, in the matter of a treaty, the people and the king were averse to contracting relations with foreign powers.

The surveying party, in the *Palos*, *Monocacy*, and some steam launches, started on June 1, 1871, making soundings and scientific observations, but, upon arriving at a sharp angle some distance up the river, batteries on either side of the stream were unmasked and fire opened upon the Americans. The vessels however soon silenced the batteries and drove the natives from their forts, after which they returned to the squadron. Some days were spent, after this occurrence, in a correspondence with the local officials with a view to a peaceful adjustment of affairs, but their stubborn reticence rendered every effort futile. Although informed that an apology for the attack upon the surveying party was expected from them, they studiously ignored the subject in their replies to the commissioners. Another expedition was therefore arranged and sailed up the river on June 10, 1871, returning two days later, after having captured five forts, which, with the munitions of war found in them, were destroyed.

Our minister, Mr. Low, now made another effort to open negotiations with the government by sending ashore a letter directed to the king, which was promptly returned unopened.

He again addressed a communication to the king and sent ashore an interpreter to deliver it and to explain to the people the necessity for its transmission to their sovereign; but this also was returned with a message that no one could be found who would dare convey it to the capital. Mr. Low finally concluded, in view of the circumstances, that any further efforts would be useless, so he returned shortly afterwards to his post. Admiral Rogers lingered for some time in the vicinity, but he too became convinced that no practical results could be accomplished and sailed with his squadron for China and Japan. Our government was duly advised of the failure of the expedition and, seeing no hope of accomplishing anything further. without a display of force in Korean waters, all plans for opening negotiations with the Korean government were indefinitely postponed.

In 1874 there was a bloodless revolution in Korea, in consequence of which the ruler, who was a usurper, was deposed and the lawful successor to the crown was placed on the throne. The tyrannies previously suffered by the people were mitigated and, although the policy of nonintercourse with other nations was still adhered to, yet public interest was excited upon the subject. The embassies annually sent to China had become acquainted with the purpose of the attempt by the Americans to establish amicable relations with the people of Korea; and the natives who visited China took with them on their return books and papers relating to foreign countries, from which was derived general knowledge of the policies that governed these nations.

In the meantime, Japan became involved in a war with Korea, and, having prosecuted the conflict to a successful conclusion, a treaty of peace was signed, by the terms of which various ports of Korea were opened to the commerce of Japan. This event marked the epoch of the opening of Korea to the outside world, since we find that the people were afterwards permitted to leave and return to their country, and were even allowed to carry their produce to foreign markets, and to take home with them the products of other countries.

The conditions for negotiations with the government having now assumed a more favorable character, the United States again made an effort in that direction. Admiral Shufeldt of the American navy was intrusted with the delicate mission, which was discharged with such success that, on May 22, 1882, he concluded a treaty of peace, amity, and commerce with Korea, the ratifications of which were exchanged at the capital on May 19, 1883. This was the first treaty made with any power except Japan. By its terms ample aid and protection is to be extended to our vessels and seamen as well as to our citizens who may travel through or reside in the country; and certain ports were declared open to the commerce of the United States. This treaty was proclaimed on June 4, 1883.

Mr. Lucius H. Foote, the first minister of the United States to Korea, arrived there and assumed the functions of his office in May, 1883. He made a favorable impression upon the government and so fully convinced the king of the friendly interest and peaceable intentions of the United States that, on July 6, 1883, it was determined, in state council, to send two plenipotentiaries on a special mission to our country. They were accordingly dispatched with credentials to our government and duly arrived at Washington, where they were received by President Arthur with cordial demonstrations of friendship and treated with the attentions pertaining to their distinguished character. Our government has been fortunate in the selection of our diplomatic representatives to Korea, all of whom have cultivated friendly relations with that people and have acquainted them with the character, resources, and policies of our government. It is doubtless due to this fact that Americans are highly esteemed there and the relations between the two governments are in perfect harmony.

The Kingdom of Samoa.

The kingdom of Samoa, popularly known as Navigator's Islands, was discovered in 1772 by a Dutchman named Rozenwein, and is composed of a group of nine islands lying in the Pacific Ocean five thousand miles southwest of San Francisco, with an area of seventeen hundred square miles, hardly as large as the state of Delaware. The population is estimated at thirty-five thousand souls.

The products of the islands are varied and abundant. The chief article of export is "copra," the dried meat of the cocoanut; cotton, coffee, indigo, corn, potatoes, arrowroot, nutmegs, mace, breadfruit, oranges, bananas, and lemons are successfully grown, but the people are too indolent to devote themselves to agriculture. The spontaneous fruits of the soil are abundant and unfailing, so that little or no effort is required to provide the necessities of life.

Relations between the United States and Samoa were first opened by Commander Richard W. Meade of the American navy, who visited the islands in the man-of-war *Narragansett* in 1872. He entered the Pango-Pango harbor and was kindly received by the natives, to whom he extended proper civilities and assurances of the friendship of the United States government. During his stay he so impressed them with the prospective advantages to be gained by the cultivation of intimate relations with our country that they readily consented to cede to the United States the harbor of Pango-Pango as port of refuge and coaling station, and a treaty to that effect was granted him. This officer also induced the chiefs of the island to form a confederation for their mutual aid and protection.

From this date the attention of our government was directed toward the affairs of Samoa, and President Grant, in response to a petition from the native chiefs, sent a special commissioner there in 1873 to collect information concerning the country and the people. This commissioner, Mr. Steinberger, sailed from San Francisco and arrived at the harbor of Pango-Pango, August, 1874, where he entered upon friendly relations with the natives and visited and inspected the various islands of the group. He prepared and transmitted to the President a voluminous and interesting report upon the topography and resources of the islands and the customs and character of the natives.

The people had been, for several years, engaged in petty warfare among themselves with the natural result that industry had been abandoned and all development suspended. They were now, however, quite wearied of strife and, to put an end to their troubles, were anxious to place themselves under the protection and authority of the United States. A petition to that effect had been signed by the chiefs of the various islands, as well as by a number of foreign residents there, including missionaries and other influential persons, and sent to the President. Under the advice and direction of Mr. Steinberger, the various chiefs assembled in council and framed a constitution and laws for their united government; and, as soon as this new government was organized, the rulers and chiefs, in response to the popular desire, again addressed the President of the United States, praying that our government might take the country under its protection. Mr. Steinberger shortly afterwards sailed for the United States and submitted to President Grant his report, together with the petition.

After the lapse of two years, during which time our government took no action whatever in reference to the subject, Mr. Steinberger became impatient and resolved to return to Samoa, with the purpose, as it appears, of taking part in the government of the island. He arrived there in 1875 and soon after, under his counsel and supervision, the government was reorganized, the chief Malietoa was chosen king, and Mr. Steinberger was appointed his prime minister. The turbulent spirit soon broke out afresh, however, among the jealous chiefs, and this government fell to pieces in the following year, Chief Malietoa having been dethroned and Mr. Steinberger banished from the country.

The new government, under the direction of a council of chiefs, started out very well and maintained peace for a considerable time. During its administration the United States negotiated a treaty by the terms of which the port of Pango-Pango was definitely secured and free commerce was granted to us. Soon after this event the affairs of state again began to assume a portentous aspect and the country reached the verge of a fresh revolution. The consular and naval authorities of the United States, England, and Germany, then in Samoa, having been appealed to, it was decided that Malietoa was entitled to be recognized as king, and he was accordingly anointed and proclaimed in May, 1879.

The history of this government for a series of years is a tale of strife and jealousies, the opposition to the king being fostered and encouraged by the German residents, who had, in many cases, acquired lands by questionable means and quite monopolized the trade of the islands. At last a crisis was precipitated in 1884, when the German consul concluded an agreement with the Samoan council providing for the creation of a German-Samoan council of government. The king refused to execute the terms of this agreement, which so exasperated the German consul that he raised his flag over Apia and took possession of the municipality in the name of his government. The rebellion of Tamasese, an aspirant to the throne, now assumed formidable proportions, and, with the aid and encouragement of the Germans, he was soon declared king. Malietoa was overthrown and carried away from the islands in a German man-of-war.

This action on the part of the German authorities justly aroused intense excitement in the United States. It was regarded by our people as an attempt to establish a protectorate over Samoa that would result in the ruin of our interests and, ultimately, in annexation to the German Empire. Decisive measures were promptly adopted by the United States challenging the conduct of Germany, the result of which was that the commissioners, appointed by the United States, England, and Germany, for the amicable adjustment of the difficulty, declared that the pretensions of Tamasese were to be discountenanced and Malietoa replaced upon the throne. The neutrality of Samoa was guaranteed, its independence was recognized, the right of the natives to choose their own ruler was established, and the citizens of the three powers were declared to have equal rights in the islands. A supreme court was created, consisting of one judge appointed by the king of Sweden and Norway, to whom are referred all suits respecting real property, all causes between natives and foreigners, and all crimes committed by the natives against foreigners. All future alienation of lands, except with certain specified exceptions, is also prohibited.

This policy, ratified by the three powers, has been promptly executed, and the government of Malietoa, thus supported and protected, has given permanent peace to the country.

Siam.

Very little is known of the ancient history of the kingdom. It is inhabited by a heterogeneous population that, in physical characteristics, customs, and manners, is closely related to the Hindoos and Chinese, and has been, from time to time, further reinforced by, and amalgamated with, a considerable emigration from those countries as well as from the islands on the south. Its boundaries, too, are as yet undefined, though its area is popularly estimated at 250,000 square miles or nearly that of the state of Texas. The number of inhabitants also is only approximately known, since there has never been an official census. Various authorities state the number of souls at 6,000,000, of which only about one third are Siamese.

The trade of Siam has been tributary to China from a remote period and is still principally carried on with that country although, in recent years, the English commerce has grown to considerable proportions. The exports in 1884, amounted to nearly $12,000,000, more than one half of which consisted of rice. The imports for the same period were valued at about $5,200,000 and were made up of silk goods, tea, opium, and English cottons. The exports, generally in excess of imports, are paid for in foreign silver, which is recoined into the currency of the country.

Although the ruler of Siam possesses autocratic power, it is rarely exercised. The code of laws is old and venerated and, though crude and incomplete, all decrees and judgments are intended to be based upon it. In cases of ambiguity, the courts are governed by precedent; and this custom is so general and strong that much of the civil and criminal procedure derives force and efficacy from the unwritten law.

Buddhism is the religion of the country and the large and costly temples, richly ornamented and stocked with grotesque and gigantic idols, form a conspicuous feature in every part of the land. The numerous religious festivals are seasons of great rejoicing and amusement. Even funeral rites are accompanied with banquets, dancing, and similar diversions, and, after burning the bodies of the dead, the ashes are preserved in urns or, being mixed with lime, serve to plaster the temple walls.

Bangkok, the capital, is a city of 500,000 inhabitants, and is located on both sides of the large river Chow Payah, about thirty miles from its mouth. The city extends for six miles along its banks and is so intersected by canals and small streams running in all directions through the city that the place is appropriately styled the "Venice of the East." Thousands of shops and dwellings, built upon bamboo floats, line the shores for miles, and boats are exclusively used for visiting all parts of the city. It is situated in a vast plain that is covered with rice fields and, although destitute of sanitary improvements, is considered very healthy. Its importance as the capital and chief commercial port of the kingdom has attracted to it a large body of European and Asiatic residents, and, with submarine cable, mail and telegraphic facilities, telephone exchanges, gas and electric light plants, and other necessary or convenient appendages of modern civilization, the city is becoming quite cosmopolitan.

The Siamese are not a literary people, yet education is generally diffused among all classes. Their system of writing, which is quite as slow as the forming of English capital letters with the pen, makes the preparation of manuscript a long and tedious process. Yet they have some printing presses, from which the natives have issued elementary schoolbooks and Buddhist volumes for the priests. The Protestant missionaries established the first printing press in Siam in 1836 and, since that date, they have printed and distributed many thousands of volumes among the people, consisting mainly of the Gospels, Pilgrim's Progress, Life of Christ, Evidences of Christianity, and other books of a similar character. Their long-continued and persistent efforts have been crowned with abundant success, their missions are in a flourishing condition and no more inviting field has been opened for the extension of the Protestant religion.

Our treaty relations with the government of Siam were first established in 1833, when Mr. Edmund Roberts was commissioned by President Jackson to visit the courts of Cochin-China, Siam, and Muscat for the purpose of effecting arrangements for the protection of our seamen and the extension of American commerce. At the time of his visit our shipping was subjected to every species of extortion that eastern avarice so well knew how to impose upon it, and American citizens were exposed to the penalties of laws that gave to the creditor power over the life as well as the property of the debtor. The success of the mission was fully attained by the abrogation of these harsh provisions and the securing of necessary and proper guarantees for the protection of our ships and seamen. Our relations with the kingdom of Siam, since that date, have been undisturbed by any untoward incident, and our commerce with the country, though inconsiderable as yet, has enjoyed all the rights and immunities which are extended to that of the most favored nation.

CHAPTER XXII.

RELATIONS WITH THE CONGO STATE AND THE HAWAIIAN ISLANDS.

The Congo State.

DURING the last decade an association was formed in Europe for the purpose of organizing a government and developing the resources of that vast portion of equatorial Africa, which Henry M. Stanley has so successfully explored. This association, called "*Comité d'Etudes du Haut Congo,*" and afterwards substantially merged into "The International African Association," had as its president, King Leopold of Belgium.

Portugal claimed this territory, or at least that part of it lying about the lower Congo, by right of discovery by her navigators in 1484. Possession was taken at that time in the name of Portugal and a colony called Zaire was founded. In various treaties with Spain dating from 1668 to 1713 Portugal's right to the Congo country was conceded. During the continental war in the eighteenth century she was dispossessed of her African colonies but by skillful diplomacy she managed to regain them in 1763. Early in this century England attempted to effect by diplomatic means, the abolition of the slave trade carried on by Portugal. The latter government, however, was unwilling to discontinue a trade which formed the bulk of her income from Africa. But in 1810 she was induced to join in a treaty to suppress the traffic. Shortly afterwards, Great Britain had reason to believe that Portugal was not carrying out the purpose of the treaty and a series of new treaties was concluded in which more stringent measures were adopted. Portugal made a proclamation expressly prohibiting the slave trade and gave England permission to overhaul and search vessels off the coast of the Portuguese African colonies. Even with such measures the slave trade continued until 1871, when the Portuguese government was able to announce to Great Britain that the inhuman traffic was at an end.

During the period from 1810 to 1871 Portuguese power on the African coast steadily declined. Commercial enterprises of various kinds had been started by Dutch, French, and English traders along the seaboard and for some distance into the interior. Over each one of these establishments was hoisted the flag of the nation to which the proprietors belonged. The far interior, into which Stanley had penetrated, was divided among many petty chieftains, who acknowledged no sovereignty save their own. Beginning in 1880 the International Association had negotiated about one hundred treaties with these African chiefs, who surrendered in consideration of "*puoents*" a territory which covers over 14,000 square miles. By these treaties the chiefs and their people were not to be actually dispossessed of their lands but were to put themselves under the protection of the International African Association. Portugal became alarmed at these encroachments upon her territory and in 1884 drew up a treaty with England which recognized the sovereignty of Portugal over the west coast of Africa between the 5th and 8th degrees of south latitude and declared the navigation of the Congo and the Zambezi Rivers free. As a remuneration for recognizing Portugal's sovereignty England received the colony of San Juan Baptista.

This treaty seemed a deathblow to the association. Portugal's dominions upon the Congo were a menace to the neutrality of the recently acquired possessions of the association. Its plans seemed impossible and its influence was fast waning when a hitherto apparently uninterested power appeared upon the scene and revived its drooping fortunes. No sooner had England by her treaty with Portugal discouraged the civilizing tendencies of the association, than Bismarck set his seal of approbation upon the movement and by his diplomacy, instead of an association under the patronage of private individuals, it became a corporation to be fostered and guided by the great powers of the world.

Bismarck had well said that the standing menace to the unity of the German Empire was the ever increasing emigration of the sturdy Teutonic stock to other countries. By what means could this mass of people be kept at home? Only by providing more extensive employment, and in order to do this, by enlarging the markets for German manufactures. To gain this end Bismarck inaugurated a regular colonial policy, which was not to encourage the emigration of German subjects but to increase the manufacture of German wares. The experiment had been tried in Samoa and in Fernando Po, of opening large warehouses for German goods and of establishing lines of German merchant vessels to supply them with the articles for which there was a demand. Samoa and Fernando Po rapidly came under German influence and exports to those ports became a considerable part of the commerce of the German Empire.

By the efforts of the International Congo Association an enormous tract of land had been opened whose population considerably exceeded a million souls. By the introduction of civilization, the wants of these people were to be increased and, as the prospects pointed to a rapid growth of population by immigration, there was an opening for German trade which would make that with Samoa sink into comparative insignificance.

Bismarck set about to gain the co-operation of France and England in support of the association. To England he wrote that Germany could not respect the right of parties who had been previously interested on the Congo. With such an announcement as this and with all of England's commercial interests demanding that the government should lend its aid to the association, the British minister hesitated to ratify, and finally rejected the treaty so lately drawn up with Portugal.

Bismarck next secured the good will of France by offering to abandon any German occupation in Africa, should it be considered prejudicial to French interests and he proceeded to show the inestimable advantage which would accrue to the French by co-operation in the plans of the association. The United States had already signified its approval of the plans of the association and on the 22d day of April, 1884, President Arthur with the advise and consent of the Senate, recognized the flag of the International African Association (a golden star on a field of blue), as that of a friendly government, avoiding in doing so any prejudgment of conflicting territorial claims that might be involved.

By this time, the association having received a strong backing, by Germany, France, England, and the United States, Bismarck issued an invitation to the powers of Europe and to the United States to a conference to be held at Berlin on the 15th of November, 1884, to consider and decide upon the free navigation of the Congo and also upon the establishment of rules which would govern future occupations on the west coast of Africa. It was expressly stipulated that all questions of sovereignty should be left untouched. Accordingly on the day appointed, representatives from nearly all the powers appeared at Berlin and, for the first time in history, representatives from the United States joined in a diplomatic conference with the powers of Europe.

After a brief discussion, the navigation of the Congo was declared free to all the powers of the world and future occupations on the coast were to be regulated by a new association, "The International Conference of the Navigation and Commerce of the Congo." This commission was authorized to maintain sufficient authority to insure peace, and Great Britain was given the supervision of it.

Although the International African Association as such did not enter into the deliberations at the conference, yet the important questions which concerned it were settled. These out of the way, the association was on a sure footing and almost immediately after the conference ended, it developed into a political entity, called the "Congo Free State." With this new power nearly all of the nations represented at Berlin negotiated treaties of recognition and friendship.

It was a novel spectacle in international politics,—a state actually created by the good will of the great powers of the world, with its recognition immediate and its independence guaranteed. Germany is, perhaps, its guardian, but the United States is its godfather. The territory of the new state was made known to the world by Stanley, and our government was the first to recognize its existence as an institution by declaring that, "in harmony with the traditional policy of the United States—this government announces its sympathy with, and approval of, the humane and benevolent purposes of the International Association of the Congo and will order the officers of the United States on land and sea, to recognize the flag of the International African Association as the flag of a friendly government."

On the first of August, 1885, King Leopold wrote to President

Cleveland, "Now that the position of the association in an international point of view, that its territorial position is established, that its mission has received valuable encouragement, I am prepared to bring to your notice and to that of the people of the United States that the possessions of the International Association of the Congo will hereafter form the Independent State of the Congo. I have at the same time, the honor to inform you that, authorized by the Belgian Chambres, I have taken the title of sovereign of the Independent State of the Congo."

The union between Belgium and the new state was to be wholly personal and President Cleveland replied, "I congratulate your majesty on being called to the chief magistracy of the newly formed government and the people of the United States cannot doubt that, under your majesty's good government, the people of the Congo region will advance in the paths of civilization and deserve the good will of all those states and people, which may be brought into contact with them."

Whatever the resources of the new state may be, and the reports on that subject are very conflicting, the method of its organization is strikingly novel and is a proof of the humanizing tendencies in nineteenth century politics.

The Hawaiian or Sandwich Islands.

The Hawaiian Islands, comprising a group of eight inhabited and four uninhabited islands, are the most important in the north Pacific Ocean, and, lying directly in the track of commerce between America and Asia and nearly equidistant from the two continents, their value to the United States as a port of refuge, as well as the seat of a profitable and flourishing trade, is fully recognized and appreciated. They are located between the nineteenth and twenty-second degrees of north latitude, nearly corresponding to the latitude of the island of Cuba, and their area, excluding that of the four uninhabited islands, is estimated at 4,250,000 acres, or about 6,640 square miles; of this amount about 2,500,000 acres, or about 3,900 square miles, are included in the area of the island of Hawaii. The population, according to the census of 1890, amounted to 90,000 souls, comprising 34,500 natives, 15,000 Chinese, 12,000 Japanese, 8,500 Portuguese, and the remainder of various nationalities, nearly two thousand of whom are Americans. At the discovery of these islands by Captain Cook in 1778, the population was estimated at 200,000, but, from official and other data, obtained at various periods since that date, it appears that the native race is in the course of gradual extinction. This is ascribed to the fact that leprosy and other diseases have been introduced from abroad as well as to the reason that the female population is much smaller than that of the other sex and that only about one of three married women bears children.

The natives of Hawaii are, in stature and development, as fine as those of any of the Pacific islands. They have a reddish-brown complexion, very black and straight or wavy hair, broad faces, thick lips, thin beards, and rather flat noses. They are naturally a good-tempered, light-hearted, and pleasure-loving people, fond of sports, swimming, and horseback riding. They are besides a brave and fearless race, though by no means bloodthirsty or revengeful; and, while they have always kindly received and hospitably entertained strangers, they have never hesitated to resent the insults and repel the attacks of those wandering buccaneers who, like the followers of Captain Cook, have sought to degrade their men and debauch their women.

The field, orchard, and garden products of the islands are generally the same as those of Cuba, except that corn, wheat, and rice are also grown in considerable quantities. Sugar, however, is the chief staple agricultural product, of which 250,000,000 pounds, valued at $12,159,585, were exported in 1890. The total exports of all products during that year amounted to $13,023,000, and the imports for the same period amounted to the sum of $6,962,000. The sugar industry was enormously stimulated by the reciprocity treaty between the United States and Hawaii that was proclaimed in 1875, by the terms of which the sugar from these islands was admitted free of duty into United States ports; and this measure, amounting to a bonus of almost ten cents per pound on their sugar, gave them a degree of prosperity never before enjoyed and diverted ninety-one per cent of their trade to the United States. The passage of the McKinley bill, however, removing the tariff upon the raw sugar of the West Indies, has proved a severe blow to the sugar interests of Hawaii; since, owing to high-priced labor, dear food supplies, and the difference in freights, the sugar planters there cannot compete with those of Cuba and Puerto Rico. In view of this desperate condition, which, if not ameliorated, must involve them in bankruptcy, the people are beginning to direct their attention to the growing of coffee. The prospect of success from this diversion of their agricultural interests is heightened by the fact that the islands are the natural habitat of the coffee plant and that, while the wild berry is of quite as good quality as that from South America, the cultivated article is fully equal to that of Java. The serious phase of the case seems to be involved in the fact that labor is thrice as dear as in South America, but this apprehension loses much of its apparent force when it is remembered that the coffee planter may cultivate his lands with one tenth of the labor that is required to till them in sugar.

The climate of the Hawaiian Islands is remarkably genial and propitious, for, although they are situated in the torrid zone, their natural isolation exposes them to refreshing sea breezes, and, for nine months of the year, to the steady blowing northeast trade winds. Scarcely a country can be found where the temperature is more equable and the elements kindlier mixed. The diurnal range of the thermometer is twelve degrees and the extremes mark fifty-three and ninety degrees. The lofty mountain peaks, some of which are covered with perpetual snows, that form such a distinguishing feature of these islands, afford a charming diversity of temperature; for at the height of four thousand feet the thermometer ranges from forty to seventy degrees and fires are often comfortable even in the month of July. The vast quantities of vapor floating up from the sea drape the mountain tops in fantastic summer clouds or, condensed by the cooler atmosphere of these high elevations, fall in refreshing showers upon the hills and valleys below.

Upon approaching Hawaii the objects that first engage the attention and enlist the admiration of the beholder are the stupendous volcanic mountains, apparently rising abruptly from the sea and lifting their summits two and a half miles into the sky. Clad in perennial verdure and isolated in their grand proportions, they appear, from the distant ships, like stupendous curtains hung up upon the azure heavens. One of these, Kilauea, is the largest active volcano in the world. Its crater, four thousand feet above sea level, is three and a half miles long and two and a half miles wide; within this and filling its area to the brim is a lake of boiling lava, which, at night, illumines the overhanging clouds and skies and which, in periods of great eruption, rolls in rapid seething rivers down through forests and over precipices to the sea.

The first Protestant mission sent out to the Hawaiian Islands, consisting of seven Americans with their families and three Hawaiians, twenty-two in all, sailed from Boston,

October 23, 1819, and, after a protracted and uneventful voyage around Cape Horn, arrived safely off the islands on March 30, 1820. It was a most auspicious moment for the success of their mission, since, King Kamehameha having lately died, his son had marked his advent to the throne by abolishing idolatrous customs, destroying the sacred images, and tearing down the temples of worship. The strangers were soon visited by many of the natives from shore and each party, in their accustomed manner, exchanged kindly sentiments of friendship and hospitality. The chiefs also, with their wives, came on board, and, after having received every demonstration of consideration, they manifested great pleasure at the coming of the party and extended to them sincere expressions of welcome and invitations to come upon shore. An audience with the king having been arranged and presents having been freely distributed among his family and retainers, he was induced, after much delicate tact and mild persuasion, to permit the missionaries to take up their residence in the islands and to disseminate their religion for the space of one year. He was averse to granting even these terms, because the idolatrous priests having hitherto weakened the power of the government, he feared that, by the admission of a new religion, similar results would ensue. Under these favorable auspices the foundations of Christianity were laid, and they were so solidly based and firmly cemented by the discreet conduct and devout life of these pious persons that the idolatrous nation was quickly and permanently converted to the Christian religion; so that now the peals of Sabbath bells and the notes of hymned praise, the Sabbath school and divine service, are settled features of the life of this interesting people.

In the year 1843, a British ship of war visited Hawaii to settle certain complications that had arisen between the

British consul and the government; and, although these difficulties were clearly traceable to the arrogance and unreasonableness of the British representative, the captain of the royal navy sent a communication to the king couched in most offensive terms and demanding humiliating concessions coupled with the threat that, if prompt and full compliance with his demands was refused, he would open his batteries upon the port of Honolulu. The king, despairing of any effectual resistance, acceded to his demands, but only to learn that this imperious dictator had framed a second series of demands, more insulting and excessive than the first. Seeing that contention was useless and that further concessions would provoke renewed exactions, the government at last determined, in the face of impending ruin, to cede the islands to Great Britain and proceeded to frame a treaty to that effect. This action, consummated under the stress of such notoriously unjustifiable circumstances, everywhere aroused public indignation and especially in the United States, in consequence of which the British government hastened to disavow any responsibility and to repudiate the cession of the islands. This was followed by a convention of the leading powers and the adoption of a treaty, by the terms of which the independence of the islands was recognized and guaranteed. American influences, always in the ascendant there, have grown so great during the past ten years that the country is now in all except government under the control of the United States.

There have been various measures in recent years, semi-official or otherwise in their nature, looking to an American protectorate over these islands or for their absolute cession to the United States, but the settled and wise policy of the government to abstain from foreign interference and the acquisition of distant and isolated possessions has prevented the consummation of such schemes, and it may well be questioned whether or not, by the annexation of such territory or by the extension of special protection to it, any compensatory advantage to the United States would result. Indeed it might be insisted, upon good grounds, that such connections might involve our government in embarrassing complications and, under certain circumstances, prove a source of serious trouble and great expense.

[*The End.*]

INDEX.

Adams, John, 150, 151, 181, 184, 225, 231, 245, 246.
Adams, John Quincy, 84, 156, 168, 210.
Adet, 181.
Alabama Claims, 166, 175-177.
Alaska.—Fisheries, 168, 169, 170, 171, 173; Purchase of, 105, 212-216; Exploration of, 213; Commercial Company, 170.
Alexander I., 168.
Amazon, Navigation of the, 82-84.
Ambassadors (see Ministers).
Amiens, Peace of, 201.
Angell Treaty, 264-265.
Argentine Republic.—Governed by Spain, 36; Revolution, 39-40; Reciprocity with the United States, 72; Independence acknowledged by the United States, 76-78; Navigation of the Rio de la Plata, 78-82; Difficulty about the Island of "Martin Garcia," 80.
Austria.—General Condition, 137, 148; War with Prussia, 145-146; Relations with the United States, 227-230; Treaty of Trade and Commerce in 1831, 227; Diplomatic Warfare in the case of Koszta, 228-229; Naturalization Treaty of 1870, 229; Citizenship of Heinrich, 229; Other Treaties, 230.
Azores Islands, 237.
Balboa, 107.
Bancroft, 226.
Barbadoes.—Reciprocity with the United States, 74.
Barbary States, The.—Relations with the United States, 244-248; Piracy, 244-248; Blackmail, 244-245; Treaty between the Dey of Morocco and the United States, 245; Decatur, 247-248.
Barclay, Thomas, 245.
Barrios, 91.
Bayard, 162, 167, 227.
Bayonne Decree, 187.
Belgium.—Relations with the United States, 231-232; Treaty of Commerce and Navigation in 1845, 231; Treaty of 1858, 232; Treaty for Capitalization of Scheldt Dues, 1863, 232; Eight other Treaties, 232; Connection with the Congo Free State, 232.
Bering, Vitus, 213.
Bering Sea Question, 168-174.
Berlin Decree, 187.
Bismarck, 227, 298-299.
Blaine, 24, 220-221.
Bolivar, 38-39; Accomplished the Independence of Venezuela, 40; Of Colombia, 40; President of the Republic of New Granada, 40; Forecast of the Condition of the American Republics, 42-46; Advocate of the Abolition of Slavery, 48-49; Proposed an American Conference, 47-48, 54.
Bolivia.—Founding, 40; War between Chile, Bolivia, and Peru, 88-90.
Brazil.—Government by an Audiencia, 36; Government by Viceroy, 36; Independence, 41; Attempt to Exclude the United States from the Navigation of the Amazon, 82-84.
British Guiana.—Reciprocity with the United States, 74.
Buchanan, 158, 214.
Bulwer, Sir Henry, 96.
Bureau of Information on the South American Republics, 68-69.
Burlingame, Anson, 261, 263.
Canal, Interoceanic, 107-118, 191-192.
Canning, 93, 150.
Canton, 252, 253; Capture by British, 255.
Central American States.—Treaty with the United States, 78; Union, 91; Independence acknowledged by European Powers, 95.
Cevallos, 201.
Champagny, 187.
Charles X. of France, 142.
Charlotte Amalie, 127.
Chesapeake, The, 155.
Chile.—Governed by Spain, 36; Revolution, 39; Reciprocity with the United States, 76-78; War between Chile, Bolivia, and Peru, 88-90; Trouble with the United States, 90-91.
China.—Diplomatic Relations with the United States, 252-272; Beginning of Foreign Intercourse, 251;

310 INDEX.

Hong Merchants, 253; Opium War, 254-255; Treaty of Nanking, 255; Treaty of Wang Hiya, 256; Capture of Taku by the French and English, 258-259; Treaty of June 18, 1858, 259; Ports opened to Foreign Trade, 259; Taiping Insurrection, 259-260; Burlingame Treaty, 263-264; Chinese Immigration into the United States, 263-269; Angell Treaty, 264-265; Scott Act, 265, 266, 267; Geary Bill, 267, 268; Mode of Reception of Foreign Ministers, 270-271; Civilization of Chinese, 271-272.

Chinca Islands, 106.
Chinese Immigration into the United States, 263-269.
Claiborne, 195.
Clay, Henry, 94-95, 99, 100, 109, 156.
Clayton, John M., 96.
Clayton-Bulwer Treaty, The, 95-99, 115-116.
Clinton, De Witt, 109.
Coahuila, 81.
Coin, International, 66-67.
Colombia, 36; Freedom, 40, 76; Ratified Proceedings of the Panama Congress, 56; Reciprocity with the United States, 74.
Columbia River, 157.
Conferences of American Republics.—Panama Congress, 49-56; Washington, 57, 62-65; Lima, 57, 58; Results, 66-75; Reciprocity between the United States and South American Republics, 70-75.
Congo State.—Founding, 296-300; Portuguese Power in Africa, 297; Bismarck's Policy, 298-299; Association of great Powers, 299-300; King Leopold made Sovereign, 301.
Congress of Vienna, 141.
Consular Service, 27-35; Origin, 27-28; Establishment of the United States Consular Service, 28; Compensations of Officers, 28, 33-34; Qualifications, 28-30; Classes of Officers, 30; Duties, 30-33, 35.
Consuls, 27-30; Duties, 30-33; Salaries, 33-34.
Costa Rica.—Reciprocity with the United States, 74; Connection with Interoceanic Canal Enterprise, 118.
Court Dress, 20.
Crimean War, 145, 148, 158.
Cuba, 52, 53; Reciprocity with the United States, 70, 74; Controversies over Cuba, 99-101; Attempts of the United States to purchase, 206; Inconvenience of Relations between the United States and Cuba, 206; War with Spain, 207; Claims of Americans, 207; Capture of the *Virginius*, 207-208.

Cushing, Caleb, 255-257.
Davie, 185.
Decatur, 247-248.
DeLesseps, 113, 191.
Democrats, 152.
De Neuville, 84.
Denmark.—Proposed Annexation of St. Thomas, 126-131; Relations with the United States, 233-236; Seizure of American Vessels, 233-234; Sound Dues, 234-236; Treaty of Christianople, 234; Treaty of 1701, 235; Treaty of 1826, 235.
Diplomacy, 12.
Diplomatic Service, 9-26; Under Articles of Confederation, 9; Under Constitution, 9-26; Intrusted to President, 10; To Secretary of State, 11; Three Classes of Diplomatic Agents, 12-13; Salaries, 13-14; Qualifications, 15; Manner of Appointment, 15-17; Credentials, 17; Duties, 17-18, 21-26; Presentation at Court, 19-20.
D'Yrujo, 200.
Ecuador.—Part of Republic of New Granada, 40; Independent State, 41; Reciprocity with the United States, 74.
Egyptian Mixed Tribunals, The, 248-250.
Emden, 224.
England (see Great Britain).
Envoys Extraordinary, 13; Salaries, 13-14.
Erskine, 155.
Exequatur, 35.
Fava, Baron, 24, 219-222.
Fayal, 237.
Federalists, 152.
Fenian Disorders, 160-161.
Filibusters, 87-88.
Fillmore, 100.
Fish, Secretary, 166, 175, 218.
Fisheries.—Atlantic Coast, 163-168; Seal, 168-174.
Florida, Purchase of, 201-204, 208-210.
Foreign Affairs, Department Established, 9.
Forsyth, John, 203.
France.—Revolution, 136-137, 138; States General, 137; Reign of Terror, 138; Directory established, 138; Government Controlled by Napoleon, 138-141; Revolution of 1830, 142; Revolution of 1848, 143; Napoleon III., 144, 145, 146; Republic, 147; Diplomatic Relations with the United States, 178-196; Extravagant Demands, 179; Recall of Genet, 179-180; Corrupt Government, 181; Treaties Declared Abrogated, 182; George Logan, 182-183; Relations Renewed, 184; Treaty of 1800, 185-186; Decrees of Napoleon, 186-187;

INDEX 311

Seizure of Vessels, 188; Commercial Treaty of 1822, 189; Settlement of Claims, 189-190; Consular Convention of 1853, 190; Correspondence regarding American Pork Products, 192; Spoliation Claims, 192-194; Treaty of Alliance of 1778, 193; Purchase of Louisiana, 194-196.
Francis I. of Austria, 137.
Franklin.—Character, 178; Negotiates Treaties, 150, 225, 230, 232, 233, 236, 245.
Frederick the Great, 223-225
Fremont, John C., 85-86.
Gadsden, James, 86.
Garfield, 89, 114.
Geary Bill, 267, 268.
Genet, 153, 170.
Geneva Arbitration, 159, 174-177.
Germany.—Holy Roman Empire, 137; War between Prussia and Austria, 145-146; Franco-Prussian War, 146-147; Relations with the United States, 223-227; Frederick the Great, 223-225; Dantzig an Asylum for United States Cruisers, 224; Treaty between the United States and German States, 225; Between the United States and the North German Confederation, 226; Samoan Conflict, 226-227; Consular Convention, 226; Reciprocity, 227.
Gerry, 181, 184.
Ghent, Treaty of, 211.
Godoy, 199.
Gordon, 260.
Gortchakoff, 129.
Grant, 112, 116, 119-126, 175.
Great Britain.—Attitude toward the Holy Alliance, 93-94; Treaties with Guatemala, Honduras, and Nicaragua, 99; Treaty with Russia, 105; War with Napoleon, 139; Diplomatic Relations with the United States, 149-178; Difficulties following the Revolution, 151-154; The Jay Treaty, 154, 156; Impressment of American Seamen, 155; War of 1812, 155-156, 159; Commercial Treaty, 156; Treaty of 1818, 156-157; Payment of Damages for Slaves, 157; Treaty acknowledging Claim of the United States to the Northwest Territory, 157; Webster-Ashburton Treaty, 158; Seizure of Mason and Slidell, 158-159; Treaty of Washington, 159, 166, 175; Geneva Arbitration, 159, 174-177; Fisheries Question, 159, 163-168; Fenian Disorders, 160-161; Arrest of Mr. Winslow, 161-162; Recall of Sir Lionel Sackville-West, 162; Bering Sea Question, 168-174; Reciprocity Treaty, 165; Treaty of 1871, 167; Treaty of February, 1888, 168; Modus Vivendi, 168.
Greytown, 90, 111, 118.
Guadalupe-Hidalgo, Treaty of, 86.
Guatemala.—Reciprocity with the United States, 74; Treaty with Great Britain, 99.
Hamilton, 152, 153, 182.
Hanseatic Republics, 225.
Harrison, 91.
Hawaiian Islands, The.—Situation, Population, Productions, etc., 301-303; Relations with Great Britain and the United States, 306-307.
Hayes, 89, 113.
Hayti, 51.
Heinrich, 229.
Holland.—Relations with the United States, 230-231; Treaty of Amity and Commerce, 230; Other Treaties, 231.
Holy Alliance, The, 93, 141-142.
Honduras, 99.
Impressment of American Seamen, 155.
Italy.—General Condition, 138, 148; Treaties, 217; Damage to Commerce of the United States, 217; New Orleans Massacre, 218-222.
Itata, The, 90.
Jackson, 189.
Jamaica.—Reciprocity with the United States, 74.
Japan.—Relations with the United States, 273-282; Founding, 273; First Intercourse with Foreign Countries, 273; Foreigners Expelled, 273; Treaty Negotiated by Commodore Perry, 274-276; Treaties of 1857 and 1858, 277; Reception of General Grant, 280; Attempts to Revise Treaties, 281-282.
Jay, 9, 154, 180.
Jefferson, 10, 151-153, 178-179, 225, 245.
Korea.—Relations with the United States, 283-289; Killing of Seamen, 284; Revolution, 287; Opened to Foreign Countries, 287-288; Treaty with the United States, 288.
Koszta, 228-229.
Lafayette, 136, 137.
La Plata, Navigation of the, 78-82.
Laussat, 195.
Leeward Islands.—Reciprocity with the United States, 74.
Legations.—Secretaries of, 14; Comparison of, 21.
Liberia, 131-135.
Logan, George, 182-183.
Logan Law, The, 183.
Louis XVI., 136-137, 138.
Louis XVIII., 140-142.
Louisiana, Purchase of, 194-196.
Marcy, 83, 190, 243.
"Martin Garcia," Island of, 80.
Mason, 158.

Maximilian, 102-104.
Meade, Richard W., 289.
Mexico.—A Spanish Colony, 36; Independence, 41; Reciprocity with the United States, 70, 74; War with the United States, 85-86; Maximilian Episode, 101-104.
Milan Decree, 187.
Ministers.—Classes, 12-13; Salaries, 13-14; Qualifications, 15; Appointment, 15-17; Duties, 17-18, 21-26; Recall, 18; Presentation at Court, 19-20.
Miranda, Francisco, 37-39, 202.
Mississippi, Navigation of, 197-200.
Modus Vivendi, 168, 174.
Monroe, 93-95, 180, 195.
Monroe Doctrine, The, 93-106.
Morocco, 244.
Morris, Gouverneur, 151, 180.
Mosquito Indians, 95-96.
Murray, William Vans, 183-185.
Napoleon I., 138-141, 185-187; Commercial War with England, 139; Waterloo, 141; Decrees, 187.
Napoleon III.—Attempt to occupy Mexico, 102; Franco-Prussian War, 146-147.
New Granada, Republic of, 40, 109; Treaty with the United States, 111.
New Orleans Massacre, 218-222.
Nicaragua.—Reciprocity with the United States, 74; Filibusters, 87-88; Mosquito Indians, 95-96; Treaty with Great Britain, 99; Negotiations for Interoceanic Canal, 111-118.
Northwest Boundary, 104-105, 157.
Nuncios, 12.
O'Brien, Richard, 245.
Offley, David, 239.
Onis, 201, 210.
Orders in Council, 186-187.
Panama, 107-118, 191.
Paris, Siege of, 146, 191.
Patterson, 108.
Peiho, The, 258, 261, 262.
Perez, 251.
Persia.—Relations with the United States, 242-243; Influence of England, 242; Treaty with England, 242; Treaty with the United States, 243.
Persona Grata, 18.
Peru.—Governed by Spain, 36; Independence, 40; Conferences, 57-58; Reciprocity with the United States, 74; War between Chile, Bolivia, and Peru, 88-90.
Phelps, 167, 227.
Pierce, 100.
Pinckney, Charles, 184, 201.
Pinckney, Thomas, 151, 189
Piracy, 244-248.
Polk, 99, 214.

Pork Products, 192, 227.
Portugal.—Relations with the United States, 236-238; Conflict at Fayal, 237; Treaties, 237.
President.—Power to conduct Foreign Policy, 10-11.
Pribyloff Islands, 171.
Prussia.—War with France, 116-147; Treaties with the United States, 225.
Puerto Rico, 52, 53; Reciprocity with the United States, 70, 74; Attempt of French to purchase, 99; Attempt of the United States to purchase, 99.
Railway, Intercontinental, 67-68.
Rambouillet Decree, 187.
Rassloff, 128, 131.
Rebellion, The, 84, 158, 211.
Reciprocity, 70; Section of Tariff Bill, 73; Reciprocity between the United States and the other American Republics, 70-75; With Germany, 227.
Reed, William B., 257-259, 261.
Reid, Whitelaw, 192.
Reign of Terror, 138.
Rousseau, General, 215-216.
Rudini, 219-222.
Russia.—General Condition, 138, 147-148; Relations with the United States, 211-216; Cordiality toward the United States, 211-212; Purchase of Alaska, 212-216; Treaty, 214-215.
Sackville-West, 162, 167.
Saint Thomas, Proposed Annexation of, 126-131.
Salisbury, 172, 174.
Salvador.—Reciprocity with the United States, 74.
Samoan Islands.—Relations with the United States, 226-227, 289-292; Rebellion of Tamasese, 226, 290-291; Adjustment of Difficulty, 227, 292; Creation of a Supreme Court, 292.
San Ildefonso, Treaty of, 84.
San Juan del Norte, 96.
Santa Anna, 85, 86.
Santana, Pedro, 105.
Santo Domingo.—Application of the Monroe Doctrine, 105; Proposed Annexation to the United States, 119-126.
Scott Act, The, 265, 266, 267.
Seal Fisheries, 168-174.
Secretaries of State.—Number and Names, 10; Direct Foreign Policy, 11.
Seward, 103, 128-130, 160, 214-216, 285.
Siam.—Population, Trade, etc., 292-294; Relations with the United States, 295.
Slave Trade.—Treaty between Great Britain and the United States for Suppression of, 156.
Slidell, 85, 158.

INDEX. 313

Sound Dues, 234-236.
South American Republics.—Founding, 36-46; Diplomatic Relations with the United States, 47-65; General Relations with the United States, 76-84, 88-91.
Spain.—Policy toward Colonies in America, 36-37; Relations with the United States, 197-210; Navigation of the Mississippi, 197-199; Right of Deposit, 200-201; Treaty of Friendship, Limits, and Navigation, 199; Recall of D'Yrujo, 200; Convention of August 11, 1802, 201; Blockade, 202; Purchase of Florida by the United States, 201-204, 208-210; Treaty of February 22, 1819, 203-204; Depredations upon United States Commerce, 204-205; Claims Convention of 1834, 205; Questions arising on account of Cuba, 205-208.
States General, 137.
Stoeckl, 212, 214.
Sweden.—Relations with the United States, 232-233.
Taku, 258-259, 263.
Talleyrand, 181, 184, 195.
Taylor, 85.
Texas, Annexation of, 84-85.

Thiers, 147.
Three-mile Limit, 165.
Treaties (see below).
Trinidad.—Reciprocity with the United States, 74.
Tripoli, 244.
Turkey.—Relations with the United States, 239-242; Treaty of 1830, 239-240; Imprisonment of American Citizens, 240-241; Treaty of Commerce, 241-242.
Tweed, 238.
Tyler, 85.
Venezuela.—Governed by Spain, 36; Independence, 40, 76-78.
Vienna, Congress of, 141.
Virginius, The, 207-208.
Vives, 203.
Walker, 87-88.
War of 1812, 155-156, 211, 236.
Ward, Frederick, 260-261.
Washburn, 191.
Washington, 153, 181, 182.
Washington, Treaty of, 159, 166, 175.
Waterloo, 141.
Water Witch, The, 78-82.
Webster, 100, 158.
Windward Islands. — Reciprocity with the United States, 74.

Treaties between the United States and Foreign Powers.

American Republics. — Commerce, etc., 78-82.
Austria.—Trade and Commerce (1831), 227; Naturalization (1870), 229; Extradition (1856), 230; Rights of Consuls (1870), 230; Convention Relative to Trade-marks, 230.
Barbary States.—For Protection of American Ships, 245, 247.
Belgium.—Commerce and Navigation (1845), 231; Commerce and Navigation (1858), 232; For Capitalization of Scheldt Dues (1863), 232; Eight Other Treaties, 232; Commerce and Navigation (1875), 232.
China.—Treaty of June 18, 1858, 259; Burlingame Treaty (1868), 263; Angell Treaty, 264-265.
Denmark.—Treaty of 1826, 235.
France. — Alliance (1778), 152; For Purchase of Louisiana, 84; Boundary (1819), 84; Treaty of 1800, 185-186; Commercial Treaty of 1822, 189; Consular Convention of 1853, 190.
Germany.—Consular Convention (1871), 226; Reciprocity (1892), 227.
Great Britain.—Peace (1783), 151, 163; Jay Treaty, 154, 180; Peace (1814), 156; Commercial Treaty of 1815, 156; Of 1818, 157; Acknowledging Claim of the United States to the Northwest Territory, 157; Clayton-Bulwer Treaty, 95-99.

Hanseatic Republics.—Treaty of 1828, 225.
Hawaiian Islands.—Reciprocity, 70.
Holland. — Amity and Commerce (1782), 230.
Italian States.—Five Treaties, 217.
Italy.—Friendship, Commerce, and Extradition (1868 and 1871), 217.
Japan.—Treaty of 1854, 274-276; Of 1857, 277; Of 1858, 277.
Korea. — Peace, Amity, and Commerce (1882), 288.
Mexico.—Reciprocity, 70; Guadalupe-Hidalgo (1848), 86.
New Granada.—Regarding Isthmus of Panama (1848), 111.
Persia.—Friendship and Commerce (1856), 243.
Portugal. — Navigation and Commerce (1840), 237; Claims (1851), 237.
Prussia.—Following Revolutionary War, 225; Treaty of 1799, 225.
Russia.—For Purchase of Alaska, 214-215.
Siam.—Treaty of 1833, 295.
Spain. — Friendship, Limits, and Navigation, 199; Ceding Florida to the United States (1819), 203-204, 210; Claims Convention of 1834, 205.
Sweden.—Treaty of 1783, 232; Of 1827, 233; Extradition (1860), 233; Naturalization (1869), 233.
Turkey.—Trade, etc. (1830), 239-240; Commerce (1862), 241-242.

www.ingramcontent.com/pod-product-compliance
Lightning Source LLC
Chambersburg PA
CBHW022045230426
43672CB00008B/1078